JEWISH FRONTIERS

ESSAYS ON BODIES, HISTORIES, AND IDENTITIES

SANDER L. GILMAN

*This volume is dedicated
to Eberhard Lämmert
whose inspiration as a teacher never faltered.*

JEWISH FRONTIERS
Copyright © Sander L. Gilman, 2003.

First published 2003 by
PALGRAVE MACMILLAN™
175 Fifth Avenue, New York, N.Y. 10010 and
Houndmills, Basingstoke, Hampshire, England RG21 6XS.
Companies and representatives throughout the world.

PALGRAVE MACMILLAN is the global academic imprint of the Palgrave
Macmillan division of St. Martin's Press, LLC and of Palgrave Macmillan
Ltd. Macmillan® is a registered trademark in the United States, United
Kingdom and other countries. Palgrave is a registered trademark in the
European Union and other countries.

ISBN 0-312-29532-4 hardback

Library of Congress Cataloging-in-Publication Data
Gilman, Sander L.
   Jewish frontiers : essays on bodies, histories, and identities / by Sander L.
Gilman.
      p.   cm.
   Includes bibliographical references and index.
   ISBN 0-312-29532-4
   1. Jewish diaspora.   2. Jews—Identity.   3. Holocaust, Jewish
(1939–1945)—Influence.   4. Post-Zionism.   5. Jews—Diseases—Genetic
aspects.   6. Multiculturalism.   I. Title.

DS134 .G54   2003
700'.45203924—dc21

                                                                    2002030304

A catalogue record for this book is available from the British Library.

Design by Letra Libre

First edition: May 2003
10   9   8   7   6   5   4   3   2   1

Printed in the United States of America.

Contents

PART III
JEWISH BODIES ON THE MULTICULTURAL FRONTIER

Preface

THIS VOLUME PLACES THE EXPERIENCE OF DIASPORA
Jewry into a post-Zionist reading of Jewish and non-Jewish history. Central to this is my claim that all diaspora societies in
which Jews live, including the State of Israel, are places of contention and complexity for Jews. This is not unique to Jewish history. The identical claim could be made for any diaspora people
that maintains its sense of identity. The situation of the moment
has required Jews to rethink the role of the center (Israel) in the
definition of what it means to be Jewish in the modern world.
This, however, is not substantially different from the relationship
of, for example, South Asians in a diaspora from national states
that have existed not much longer than the modern state of Israel.
South Asians have come to identify with those new national
(postcolonial) states—India, Pakistan, Sri Lanka, Bangladesh—in
which they often have never lived, but to which they can and do
return. This is equally true of the vast Chinese diaspora. Is the
China with which they identify the People's Republic, Taiwan,
Hong Kong, or Singapore? Is it classical Chinese culture beyond
the politics represented by the identical statue of Confucius that
graces the Chinatowns in New York City and in Manchester,
England. Or is it, as with many South Asians, a vaguely conceived
historical or cultural homeland that exists in cultural artifacts
such as art, literature, food, and the echoes or realities of religious

practice? This agglomeration of cultural elements, at least in Chicago, means that it seems easier to speak of South Asian culture in the diaspora than within the national states in South Asia—or indeed in an amalgam of all of these, once or twice removed from the daily realities of a distanced, real homeland.

What binds together these diasporas (and others such as the Greek or the Irish) is their identification with a nationalist project that is quite modern. This nationalist project demands that the national states of the nineteenth and twentieth century be seen as a natural or divine continuation of a longer mythic history. This is nowhere more true than in the history of the idea of Greece from the eighteenth century through to the creation of the modern Greek state as we see it at the beginning of the twenty-first century. The move from an imagined community to a national state seems seamless, especially when it is viewed from the diaspora. New national states build their mythologies into their creation. We are at a point where we can begin to examine the conflicts and compromises that exist in a diaspora situation that is always oriented on a homeland. This homeland itself has been transformed with the creation of a modern national state and, often, with the demand for a return to build or rebuild the new state. For Jews, nineteenth-century Zionism was the articulation of that demand. In our post-Zionist age, the radical claims of Zionism for a Jewish state to end the Diaspora of *all* the Jews of the world have been drawn into question. It is possible to examine how the life on the "frontier," in which such diasporas always exist, shaped not only the intellectual and cultural work in the diaspora but also the very formation of a new national culture in the new national state.

One further common denominator of these dispersed peoples should be noted: the success that such groups have had in their diaspora experience. Success is a word rarely spoken in discussing the Jewish experience. The focus has been (quite correctly) on the horrors of anti-Semitism and the Shoah in the

Jewish diaspora in the United States. The reduction of modern Jewish history to a history of victimhood is possible only in societies such as that of the United States, where Jews have become successful as formers and shapers of culture. By contrast, it was virtually impossible to produce major texts that dealt with the Shoah in the state of Israel during its formative years. Only over the past few decades have major writers, such as Yehuda Amichai and David Grossman, produced such texts that appealed to a broader audience in Israel and beyond. This shift in Jewish cultural production and identity is a reflex of the very notion of the frontier, which is not seen as a displacement from the center but as a new beginning. It is similar to the attempt of eastern European Jews coming to North America in the late nineteenth century to reshape themselves as new Americans, and in so doing they stripped themselves of any identification with Russia or Russian Poland. They were Jews and chose to reformulate their identities as they felt only antipathy to their "homeland" and saw America as the "Golden Land" of promise. Virtually no Eastern European Jews or their progeny feel any identity with Russia or Poland as national states. Likewise, Jews escaping (or having escaped) Central Europe before, during, and after the Shoah felt little compelling identity (except perhaps on the level of cultural practice) with their land of national origin.

The first essay in this volume presents a theoretical argument for dealing with a post-Zionist idea of Jewish culture that includes contemporary Israel as well as Jewish cultural production through the world. Cultural production (in this book, represented by the writing of novels and the making of films) is for me a litmus test, as it is the means by which one can present thought experiments about identity formation in the most easily packaged way. To actually experiment with real human beings in the manner that a novelist or filmmaker creates characters and contexts is virtually impossible, but the thought experiments that are fixed in cultural objects reflect how these creative individuals think about identity in their world.

This volume concentrates on a series of questions. First, how do Jews and non-Jews imagine the idea of the Shoah within the mass media at the end of the twentieth century? The first two essays examine two different frontier situations in which individuals find themselves displaced and reconstituting an identity in a new cultural space. The first sketches the development of a Jewish identity in postwar Communist East Germany and the creation of the first major comic novel (and film) about the Shoah, written by Shoah survivor Jurek Becker. The second examines the appropriation of the victim status, attributed to the Jews in the post-Shoah world, by the non-Jewish Italian filmmaker Roberto Benigni and the unparalleled success of his comic film. Both essays show the struggle for control of a medium of mass culture (film) over representations of the Shoah. How and why the films take the form that they do, and how each of necessity wrestles with the idea of the Jew in the culture of post-Shoah East Germany and Italy, is the subject of the first section. The frontier experience is that of a global culture of the cinema with truly localized origins in which the competition for the attention of the public often masks the local needs and demands of the writer or filmmaker. This is not a Jewish problem, even if the theme of the Shoah is the most intensely Jewish theme of the latter half of the twentieth century. Rather, the question remains: Who owns the Shoah? Who can (or cannot) use it, and are there acceptable or unacceptable ways of representing it? Perhaps more elegantly put: How does the local context of any presentation of the Shoah make it more or less acceptable and for which audiences is it not acceptable? Each interpretive community constructs an identity that claims the right to represent (or deny) history and make it its own.

Second, my exploration of Jewish fantasies on the frontier of Diaspora existence addresses the fantasies of the Jewish body both within and outside the Jewish community. No better example is the century-old association of Jews with the smoking of tobacco. Here the question arises of the "special nature" of the Jewish body, as debated by Jews and non-Jews alike, around such practices as the smoking of cigars that have multilayered meanings in modern society. These fantasies shape Jewish self-representations in many ways, even in the work of writers who are only tangentially Jewish, such as Marcel Proust. Third, how do traditional ideas of the Jewish body and modern ones, such as the most recent findings about the human genome, shape the science associated with studying the Jewish body? Proust and Franz Kafka are two embodiments of the preoccupation with fantasies about a Jewish body being marked, being inherently different, being corrupt and diseased, that dominated the rise of anti-Semitic pseudoscience in the nineteenth century. Both are aware of the power of these images. Each deals with this fantasy in his own manner, and each grapples with it in ways that are typical as well as atypical of his time. The final essay in this section looks at the close of the twentieth century and the reappearance of a discourse about Jewish illness that echoes and yet is very different from that of the late nineteenth century. Now the science is better (if not perfect) and the construction of an "ill" Jewish body seems to be simply a consequence of the reality of genetically transmitted illness in groups. Yet, it is clear that contemporary Jews grapple with the notion of their identities as Jews and as individuals with the possibility of transmitting illnesses in equally ambivalent ways. These concerns are not uncommon among diaspora communities; this is not a Jewish problem. The nineteenth-century pseudoscientific idea that the Irish body or the Chinese body was diseased and dangerous, as well as the discovery of other genetic cohorts that are more or less conterminous with patterns of genetically transmitted illness in the past decade, parallels the situation of the Jews. But modern Jewish culture, more than most, became a medicalized culture, as the body of the Jew was more often than not the case study for racial or genetic difference.

Finally, what happens when everyone knows what is going on with images and their history, as in modern multicultural writing? What happens when the interpretative community seems not to be hostile to the Jews (as a conceptual structure) but to embrace diversity, including the Jews? Today we all seem to agree that groups have a specific or a particular culture related to their ethnic or religious or class definition. Today identity is so widely assumed, even in casual conversation, and culture is taken for granted in explaining identity and behavior. Does this actually change the function of the image of the Jew in the thought experiments of multicultural writers? The image of the Jew, even when it is self-consciously placed against traditions of anti-Semitic rhetoric, comes to fill the contours of that rhetoric. Notions such as hybridity that were supposed to answer the pressures on Jewish "difference" (whether that of the stereotyped "Oriental" Jew or the "cosmopolitan") reveal themselves to present another case of conflict on the frontier of multiculturalism. The Jewish self-image in high and mass culture shows the ongoing struggle with Jewish cultural success, as demonstrated by the work of Jews using Jewish themes (for example, Saul Bellow and Steven Spielberg in the United States). Coupled with the normalization of Israel as a national state, with all of the difficulties of a simple identification of Jews with the contemporary Israeli project, the image of a Jewish culture on the frontier points toward a productive set of cultural exchanges in the postcolonial world.

These essays were written over the past two years. The first chapter, used with permission of the University of Illinois Press, appeared in a different form as the introduction to *Jewries at the Frontier: Accommodations, Identity, Conflicts* (Urbana and Chicago: University of Illinois Press, 1999, edited by Milton Shain and me); the chapter on Jurek Becker in a much different form as "Jurek

Becker and Cultural Resistance in the German Democratic Republic," the inaugural Heinz Bluhm Memorial Lecture (Boston
College, 2001); the chapter on Benigni as "Is Life Beautiful? Can
the Shoah Be Funny? Some Thoughts on Recent and Older
Films," *Critical Inquiry* 26 (2000): 279–308; the Proust chapter as
"Proust's Nose," *Social Research* 67 (2000): 61–80. They were revised as a volume and the additional essays were written while I
was a Berlin Prize fellow at the American Academy in Berlin. I
wish to thank the academy's director, Gary Smith, as well as the
staff for their support.

Berlin
June 1, 2001

INTRODUCTION

THE FRONTIER AS A MODEL
FOR JEWISH HISTORY

THE PROBLEM OF A CENTER OR
CORE-PERIPHERY MODEL

NINETEENTH- AND TWENTIETH-CENTURY ZIONISM PROM-
ised to solve the "problem" of Diaspora Jews. The problem was
defined as the inevitable alienation experienced by Jews attempting to become citizens in nations that designated them inherently
unassimilable. Zionism promised to provide a constant, uncon-
flicted identity for them by making them citizens of a new nation
state during an age in which national citizenship provided the primary point of identification. At the beginning of the twenty-first
century this promise has now been shown to be problematic. We
live in an age where national states themselves are of lesser importance for identity formation. The very fabric of state-based identity has been shown to be a composite resulting from the willing
or unwilling movements of people over time and across space. All
individuals create their sense of themselves out of this composite
whose global scope is now quite evident. The promise of a stable
identity for all Jews rooted in a specific Jewish (but also democratic and multiethnic) state has given way to the renewed importance of a complex Diaspora identity. Israeli identity is just as

conflicted as any other national identity with its various undercurrents and tensions. Indeed, part of the Diaspora in the twenty-first century is the new presence of Israeli Jews, with all their conflicted, multiple identities (secular, religious, ethnic, class) throughout the world.[1]

Let me share an epiphany with you. I found myself one day at *Bet-Ha-Tefutzot*, the Museum of the Diaspora in Israel, a space devoted to the documentation of the cultural achievements of the Diaspora. It is a self-conscious parallel to *Yad Vashem*, the memorial and museum of the Shoah, which documents the victimization of Diaspora Jews. Inscribed at the entrance of the Museum of the Diaspora, as Arnold Eisen in *Galut: Modern Reflections on Homelessness and Homecoming* imagines, is the implicit admonition: "Remember where you stand. Only the Land around you is real. The rest is not. If you come from a Diaspora of the present, know that sooner than you think, your community too will be part of our past, a room in our museum."[2] When I first experienced this, my sense was that the foundation of the state of Israel had made the life of Diaspora Jews somehow simpler, if more stressful. Today this epiphany of a Diaspora Jew reading such a statement in what still claims to be a non-Diaspora, Zionist space brings home to me that the overarching model for Jewish history has been that of the center, or core, and the periphery. Used extensively by sociologists in the late nineteenth and early twentieth century, this model had been reinforced by the role that Israel has had in reshaping the narrative of Jewish history. It was (and remains) the model of "you" and "us." It is the imagined center that defines me as being on the periphery. Israel, the lost Garden of Eden, the City on the Hill, is the center; all the rest of Jewish experience is on the periphery. Recently the so-called revisionist historians of Israel (such as Zeev Sternhell and Yael Zerubavel) have pointed to the necessary mythmaking that went into the construction of the very idea of Israel in the course of the twentieth century.[3] But even they still assume a central role for this mythic identity in writing the history of the Jews. Today such a model no longer seems adequate for the writing of any aspect of Jewish history, including that of Zionism and of the state of Israel. I want to argue in this volume that a new model, that of the frontier, would be more appropriate for a reading of modern Jewish experience. The frontier model also exists as an imagined space and often intersects and coexists with the center-periphery model, but overall offers a more nuanced reading of Jewish experience.

The complexities of the models for Jewish identity and historiography rest in part on the links between knowing who you are (identity) and knowing how you came to be who you are (history). The links between questions of identity, identification and history, and historiography rest on the construction of organizational categories by the authors and the readers of texts. We inscribe who we believe ourselves to be and where we believe we came from in these texts we call history. Identity is what you imagine yourself and the other to be; history and historiography is the writing of the narratives of that difference.

Since the post-Egyptian biblical narrative, the reader finds the center defined as the God-given space of the Jews speaking the authentic language of the Jews; all other Jewish experience lies beyond. But beyond is a space poisoned by the very notion of the center. The competing notions of Diaspora and Galut that structure Jewish historiography presuppose a model of center and periphery and condemn the periphery to remain marginal. These concepts can be understood as either cosmopolitan (good) or rootless (bad) in their expression. The Jews are either the exemplary people at home in the world or are so isolated from any natural attachment to place that they become the consummate mimics of everyone else on the frontier.

After the founding of the state of Israel, one of the great difficulties facing Jews (and non-Jews) is that they have had to understand the existence of Jewish life beyond Israel or the Holy Land.

How can this be seen as a valid life experience authentically expressed in an adequate language or discourse when only Hebrew
and the idea of return seems to be an authentic model for Jewish
identity? For a millennium this had been the distance from an
imagined, textually based center—Torah as the symbolic topography of the missing center. Following the founding of the state of
Israel, though, exile has meant exile from a real, geographically
bounded place, while the act of returning, endlessly postponed, is
now a possibility. The traditional center-periphery models of the
meaning of the exile experience for Jews still provide good ways to
understand this Jewish experience.

The contradictory yet overlapping models of a Diaspora as
opposed to a Galut has formed the Jewish self-understanding of
exile. The voluntary dispersion of the Jews ("Galut" or "Golah") is
articulated as inherently different from the involuntary exile of the
Jews ("Diaspora"). These two models exist simultaneously in Jewish history in the image of uprooted and powerless Jews on the
one hand, and rooted and empowered Jews on the other. It is possible to have a firm, meaningful cultural experience as a Jew in the
Diaspora or to feel alone and abandoned in the Galut (as well as
vice versa)—two people can live in the very same space and time
and can experience that space and time in antithetical ways. Indeed, the same person can find his or her existence bounded con-
ceptually by these two models at different times and in different
contexts.

The notion of a dispersion of the Jews is inscribed in the
Torah in a specific manner with negative, punishing overtones.
This dispersion represents punishment for the transgression of
specific boundaries. (Here the very sense of the boundary is linked
to clear definitions of what is taboo within the belief system of
rabbinic Judaism.) The idea of a textual model for the Diaspora
rooted in the Torah and reflected in other writings is important to
any comprehension of a Jewish articulation of the meaning of

exile. The very assumption of the Diaspora, however, is ambiguous and contradictory even though it carries the force of divine revelation incorporated in texts. Is God's punishment part of the covenantal relationship He creates with the Jews? It is an abstraction read into Jewish (and human) history from the expulsion from the Garden of Eden to Moses' death outside of the Promised Land.

The Galut, on the other hand, is often understood as the experienced reality of being in exile, structured, however, by the internalization of the textual notion of the Diaspora, tempered by the daily experience (good or bad) of life in the world. The Jew experiences the daily life of exile through the mirror of the biblical model of the expulsion, whether it be the expulsion from the Garden of Eden or freedom from slavery in Egypt. If these two experiences are parallel, if life in the Galut is harsh and painful (as it often was), it seems a further proof of the validity of the model of the Diaspora. The South African Jewish writer Sandra Braude has stated this succinctly: "But Jews tend to forget that there is only one promised land, and that they seldom are permitted to remain in any one place for longer than three generations."[4] It is the "land" that shapes the center-periphery model. Historians, such as Jacob Neusner in *Self-fulfilling Prophecy: Exile and Return in the History of Judaism*, have argued for a material understanding of this notion of Diaspora.[5] For him it is the model of wilderness and land, the dialectic between tent and house, nomadism and agriculture, wilderness and Canaan, wandering and settlement, Diaspora and state. W. D. Davies has argued, in *The Territorial Dimension in Judaism*, that this dichotomy is well-balanced in the Bible, that for every quote praising wilderness as the decisive factor in Judaism, there could be found a counterpart praise of the Land of Zion.[6]

Such a model has different readings from different positions. Certainly a gendered reading of the center-periphery would and does provide quite different inflections of the model. But the domination of the model even levels the implication of gender for the writing of a history of Jewish culture and life.[7] For center-periphery models demand a specific type of hegemonic orientation. In the writing of women's history, the core becomes the family and the periphery, the world. Such models in the writing of the history of Jewish women tend to recapitulate the complexities of the role that the center-periphery has for the writing of all aspects of Jewish history. No place is this more clearly seen than in the writing of the history of the Jews after the Shoah.

If there is a postmodern reading of the center-periphery model that dominates the writing of Diaspora history in the 1990s, it is the shift of the center from Jerusalem to the Shoah. Such a reading of the Shoah, Holocaust, Churban—the Yiddish term for the murder of the Jews—as the new center of Jewish history and historiography places the rest of Jewish history into a new periphery. In light of this it becomes necessary to define Jewish history either teleologically or metaphorically in terms of this new center. Readings of Jewish history from the Middle Ages to the 1920s become nothing more than preparation for the appearance of the Shoah. Studies of anti-Semitism as a European phenomenon come to make sense only in terms of its relationship to the new center, the Shoah. Indeed, even studies of the origin and meaning of the state of Israel in all its forms are read in terms of the Shoah. Given the power in the writing of Jewish history that understands the center-periphery model to be normative, its translation into a Shoah-centered model with its intimations of meaning and punishment seems frighteningly logical.

Thus Daniel Goldhagen's *Hitler's Willing Executioners* postulates a relatively straight path from medieval Jew hatred to the Shoah.[8] The center of Jewish history becomes the Shoah and all Jewish experience comes to prefigure it. Unlike Goldhagen, I understand that there is a complicated history of anti-Semitism (for me a blanket term for Jew hatred) in the Christian West which is different than simple ubiquitous xenophobia. I see this as stemming from the very origins of Christianity and its constant need to distance itself from Judaism and the Jews. What Goldhagen views as eliminationist anti-Semitism, the desire to destroy all Jews everywhere, is present even in the early church. Goldhagen provides a model for anti-Semitism in Germany that explains the Shoah, the very center of his argument. Germany becomes a limited, specific case that in a complex way absolves all other nation-states of anti-Semitism. Given the specificity of the self-conscious construction of a German *Staatsnation* (in the sense of Friedrich Meinecke) in the place of a *Kulturnation* and the movement from the status and power of religious anti-Semitism to the new status of scientific racism at the close of the nineteenth century, the function of anti-Semitism in Germany is clearly different from that in France or Austria. The *Sonderweg* debate was whether Germany and "the Germans," however defined, were different from other European "nations" or "peoples" at the end of the nineteenth and beginning of the twentieth centuries. Indeed, comparative studies are beginning to pinpoint specifically the function of such stereotypes in understanding German culture in contrast with other self-consciously constructed national and local cultures in Central Europe. This is not to say that nineteenth- and early twentieth-century German culture in its construction of Germanness, the Germans, and the Jews was better or worse than in other national cultures; only that it fulfilled a different function. All of this means that, in my reading, the presence of what Goldhagen labels "eliminationist" (rather than exclusionist) anti-Semitism in Germany was necessary but not sufficient for the Shoah to take place. However, if we employ the model of the frontier rather than of the center-periphery, then a reading of the experience of the Jews at the German frontier would eliminate the seeming centrality of the Shoah for an understanding of Jew hatred. It would allow for a new reading of anti-Semitism as endemic rather than as teleologically resulting in the Shoah.

The center-periphery model in the writing of Jewish history is in truth a symbolic structure for the understanding of the impossibility of a Diaspora life. Such a definition demands the existence of a real center and thus defines the Jews in terms of their relationship to that center. An alternative model would be that of Jonathan Boyarin, who comments that "postmodern sensibilities allow us to recuperate the alternative (and in this sense traditional) resource of identifying with Jews as a collective through continuity (coextension in time) at least as much as through contiguity (coextension in space)."[9] This partial rejection of "land" means that "Jews can only constitute themselves as such in relation to others who are both like and unlike them" (128). In spite of his insight into the redefinition of the Jews as a temporal rather than as a topographic category, Boyarin himself falls into an attenuated center-periphery model in his suggesting "a postmodern ideal of Diaspora" (124). I would see this as transcending rather than inscribing the center-periphery model which cannot be postmodern in any way.

If Jewish experience contradicts the expectations of the Diaspora model, for example in the Golden Age of the Jews in Spain or the exile of Jews in the United States, the meaning of the model becomes muddled. This is certainly the case in the late twentieth century. Today, the pervasiveness of the center-periphery model (Diaspora, borderlands, margins, and the like) for a conceptualization of Jewish history is fraught with difficulties. We experience the simple reversal of the condemnation of the periphery as the place of failure and punishment. The margin becomes either the space of alienation from *Yiddishkeit* (as the inscription at the Diaspora Museum notes), or it becomes the pure site of Jewish radicality, creativity, intellectual empowerment. Today we have seen a radical transvaluation of the meaning ascribed to the periphery. Diaspora has come to mean deterritorialized; homeless; rootless; displaced; dispersed; nomadic; discontinuous; hybrid; plural; incommensurable; interstitial; minor. All of these terms have permeated the critical and historical appropriation of the center-periphery model. In a world defined as multicultural, they have reversed their traditional meanings and have come to mark the desirability of life at the margin rather than its failure. This romanticization of the periphery is just as deadly dangerous as it presents only the margins as the space for cultural success. By abandoning both center and periphery and by focusing only on the frontier experience without any positive or negative reference to an assumed center, a new Jewish history can provide more adequate models for the interpretation of Jewish identities and histories.

Both positive and negative readings are inherent to the center-periphery model and both point up its problem—authenticity. Either the authentic is at the center and only at the center; or the flight from the center is the hallmark of the authentic. The one marker that seems constant is that of language—whether it is Hebrew at the center and the false, base Diaspora languages of the Jews at the margin; or Yiddish at the center and the false lapse into languages of acculturation or assimilation at the margin; or German, Magyar, English at the center and the peripheral and false languages of victimhood (Yiddish or German) at the margins. Our center-periphery is always articulated in terms of the struggle for an authentic Jewish language.

LANGUAGE AS KEY

"Next Year in Jerusalem?" asks the Israeli, American Jewish philosopher Richard Schusterman in his paean (while in exile in America) to the formative power for creating an authentic Jewish identity only in relationship to a mythic center.[10] Having returned to the United States (also a real and a mythic space), he finds himself "no longer one of the redeemed ascenders to full Jewish national identity (*olim*) but one of the fallen (*yordim*) who lives in what is termed 'exile' (Galut). However, I'm not yet sure whether I should be written off as a *yored*. For not merely do I maintain a love for Israel, whose experience and way of life have structured so much of my own that it is an inalienable part of me; but I have not renounced the option of going back to resettle there and thus to reenact the myth of return, that, I argue, is quintessential to Jewish identity. But such a return, in contrast to my official *aliyah*, will indeed be an actual return as well as a mythic one, for I will have already been there before." (295) And Schusterman tags his Jewish identity in his American text by interpolating the authentic language and/or discourse of the center-periphery model, Hebrew, into his parenthetic model, saying in effect, I write in English, the language of cultural hegemony, but within me resides the true Jew, whose language "is quintessential to Jewish identity." Language is a primary marker of the center-periphery model in the understanding of Jewish identity and the writing of Jewish history.[11]

In the same volume of philosophical discussions of Jewish identity in which Schusterman's essay appeared, Gabriel Josipovici bemoans the problem of the meaning of language by evoking his models of margins. He is quite a different Jew by his own definition ("not circumcised, have not taken my bar mitzvah, do not attend synagogue or celebrate any of the feasts" [309] and, one might add, living in England, not Israel). He quotes Kafka's diary entry "in which he examines why the German language, which is the only one he really knows, is incapable of expressing in the word *Mutter* his own (Jewish) sense of his mother; or Proust's description of Marcel's despair at not being able to express his sense of joy at the way the sunlight strikes the river and being reduced to banging his umbrella on the ground and crying 'Zut zut zut'"[12] (314). Here Josipovici interpolates Kafka's "Jewish" response to his German into his own English, for him, now a language that can only approximate his exilic condition; yet Proust's inarticulate sounds are not at all labeled as Jewish. Who is more Jewish? The writer who reflects on the inability of his language to carry meaning (while showing that it does) or the one reduced to describing the inarticulate banging of the umbrella? Both are, of course, merely enactments of modernist conventions about language. Proust's language is certainly as expressive as Kafka's in stating its inexpressiveness. As Josipovici himself notes, all writers doubt the power of their own language and/or discourse to express the world that they imagine. But for the Jew (self-defined and temporally defined as the other—whether Kafka, Proust or Josipovici), language on the margin becomes the testing place for the notion of an authentic language of the Jews: even the language that one does possess is drawn into question.

The authentic is tied by the center-periphery model in Jewish history to language. It is clear that such a symbolic model has structured the writing of Jewish history—or perhaps better, the history of the Jews—from at least Flavius Josephus. Even insightful historiographers, such as Arnaldo Momigliano, share the model while being quite clear in their understanding of its limitation.[13] It is striking, however, that the hidden litmus test for the center-periphery model is a quality of the Jewish experience that is ambiguous in its very nature: the function of language and/or discourse as a marker of Jewish identity. Thus, Momigliano writes that modern ideas of the Diaspora, such as those held by the historian Pierre Vidal-Naquet, overlap with that of Flavius Josephus: "Flavius Josephus, the historian of the war of 70 A.D., is a Jew who speaks Aramaic and writes first in Aramaic. It is only after he has acquired Roman citizenship and settled in Rome that he begins, with some difficulty, to write in Greek. By adopting Greek patterns of thought Flavius signified his distance from Palestinian Jews, but at the same time wrote an apology of Judaism" (69). In all cases Josephus remains essentially Jewish: "Flavius Josephus is far from secularizing his categories of judgment" (75). For Momigliano the key to his reading of Josephus is the fact that

Josephus ignores the synagogue and the tradition of the apocalypse. Both are linked in the notion of the center of the Jewish experience to Jerusalem but also to Hebrew as the liturgical language of the Temple (not the Aramaic of everyday life). Since Josephus is on the margins—in both historical and geographic terms—of the Roman empire, his sensibilities come to represent the Diaspora tradition for Momigliano. Rome or Paris or Chicago can be understood as the periphery if the Diaspora is taken only in relationship to the unarticulated center (Jerusalem). Further, that center must be timeless, unlike the world of the Diaspora, which is defined as temporally bound. Thus in Momigliano's model, Josephus's retelling of the Torah for his Roman readers binds it to the world of Greco-Roman culture while the purity of his mental construct shows his relationship to transcendental Jewish conceptual categories.

Josephus is also the prime example of problems perceived when Jews live at the symbolic margin. It is not that all Jews became Hellenistic critics of Maccabean power—not all Jews so overidentify with Rome while writing in Greek—but the line between the poles of the religious fanaticism of Masada and total acculturation became a permanent marker of the Jews in the Diaspora. Josephus's position, according to Momigliano, came to be marked by a need to repress the center-periphery model and its language in his conceptualization of the historical process of the Jews and to replace it with a new center, the language of Greco-Roman historiography.

For Momigliano, the patterns of thought of the Franco-Jewish historian of the Holocaust Pierre Vidal-Naquet and his use of French come to represent the "good" Jew using the languages of the Diaspora to reveal rather than disguise his Jewishness. Vidal-Naquet represents in his estimation the positive values of a Jewish historiography on the periphery, one that is conscious of its Jewishness. But there is still a specter that haunts

Momigliano's notion of the authentic Jewish historian: it is the distance from the center, a center now real, existing in Israel rather than symbolic, existing in the Jewish (read: Hebrew) texts that uniquely formed his Jewish Italian identity as a child. In a complicated way, Momigliano uses Josephus as the negative image of acculturation and Vidal-Naquet as the positive one. Vidal-Naquet represents the world of Romanic Judaism which Momigliano identifies as his own: "Vidal-Naquet has not forgotten and will not forget that he is Jewish, one of the Jews from the Arba' Kehillot, from the 'four communities' of the Contado Venassino, whose center is in Carpentras; ever since the Middle Ages, generations of rabbis and doctors, and more recently musicians, politicians, writers, and scientists, have come from Carpentras in very high proportions compared to their small numbers. Both Vidal-Naquet's father, who participated in the Resistance in 1940, and his mother, were deported and killed at Auschwitz by the Nazis" (68). This is a biography that echoes the autobiographical account of Momigliano's youth and upbringing that prefaces the volume of his essays on Judaism (xxv–xxviii).

Momigliano's town Caraglio is a space for Jews and his Jewishness is that of text, including the Jewish mysticism of the Zohar. He is raised in a religious orthodoxy unusual among his peers and he remains conscious, unlike Josephus, of synagogue and language. His "father and mother were among the victims" of the Nazis (xxvii). Momigliano comes to represent the problems of the Diaspora model that seem to end in the Shoah, the ultimate condemnation of the periphery, and yet, as in his work and that of Vidal-Naquet, continue at the margins after the Shoah. Josephus's Greek, Vidal-Naquet's French, and Momigliano's Italian come to represent languages and cultural traditions on the periphery rather than the new site of cultural dispute. And yet, in Momigliano's words, there is the desire for the traditions of Diaspora Jews to be unbounded in terms of time. His genealogies show the continuity of Jewish life before and (in his own work) after the Shoah. It is the dream of a new center on the periphery.

Recent non-Jewish critiques of the use of the Diaspora model, such as that by the Irish American anthropologist Benedict Anderson, point to the need for an alternative manner of imagining the historical movement of people.[14] Anderson's stress on "today's long-distance nationalism," the globalization of national identity, is seen by him as a reflex of "capitalism's remorseless, accelerating transformation of all human societies" (327). He too sees the process of national identity as a process of interaction on the margins. He comments that the construction of the "native" is a white-on-black negative. "The nativeness of natives is always unmoored, its real significance hybrid and oxymoronic. It appears when Moors, heathens, Mohammedans, savages, Hindoos, and so forth are becoming obsolete, that is not only when, in the proximity of real print-encounter, substantial numbers of Vietnamese read, write, and perhaps speak French but also when Czechs do the same with German and Jews with Hungarian. Nationalism's purities (and thus also cleansings) are set to emerge exactly with hybridity" (316). The collapse of the Diaspora model in the contemporary world (in contrast to Momigliano's romanticization of its tenacity) is the result of the ability to shift language. Momigliano makes Hebrew and the synagogue the touchstone of identity. The true center was replaced by French as the cultural equivalent of Hebrew, following the accepted model of the *Alliance israelite universelle*, or by German following the lead of the *Hilfsverein der deutschen Juden* (the Welfare Society of the German Jews) as the cultural center for German Jews in the nineteenth century. This language hegemony extended into the United States, as Michael Meyer has shown.[15] Remember, German and French were the languages of the schools founded to turn the Jews of the Orient into Western Jews. It is the modern mobility of language (for Anderson, tied to modern technology and print) that

now defines hybridity—and it is of course an older and more ideo-
logically suspect maker than even he credits. Anderson is thus an-
swering to a degree James Clifford's image of all of those exiles,
migrants, displaced peoples caught up in a margin of nonmove-
ment within a tyrant economy of movement.[16] Clifford's vision of
the periphery, unlike those of Momigliano or Anderson, is totally
disempowering. He is aware that the romanticization of the periphery creates a new center and perpetuates the model of the
marginal. It is language that marks all of these readings of exodus
and the periphery. It is language that can also provide a key to an
alternative model for viewing Jewish history, the model of the
frontier.

THE FRONTIER AS AN ALTERNATIVE

Let us imagine a new Jewish history written as the history of the
Jews at the frontier, a history with no center, a history marked by
the dynamics of change, confrontation, and accommodation, a
history that focuses on the present and in which all participants
are given voice. The frontier is not the periphery, as it relates only
to itself. It is the conceptual and physical space where groups in
motion meet, confront, alter, destroy, and build. It is the place of
the "migrant culture of the in-between" as both a transitional and
translational phenomenon, one that "dramatizes the activity of
culture's untranslatability," according to Homi Bhabha.[17] It is
clear that the *frontier* is a modern, if not a postmodern, concept.
The word itself is not to be found in the King James Bible. And
yet by the Revised Standard Version of the mid-twentieth century,
the concept of the frontier begins to infiltrate an English reading
of the text.[18]

Passages in the Revised Standard Version reflect a postcolonial English reading of the sense of place, a place not defined by a
center and a periphery but by a constant sense of confrontation at

the margin. The Jews go out and confront others at the margins—
where they too become marginal. Is it war? avoidance? intermarriage? accommodation? acculturation? that can result on the
frontier? All, of course, are possible when the inhabitants of Israel
meet the Jewish others, "the Reubenites and the Gadites and the
half-tribe of Manas'she," or the non-Jewish others, the Moabites
or even the sons of Lot at the frontier. It is the focus on this space,
a rupture of the frontier from the center, that can provide the
space not only of confrontation but also of accommodation (both
concepts having negative and positive valances).

The frontier is a colonial and a postcolonial concept that is
applicable in complex ways to the writing of a new Jewish history.
Today we should move from the King James Version, with its
missing "frontier" and its evocation of London as the new
Jerusalem, to the New English Bible, not because it is aesthetically
superior, but because it reinscribes a series of colonial and postcolonial images onto the language of the Hebrew Bible which may
well clarify a new reading of Jewish history. If language, even the
language of the Bible, can be viewed as a litmus test of the formation of a Jewish identity however defined, the submerged model
for the writing of Jewish history, which also is present in Tanakh,
is that of the frontier.

This is not to advocate the reduction of the Jew to a symbolic
figure on the new stage of the frontier. I am quite attuned to the
problems of symbolic representations of the Jew as an abstract figure beyond history. The cultural critics Daniel and Jonathan Boyarin were quite right to call our attention to the political
challenge implied in Jean-François Lyotard's act of allegorizing
the Jew as liminal man.[19] It is equally false to separate the internal
and external definitions of the Jew. It is the center-periphery
model that enables this separation to seem natural as it presents
one extreme as positive and the other as inauthentic. Once this
model is suspended, the frontier becomes the space where the

complex interaction of the definitions of self and other are able to be constructed. Once we understand that the bipolar structure of center and periphery maintains the separation between real and symbolic definitions of the Jew, then the model of the frontier can lead to a new reading of Jewish history of the modern era. In this new reading, the symbolic becomes a meaningful function of both internal and external identity, an extension of the network of meaning into all aspects of our understanding of the Jews.

The frontier in biblical terms is also marked by a specific relationship with all the inhabitants found there. The land (space or topology) that God gave to the Jews is as much Moses' frontier as it was Abraham's. In the King James Version of Genesis 17:5: "Neither shall thy name any more be called Abram, but thy name shall be Abraham; for a father of many nations have I made thee." Abraham's story is a tale of the frontier, for he "journeyed from thence toward the south country, and dwelled between Kadesh and Shur, and sojourned in Gerar" (21:1). Abraham's being caught between Sarah (whom he disguises as his sister to stop Abimelech, the king of Gerar from raping her) and his bondwoman Hagar the Egyptian is typical of the experiences on the frontier, for which language, culture, and even sexuality are markers. Sexual conflicts and accommodations on the frontier mirror cultural ones. These biblical nations are nations in conflict and change, ever shifting in their cultural definition and space. What language does Abraham speak? Hebrew, Chaldean, Ugric, Gerarian, if indeed such a language actually existed? He had to negotiate with people who spoke different tongues, had different social systems, saw him as enemy or ally. The tale of Abraham is the tale of the frontier, a frontier still without a true center. It is, as all biblical narratives are, repeated with variations throughout the Bible, each variation proving the truth of the original model. Just as the center-periphery model begins with the tale of the expulsion from Eden, so too the model of the frontier begins with

Abraham and his confrontations during his wandering. Both models (like those of Diaspora and Galut) exist simultaneously in the symbolic space of the Bible, and yet each functions separately to provide different narratives for the history of the Jews. As in Talmud, it is not necessary to fix one single model or meaning as the authentic one. Rather, it is from the competition of multiple models that some sense of a pattern can be found.

What if we heuristically assume the existence of this sub-merged biblical model of the frontier and apply it to modern Jewish history? Always at a frontier, often a material frontier, the Jews (however defined) understood this material frontier symbolically. Indeed, it becomes the space in which the Jews are defined and define themselves. Here we must move from Flavius Josephus, the first century C.E., Greco-Roman Jewish historian, to his contemporary, the Roman historian of the German frontier, Tacitus (who did not like Jews very much), to examine both sides of the image. From Roman Germany through medieval Poland to nineteenth-century South Africa and the United States, Jews have always functioned on a permanent symbolic frontier. Israel itself was and remains a frontier state and so can be read outside of a center-periphery model. It is a place of the constant negotiation of identity among Jews and between Jews and the other peoples who live there. It is a multicultural nation with a mandate as a Jewish state. It is a democracy that does not give innate political primacy to Jews, even though that is the reality. It is a land in which being Jewish has multiple meanings and yet one in which a narrow definition of the Jew is mandated by the religious authorities who were given this right by a secular state. It is a land of multiple languages and discourses. The very creation of modern Jewish identity demanded a frontier sensibility at its core.

The model of the frontier I imagine is not Frederick Jackson Turner's model of the American frontier with its reliance on the manifest destiny of American expansion into the lands of the West.

My model is analogous to the stress on the materiality of the land that Jacob Neusner understands as the basis of the center-periphery model of Jewish history. One must think of the very concept of frontier as a structure of communal fantasy, as a model of imagining oneself in the world. The best example of such an imagining is the "New Western History," that new model of understanding the American frontier. Stephen Aron notes that the New Western History began with Patricia Limerick's casting off of Turner's notion of the frontier as an "unsubtle concept for a subtle world." But, Aron argues quite correctly, the frontier is the very center of a New Western History: "Rather than banishing the word for past offenses, western historians need to make the most of the frontier. Reconfigured as the lands where separate polities converged and competed, and where distinct cultures collided and occasionally coincided, the frontier unfolds the history of the Great West in ways that Turner never imagined."[20] Turner, who used the idea of the frontier to define his understanding of America, would not have recognized the notion of the frontier today. For North American historians it is the new "F" word, according to Kerwin Lee Klein, for it seems to want to construct a new regionalism at the expense of a national identity.[21]

Yet this new regionalism is precisely the type of focus that a new Jewish history needs as it would take the various Diasporas seriously on their own merit. Charles Taylor has suggested that group recognition is the primary means of creating and discriminating among groups in a multicultural world.[22] It is in this light that the frontier becomes a useful concept replacing the finite and contested notion of the boundary. This process of recognition, however, can have negative as well as positive ramifications, as we become aware of the complexity of the interactions possible at the new frontier. However, it is the ability to balance the moment of the frontier experience with the general sense of integrative histories of peoples that makes the frontier a useful category for the writing of the new Jewish history.

The frontier is, to use a poetic evocation as the German-language poet Hilde Domin did in an interview in the 1970s, a Jewish borderland. It was a way of seeing herself as a Jew as a "border dweller" and Jewish history as a *Grenzfall*, a case at the margins: "It is true," she wrote, "that I see the fate of the Jews as only the extremist case of the general. The specific, the marginal case (*Grenzfall*) is sublimated into fate, especially by the poets."[23] But it is at the real and at the imagined frontier that the shaping of Jewish identity takes place. Such a sense of the frontier as a contested space rather than as a border between constructed identities runs counter to Homi Bhabha's claim about the Jews as the force of cultural translation.[24] For Bhabha, the Jews are seen as one of the "wandering people who will not be contained within the *Heim* of the national culture and its unisonant discourse" (*Location of Culture*, 164). Instead, such peoples:

> are themselves the marks of a shifting boundary that alienates the frontiers of the modern nation. . . . They articulate the death-in-life of the idea of the "imagined community" of the nation; the worn-out metaphors of the resplendent national life now circulate in another narrative of entry-permits and passports and work-permits that at once preserve and proliferate, bind and breach the human rights of nation. (164)

Bhabha's notion of the frontier is suddenly no longer imagined but concrete. It is the border that is maintained as the illusionary mark of difference, rather than the frontier as the site of dispute and accommodation. It is a real border rather than an imagined frontier. On the other hand, discussions of the imagined border, such as that by Gloria Anzaldúa in her *Borderlands/La Frontera: The New Mestiza* and others already mentioned, have tended to romanticize the border as the ideal space of meeting and merging.[25] Both aspects are certainly present, but one should not be privileged over the other.

The border can also be the frontier where competition can lead to destruction and devastation, to the commission of abominable acts in the eyes of all parties. Terrible things can happen at the frontier—massacres, banishments, rapes, and murders. The destruction of the Amalechites, of the Jews of England, of the Native Americans in the expansion of European colonialism can all occur at the frontier. But it is in this liminal space that all parties are forced to understand and define themselves in the light of their experience of the other. It is not a space in which liminality is always rewarded by its movement to a new center with the forces of power now at the periphery. This view, the view of much multicultural argument over the past decade, simply constitutes a new center-periphery model with those who were powerless now redefined as the center of power.

Richard White's writing on the frontier can serve as a model for how such a history can be undertaken. White's greatest historical work is *The Middle Ground*.[26] This work began as a rather straightforward rewriting of North American Native history in the Great Lakes region. White, too, was surprised when he found the frontier a useful concept. In his detailed, often horrific, often fascinating account of the long eighteenth century in lower Canada and the adjacent British colonies to the South, the idea of a space of contest and accommodation is developed. His idea of the frontier as the middle ground, as the space of compromise, is helpful in shaping a new vision of Jewish history. For it neither privileges any group nor does it see a clear-cut distinction between victims and oppressors. All roles are relative and all roles can be reversed over time.

The middle ground in North American history is, of course, different from the numerous middle grounds of Jewish history. But the potential values and horrors of the compromise position with the confrontation between and among cultures and peoples can provide a new multivocal account of the histories of a people.

The frontier as imagined by White is not a pure space, an absolute answer to the center-periphery model of history. White's model is an attenuated center-periphery model that focuses on the distance from the presumptive center as a factor in the ability of the middle ground to serve as that place of accommodation and confrontation. Yet the center (London or Paris in White's history of the Great Lakes region from 1650 to 1815) truly vanishes in his account, while the real markers of the middle ground in his narrative are the languages spoken. Certainly English and French are the contesting languages, but it is the wide range of Native American tongues that dominate his account. Indeed, his marker of the mediator is the hybrid, which White defines in terms of the offspring of Europeans and Native Americans. Stories that replicate those of Abraham, Sarah, Abimelech, and Hagar constantly reappear in White's narrative of the frontier. In fact, the true hybrids, to use the term most favored in postcolonial theory, are those who can negotiate between languages. Language, as much as sexuality, is the marker of hybridity as well as the source of conflict. This is the true marker of the frontier in White's account.

I know that the middle ground is a controversial term and that my linking it with language will evoke a critical response. This Aristotelian term comes to play a central role in the construction of ideas of liminality. It is a term that shows up within Bruno Latour's work as the object of one of his critiques of the modern.[27] The middle ground is one of his answers to the "illusion" of the "totalitarian center" and its counterpart the "ridiculous" claims for the margins (124). He too understands the preoccupation with the hybrid as a fault of such a conceptualization of the center-periphery model: "the less the moderns think they are blended, the more they blend" (43). One assumes the reverse is also true. Here too the center-periphery model disguises its intent. Those constructing the modern, according to Latour, could have as one strategy "seized the middle ground, whose dimensions were continuing to expand. Instead of concentrating on the extremes of the work of purification, this strategy concentrated on one of its mediations, language" (62). For Latour, such a strategy lost the networked complexity of his understanding of how material and symbolic structures interact. He, however, misjudges how language and discourse reflect the problems of identity formation, enabling each of us to construct multiple worlds of words. Even Latour's critique of the middle ground and its appropriation of language is clothed in a language of confrontation rather than accommodation. It too holds the middle ground.

If there is a Jewish pendant to Latour's anxiety about the function of language or discourse as a contested space, it is Zygmunt Bauman's claim that the very culture of modernity is "a 'project' of postmodernity in a prodromal stage."[28] Jewish art and culture are the essential representation of the modern: being Jewish means, for Bauman, being avant-garde in all senses of the word. (This is Bauman's reworking of the notion that the Jews are a pariah nation in the Diaspora where they serve as a catalyst for change or a measure of change. This is his version of the argument as presented by Max Weber and Hannah Arendt [Momigliano, 171–7)]). Thus, the "Jewish struggle with modernity" is merely a by-product of "modernity's struggle with itself," according to Bauman (154). And, the language of the frontier, of the confrontation of the Jew and the other, comes to constitute "the seminal contribution of the obstreperous, critical and rebellious culture of modernity" (195). There is no Jewish particularism; it is all a function of the strains and claims of the modern. (This is very much in line with Gabriel Jospovici's desire to see the alienated language of the modern European Jew as a sign of the modern condition.) This is the romanticized version of the frontier that assumes each group's confrontation will be creative within the model of an avant-garde. But what if it is not Sigmund Freud and Georg Simmel and Franz Kafka that one takes as one's witnesses, but J. Robert Oppenheimer and Friedrich Gundolf and Walther Rathenau, the conservatives at the frontier, whose confrontation resulted in accommodation, or Gershom Scholem and Abraham J. Heschel, whose modernism is to be found within traditional religious forms of argument and language. It is not only "metonymic, iterative temporality" that is the counternarrative of the nation, as Homi Bhabha claims (55). Are these other voices not also representatives of this prodromal stage of postmodernity? Are they not hybrids of a not very exotic type? In *Displacements: Cultural Identities in Question*, Angelika Bammer has noted that the Diaspora experience may be one of mobility, plurality, alterity, but is eventually also one of fixation, of the need to settle upon certain symbols, of assimilation.[29]

It is vital to understand that the middle ground is not equivalent to the nomadic, seen by Gilles Deleuze and Félix Guattari as the definition of the modern Jewish experience. They sketch the process of identity formation in their description of "becoming-Jewish." They wrote in *A Thousand Plateaus*:

> Jews . . . may constitute minorities under certain conditions, but that in itself does not make them becomings. . . . Even Jews must become-Jewish (it certainly takes more than a state). But if this is the case, then becoming-Jewish necessarily affects the non-Jew as much as the Jew. Becoming-woman necessarily affects men as much as women. Conversely, if Jews themselves must become-Jewish . . . , it is because only a minority is capable of serving as the active medium of becoming, but under such conditions that it ceases to be a definable aggregate in relation to the majority. . . . Becoming-Jewish . . . therefore implies simultaneous movements, one by which a term (the subject) is withdrawn from the majority, and another by which a term (the medium or agent) rises up from the minority.[30]

This merging of the identity of the majority that defines and the minority that is defined and thus redefines the majority is a process of constant construction and reconstruction of identity.[31] Such identity transformations have been understood as being internal, purely psychological in their representation. "Becoming-Jewish," in the sense of Gilles Deleuze and Félix Guattari, is understood as a process of identity formation. And yet this too presents a problem, the problem of the loss of specificity in time.

In all of these critiques, the struggle with the modern comes to evoke and use the Jews and the problem of a Jewish historiographic model as the touchstone for the specific problems of the modern or the illusion of modernity. The Jews in each case are defined ahistorically rather than temporally. Here is where the error lies. For it is in the radical temporality of Jewish existence that one can find the answer to the atemporality and ahistorical nature of the center-periphery model. Who are the Jews? Those who understood themselves as Jews at specific moments in time. Does this definition change? It is constantly shifting and constantly challenged, which is why absolute boundaries *must* be constructed for the Jews within and without Jewish culture and ritual. The less possible a definition is, the more rigid it appears. This is true in Felix Theilhaber's and Bernard Wasserstein's complaints about the vanishing Jews of Europe[32] (one written substantially before, the other substantially after the Shoah); this is true within debates in Germany and Israel today about who the real Jews are. Over and over, one group comes to be defined as the authentic Jews.

On the frontier, it is vital to hear all of the voices—both those voices defined and self-defined as Jewish and those understood by the Jews as "other." R. Po-chia Hsia has shown how vital it is in the history of the Jews in early modern Germany to understand both sides of the history[33]; and any understanding of the Haskalah, the Jewish Enlightenment, and modern Israel needs both sides too. The sides are marked by the languages of the protagonists. And this language actually marks the frontier. It is the middle ground, the space in which confrontations take place—and, if

White's balanced account is any indicator, true horrors as well as accommodations take place on both sides. Horrors, because motivations are not comprehended; noble actions because the very fabric of the culture observed is never quite comprehended. Language serves as the marker.

Why do Jews in Central and Eastern Europe speak Yiddish as their Jewish secular language (as opposed to the liturgical language of Hebrew or the language of the population among whom they lived)? They speak Yiddish because in the Rhineland before ghettoization they spoke the German dialect of the area. They moved from whatever language they had brought with them from the south—whether Latin or Greek or Aramaic—to German because they were on the Roman frontier, a frontier marked by its distance from Rome. They spoke the language of their neighbors. When they moved to Poland and the east, they continued to speak German (or now proto-Yiddish) because it was a language of hegemonic value, given the role of the German knights in the east. This identification of Yiddish with German reappeared during World War I when German politicians wished to win Jews in Russia to their cause. It reappeared after 1989, when the claim was made that Yiddish-speaking Jews were indeed displaced Germans who should be able to claim German citizenship under the German parallel to Israel's Law of Return. The meanings attached to language shift based on their context.

This is also the pattern of the history of the Jews: the Jews are to be understood as a multiple yet single entity. Multiple because of the cultures manifested under that label and yet unitary because of the common archeology or cultural identity they believe they share—even those who are never self-consciously part of the Jews. This is not to say that the center-periphery model is wrong or even incomplete given its power, only that among the models for Jewish history, the frontier model with language as its central marker can have powerful, heuristic value. It is clear that neither one of these models are found in their pure state. The center-periphery model can be read as a frontier model, and the frontier can be understood as *merely* an isolated aspect of a center-periphery model. It is the tension that is of real interest.

It is not the real frontier, the actual land that concerns the new Western historians, but rather the fantasy topography of the frontier that Turner actually constructed. It is the frontier as that contested space beyond the world of the self, a frontier of fantasy. It is a notion of the frontier (as Francis Parkman's *History of the Conspiracy of Pontiac* shows) where one imagines oneself teleologically as the center and end of history and where one understands one's own physical position in the world as that cutting edge of (divine) history. Clearly, Parkman created his Pontiac as the Native American whom he needed for his dramatic confrontation between "world historical personalities" on the frontier. But Jewish history in the center-periphery model tends to provide such concrete figures in a similar manner. Sigmund Freud's Moses, in his *Moses and Monotheism*, becomes much the same type of surrogate for the Jews as a collective as Parkman's Pontiac is for the Native Americans. Such acts of concretization seem to be needed as long as one imagines a center, even the author's self as center.

To answer this move to the concrete, one must therefore imagine the frontier as a constructed, psychological space. It is the structure that underlies all of colonial expansion, whether cultural expansion from China into Japan, or the mercantile expansion of British might into Africa, North America, and India, or the political and cultural hegemony of America in the contemporary world. In each case, a frontier populated by indigenous people must be confronted in order to establish the identity of the group entering into the established order—and that established order can be "primitive" as in Francis Galton's Hottentots or can be "cultured," as in Marco Polo's Moguls. Such a frontier is seen, however, from only one narrative perspective. My sense of the frontier, like that of the new Western history, is one in which multiple voices can be articulated. Language as the medium and the stuff of dynamic interaction needs to be seen from both sides—the speakers of different languages, speech peculiarities, discourses come together and therefore all sets of texts become imperative in understanding the contact between and among groups.[34]

Such linguistic and cultural interaction and conflict takes place within the psyches of those crossing the frontier. It is the notion of violation and transcendence of boundaries that is inherent in such a construction of the frontier. No frontier exists unless this notion of violation is present. Thus, the notion of the frontier is that it seems to be inscribed on the land but is actually a narrative tradition superimposed on a landscape. It is defined by the very notion of violation and this notion can be read as positive or negative. It is a means of organizing the world, rather than the world itself. It creates the markers even if the markers rely on phenomena of the world. Language is the constant marker of difference for the frontier. Some at the frontier are understood to speak a language perceived as crude and deceptive. But it can be equally true that those at the frontier are imagined to speak a tongue understood as complex and revealing. The language of the other is not the language of the self.

The Jewish experience as imagined on such a frontier is thus complex; indeed, more complex than most. It is not the colonial or postcolonial experience as understood by contemporary theory, but it is certainly impacted by the notion of the frontier that haunts postcolonial theory. The borderlands are where Jews, like all people, perpetually live. The margin is defined by the presence of those who identify themselves as Jews or where Jews are imagined to dwell. Jews may accompany or create colonial expansion, whether cultural as in Hellenistic or Roman culture, or mercantile as with the European expansion, or cultural-political as with the globalization of American popular culture (such as films shaped by a Jewry at the U.S. frontier, California). America as the frontier is a space where various languages and discourses meet and match and transcend, as Marc Shell has commented.[35] This is not the America of Frederick Jackson Turner, but of a permanent frontier in which peoples enter and mix and change and confront one another, producing a constantly new and revitalizing culture.

Jews confront and are confronted by the inhabitants of each land, from medieval Britain to Poland to China to India to Palestine. The options open to them are defined in terms of the experience of the frontier, including imagining that the frontier no longer exists. The frontier can be either the golden paradise or the place of torment. It is a place of perpetual contact at the margins.

This is the Jewish construction of the frontier. It is to be found in models such as the commonplace about "land without people for a people without land." Here is the notion of the frontier without conflict that marked the fantasy of the Jewish desire for a space different from the frontier experiences in Europe. Such a notion of the Middle East marks the transgression of one frontier by Jews from another frontier experience—Europe, North America, South Africa—who imagine the Middle East as without the conflicts that marked their own experiences. The Zionist fantasy of Israel as the frontier is tied to language and in a most powerful manner. Theodore Herzl's Israel in his *Der Judenstaat* was to be a linguistic Switzerland, a compromise without conflict at the borders of his fantasy. All languages would be welcome there and all cultures from the other frontiers preserved with the sole exception of Yiddish. Yiddish was for Herzl the mark of the failure of the Jews at the old frontier. Although it was not German, it was the linguistic marker of the failure of the Jews to create a real cultural space. Thus, Jews who moved into the imagined space of Israel with the first and second *aliyah* (emigration) clearly could not identify with the language of the majority (Arabic) or with that of the colonial forces occupying the land (Turkish or English), but could relate to the language of a present minority, the Hebrew-speaking Jews. Hebrew becomes the identifying marker of Jewish particularity at the frontier. It is a language that is given virtually miraculous powers as the sign of Jewish cultural resurgence at this frontier, yet it is clear that Hebrew and Jewish identity are not interchangeable even here. With the rise of a Hebrew-speaking and -writing Arabic minority, the age of post-Zionism begins. For the magic nature of Hebrew as the new language of a new people gives way to the more utilitarian understanding of Hebrew as the language of a frontier experience, which produces boundary-crossers of a most complex nature. The construction of Dugri speech as the language of the Sabra, a language that was to capture the new psychology of the tough Jew at the frontier, now admits others than Jews into its pantheon of language use. Hebrew in a post-Zionist world has become a normal language, a language at the frontier space of accommodation and conflict, as Benjamin Harshav has recently noted.[36]

The model of accommodation and conflict at the frontier can be found in the acculturation of Jews in the Middle East today, as well as in the Rhine valley in the High Middle Ages and in modern North America. Such a conceptualization shows how language becomes a marker for the movement across the frontier and the establishment of a complex relationship with the inhabitants. Such movement does not have to integrate the Jews into frontier society. It can result in a self-conscious distancing of the Jews into rigidly defined communities, characterized by self-interest and delimited by hostility. It can also result in the destruction of the Jews or, if one evokes certain biblical moments, of those peoples with whom the Jews came into conflict at the frontier.

The temporal frontier as the topography of Jewish history has, as does the center-periphery model, a biblical model, if the model of the frontier is applied to a reading of biblical history from Abraham and Moses to the expansion of the kingdoms of

Judah and Israel into the frontier. Before the construction of Jerusalem, there is no center and therefore no periphery. Israel exists only retrospectively in the narrative of the Bible, as the center superimposed on the Abrahamic search for God. For it was "Abraham [who] planted a grove in Beersheba, and called there on the name of the Lord, the everlasting God. And Abraham sojourned in the Philistines' land many days" (Genesis 21: 33–4). As do we all.

PART I

REPRESENTING THE
SHOAH AT THE FRONTIER

CHAPTER ONE

THE FIRST COMIC FILM
ABOUT THE SHOAH

Jurek Becker and Cultural
Opposition within the GDR

FOR JEWS AFTER THE SHOAH, NO WORLD COULD HAVE
been more of a frontier experience with all of the horrors, advantages, and contradictions than occupied Germany after 1945. In
both the Western and Eastern zones of occupation, Jews found
themselves in a conflicted role with the creation of state socialism
in the Soviet zone after 1945 and again after 1949 in the German
Democratic Republic (the GDR). The conflict between communism, defined by the party as universalism, and a Jewish identity,
demonized in all of its forms as particularistic, marked this German frontier on which Jews did indeed function, especially within
the world of culture. The Jews who became part of this world returned from life in exile and from the camps. The *she'erit hapleyta*,
the remnant of the saved, some 200,000 Jews from the Jewish
communities of Central Europe were the core of the survivors.
There had been some 500,000 in the various camps and ghettos
before the beginning of the death marches west from the camps in

1945; 60 percent died on the marches.[1] This small fragment of the once flourishing Jewish life of Central Europe all but vanished among some six to nine million "displaced persons" (DPs) by 1946, who were ethnic Germans from Poland and Bohemia; forced laborers from throughout Europe; Russian soldiers who had fought for the Germans; peoples simply displaced by war and moving west before the Soviet army.[2] Officially there were no displaced persons in the Soviet zone of occupation, as the term refers only to those in the Western zones.[3] From among the exiles and the survivors came the generation of Jews who became part of the intellectual elite on the frontier that marked the boundary between the West and the East in the Cold War. By the 1960s, the Jewish writers—as different as the exile Stefan Heym, the hidden child Günter Kunert, and the daughter of Communist party returnees Barbara Honigmann—formed part of the covert cultural opposition to the official party views of the GDR.

The tale related here is one about a moment of contention on the frontier of the GDR. It is the tale of a development of a sense of opposition to the cultural norms of the state, a development that takes the form of a survivor of the Shoah defining himself as oppositional through the creation of the work of art that gives voice to the victims of the Shoah for the first time in the cultural world of the GDR.[4] It deals with the subtle creation of a film and a novel, both of which embody a sense of identity formation in the GDR as well as the personal reeducation of a member of the opposition, one of its major literary and film personalities, Jurek Becker. Becker was more than a member of the cultural elite; he was also the most visible Jewish survivor-author of that elite of the generation raised and educated in the GDR. He repeatedly changed identities, languages, political ideology. His is an exemplary case of a Jew on the frontier.

Jurek Becker, born in Lodz in 1937, had survived the Lodz ghetto, and was then sent with his mother to Ravensbrück-

Sachsenhausen in 1944. His mother died of tuberculosis. He was eventually placed in a United Nations Relief and Rehabilitation Administration children's camp where the Red Cross reunited him with his father, who had survived Auschwitz after the family was divided in 1944. After the Shoah and his move to Berlin, Becker's father observed over and over to his young son that he was simply more comfortable in Berlin: "It wasn't the Polish anti-Semites who lost the war."[5] Polish-speaking in his youth, Becker was raised as a German-speaking "young communist" in the Soviet sector of Berlin. He loyally belonged to the Communist Youth movement and strongly identified with the universalist claims of Marxism-Leninism as articulated under the Stalinist leader of the GDR, Walter Ulbricht. In the German Democratic Republic, he became the most important Jewish literary voice of the younger generation. Being "Jewish" in Becker's sense was an external label. The Beckers had neither religious affiliation with traditional Judaism nor any political affiliation with causes such as Zionism. The universalist claims of Marxism-Leninism made being Jewish one of the few ethnic identities not acceptable to a good communist.

Being Jewish became a public and political sign of a dual loyalty in a world in which the claims for a universal Marxist identity beyond national and religious definition permitted only one level of identification, and that was with the new state. It was a consequence of the establishment of a new socialist German identity in the GDR. This GDR was, at least after the beginning of the anti-Zionist campaign of the 1950s, incompatible with a Zionist identity, and all Jews were assumed to be Zionists. The impact of this view was powerful (in both the GDR and among the left in the FRG, the Federal Republic of Germany.) Thus, by the 1960s it was possible to state that there was no anti-Semitism in the GDR, for even Jews were forced to renounce Zionism, which became the catch-word for all the classic anti-Semitic stereotypes. No dual loyalty was permitted in the new socialist state. Becker, as late as

1977, dismissed the Zionist project with the rhetoric of the GDR, as Nazi-like and therefore criminal.[6] He withdrew this comment in 1996 as "exaggerated and false." He had come to understand that in this specific context anti-Zionism was anti-Semitism, as it did not permit the identification of oneself as a Jew in the public sphere of the GDR.

Jurek Becker's 1974 film *Jacob the Liar* was the first Jewish film about the Holocaust in the GDR. It was Jewish because its author (Becker) was understood as "Jewish" and the film focused solely on the Jewish aspect of the Shoah in Eastern Europe.[7] Directed by Frank Beyer, it was produced by DEFA (Deutsche Film-Aktiengesellschaft), the official studio of the German Democratic Republic, which produced over 750 feature films and countless documentaries and shorts between 1946 and 1992.[8] Major directors such as Slatan Dudow, Wolfgang Staudte, Kurt Maetzig, Konrad Wolf, as well as Frank Beyer worked for DEFA. In the United States, *Jacob the Liar* was nominated for an Academy Award as the best foreign film in 1977. Its worldwide reception was extremely positive and extremely broad.

How can Becker's process of writing in a state with which he strongly identified be understood as contributing to his movement from a loyal citizen and artist of the GDR to an oppositional figure? By its very nature, the very act of representing difference, in the form of Jewish characters and the Shoah, becomes an oppositional move. The Shoah was a moment in time that becomes in the GDR a silent space peripherally inhabited by Jews.[9] The state and the public responded to this work in its three incarnations: as an unmade film script, as a novel, and as a completed film. This provided Becker with a vocabulary within the state ideology of reeducation by which he could imagine himself as an oppositional voice engaged in the reeducation of the state and of the general population. His content, however, drew on his own experiences as a "victim of fascism."

Becker had thought about what opposition was as early as 1959 when he began to write a column on film criticism for the journal *tua res*. In 1956 students at Humboldt University in the GDR started a magazine, which was also distributed in the western sectors, called *tua res*, after a quote from Horace that it is in your interest, too, to put out the fire when your neighbor's wall is burning. It was edited by Hermann Kant, who later became a major official novelist in the GDR. Jurek wrote columns under the pseudonym given to him by Kant, "Lola Ramon," a name Jurek was very unhappy about.[10] He also distributed the magazine at the West Berlin universities during which the West Berlin police arrested him.[11] His account of this in his 1973 novel, *Misleading the Authorities*, has him defend himself against a young West Berlin policeman who arrests him, not through logical arguments but by simply knocking him down. The protagonist thus frees himself to "escape" back to the safety of "Berlin—the Capital of the GDR," wondering that his very act mirrored the films he saw in the movie houses of West Berlin.[12] Acting like the movies becomes part of the way that Becker understands himself. (And, of course, this notion of the false face, the merely acting like something you are not, is a central part of the repertoire of German anti-Semitism. Indeed, one of the often-repeated questions in Weimar Germany was, why were Jews such good actors?)

What Becker chose to write about in *tua res* was the film politics of West Berlin. Becker's position then and there was clearly socialist and antagonistic to the public film policies of the West German government. But his sense of what criticism had come to mean in that environment can help frame his later views:

> It is not sufficient simply to be opposed to something. The scale of opposition runs from being obstinate to being indignant. This scale is too crude to express the necessity of not being in agreement. This necessity is only ever partially understood. One

negative side effect is that when one obsesses about this one easily becomes labeled as an "angry young man." Purely destructive
criticism, not unlike griping, gives rise to the suspicion that the
critic does not know any better. Such critics seem to have no or
only a vague sense of the changing circumstances (which is
probably the case). Or they refrain from any constructive criticism with positive countersuggestions on the basis of pragma-
tism or from a sense of personal valor (or fear). Or they write
out of pure joy in (a limited) opposition against the trivial and
quotidian, seeing this as a pleasant occupation, as other people
like to fish or look in a mirror. It is with such critics as it is with
many other prophets: either you kill them or they kill you.

　　Few critics, if I can so say, have the slightest sense of reality.
Such critics should hope to remedy through their revelations
such misunderstandings. The point of most criticism is that
while the present state of things is to be bemoaned, one would,
if one tried to attack it, become an *enfant perdu* (lost child), because one cannot really do anything to remedy them. Resigna-
tion is appropriate for these clever critics.[13]

Becker does not see criticism as negative but as constructive, as
reeducative. He is able to see these West German voices as trans-
parently vacuous: "There is something comic about opinions. One
needs only to repeat them accurately in order to destroy them." It
is the accurate reproduction that is the best criticism, a view es-
poused by earlier critics such as Karl Kraus. Becker sees the artistic as well as the creative process as rooted in individual vision and
commitment: "The true artist must seek a path in order to carry
out his individual monomania. In other words, the collective
should be the means to hide his schizophrenia. But precisely in the
collective does this appear most clearly." Thus, it is the voice of
the artist that articulates the desires of the collective. But for
which collective can the artist speak? The socialist state in which
all art is perceived as being equal or only in older collectives, such

as the one that he had been assigned to by history? Can Becker only speak as a Jew?

In the spring of 1963, at the age of 26, Becker had begun drafting the first film script called *Jacob the Liar* for Frank Beyer. Beyer's earlier film *Spur der Steine* (*Trace of Stones*) vanished after a week in the cinemas. Political considerations in the GDR in 1966 following the domination of the eleventh Plenum of the Central Committee of the Socialist Unity Party (SED), the ruling party of the GDR, by antireform forces inhibited any cultural thaw in the GDR, such as that represented by Beyer's film. But Becker's screenplay was to be filmed after the withdrawal of *Spur der Steine* in spite of Beyer's having fallen out of favor. Beyer had intended to film the script in Krakow, but the Polish studios refused to film it once they saw the story. Becker—like Ulrich Plenzdorf, whose film script *Das Leiden des Jungen W.* (*Sorrows of Young W.*) was also left unfilmed and was then turned into an oppositional novel in 1972—then decided to redo this script and transform it into his first novel.

In the GDR, the novel had a greater impact as an agent of social opposition and change than did the cinema, which was seen, even by writers and directors, as more of an extension of state power and socialist ideology. In 1968 Becker was made a member of the state union of authors, the *Schriftstellerverband*, as a film writer. He presented a chapter from his novel that year in a collected volume (*Neue Text* 7) as his literary debut. Suddenly the scriptwriter was a novelist with all of the status that label brought in the GDR. The writing of the novel was both his response to the cancellation of the film as well as a means to establish his credentials as a member of the intelligentsia of the GDR.

Becker's project of making a film about the Shoah with a Jew as its protagonist and written in a comic mode was an anomaly. Films about fascism and its opponents or supporters had a central role in the reeducation of the GDR citizen as a good socialist. It was used as a means of dealing not only with the Nazi past but also with the West German present. The FRG became a surrogate state for Nazi Germany. The filmmakers, too, were simply seen as "citizens of the Workers' and Peasants' State," without any ethnic or religious or cultural specificity. The idea of such a film being written by a Jew—for in the GDR, as Becker and his father were officially designated "victims of fascism"—had specific positive (and therefore potentially exploitative) implications. One had social advantages, a pension, and visible status in the society of the GDR, a sort of affirmative action for survivors, but one was also perpetually labeled as the victim.

In early feature films in the GDR, there had been a few exceptions to the rule that one did not represent the "victims of fascism" but rather the heroes of socialism. No novels *centrally* about the Jewish experience in the Shoah had been created in the GDR by the 1960s. There were certainly none about the experience of the Jews in the East, in what were now the "brother socialist countries." There were a few exceptions in the realm of the early feature film in the Soviet zone and in the early GDR that recorded the impact of Nazism on *German* Jews. Kurt Maetzig's *Marriage in the Shadows* (*Ehe im Schatten*) (1947), based on Hans Schweikart's novella *It Won't Be So Bad* (*Es wird schon nicht so schlimm*), shows how the Nazis force a Jewish actress to give up her career and insist that she divorce her German husband. When he is ultimately unable to protect her, the two resort to suicide. The novel was based on the actual triple suicide on November 7, 1941, of the Berlin Volksbühne actor Joachim Gottschalk, his wife, and his daughter. Like so many of these "Jewish" films, it reflected a strongly autobiographical moment. Maetzig's own mother committed suicide in 1944 rather than be deported to certain death in the East.

Erich Engel's *The Affaire Blum* (1948), based on a well-known 1926 murder trial with Dreyfus-like overtones, also represents a

German post-Shoah reflection on anti-Semitism and the pattern of thought and action that led to the Shoah. Blum, a Jewish manufacturer living in Weimar Germany, is falsely accused of killing his bookkeeper. Even when the real killer's identity becomes evident, the state prosecutor refuses to accept Blum's innocence. The film explores German reaction to the trial and investigates the relationship between the legal system, anti-Semitism, and fascism, providing insight into the historical context that allowed Nazism to flourish.

Later in the history of DEFA, the theme of the Shoah, or at least the theme of anti-Semitism as an aspect in the German past, reappears in a modified manner. In the work of perhaps the best known director in the GDR, Konrad Wolf—the (Jewish) brother of the head of the GDR's spy agency, Marcus Wolf—the Shoah appears in *Stars* (*Sterne*) (1959). *Stars* deals with Jewish survival in Nazi-occupied Europe and presents a love story between a German soldier and a Bulgarian-Jewish girl who is deported to Auschwitz. In addition, in 1961 Wolf filmed a 1935 play by his father, Friedrich Wolf, *Dr. Mamlock's Escape* (*Doktor Mamlocks Ausweg: Tragödie der westlichen Demokratie*), a dramatization of Arthur Schnitzler's "comedy" of assimilated Jewry, *Professor Bernardi* (1912). The film, titled *Professor Mamlock*, starred Jurek Becker's lifelong friend Manfred Krug. *Professor Mamlock* deals with anti-Semitism and the problematic position of assimilated Jews in the prewar period. In all cases, the representation of the actual events of the Shoah, of the concentration camps, of the ghettos, of the death camps, is avoided. The "Jewish problem" is rooted in the capitalist past of imperial or Weimar Germany. Jews in the Shoah could be victims to be rescued, but they could not be actors in their own stories.

In novels about the Jews of Europe, written to sketch the world that led to the Shoah, the Jews remain marginal. In perhaps the most striking avant-garde fiction on this topic, the Shoah too seems to vanish. So also in Johannes Bobrowski's *Levin's Mill* (1964), a historical novel set in the nineteenth century and later filmed by Horst Seemann for DEFA (1980), the Jews are distanced into the past. In the realm of fiction, Franz Fühmann's *Jew's Auto* (1962), a first-person account of a series of days in the life of a "normal German" spanning twenty years, the Jew is seen literally on the horizon line of the historical picture. Even Jewish writers, such as Günter Kunert, had little better luck. Kunert's novel about the repression of the Holocaust in postwar Germany, *In the Name of the Huts* (*Im Namen der Hüte*), published in West Germany by Hanser in 1967, was only able to be published in the GDR by the Eulenspiegel Press in 1976.

Such an avoidance of any direct representation of the Shoah in the GDR is a reflection of the claim in the socialist reconstruction of the past that the anti-Semitism of the Nazis was a marginal aspect of their ideology. There are several DEFA films of the 1950s and 1960s about the aftermath of the Holocaust, such as Janos Veizi's *Incident at Benderath* (*Zwischenfall in Benderath*) (1956), which used an actual anti-Semitic incident at a West German gymnasium to criticize that country's insufficient dealing with the past (*Vergangenheitsbewältigung*). Joachim Hasler's film, *Chronicle of a Murder* (*Chronik eines Mörders*) (1964), in which Angelika Domröse plays a Holocaust survivor who murders a former camp official who has become mayor of her West German town, likewise places the legacy of fascism in the West.

Few DEFA films actual dealt with the Jewish question as directly as did in at least two West German films. Both Artur Brauner's film *Morituri* (1947), based on his own experiences in the Lodz ghetto, and Marek Goldstein's and Herbert Fredersdorf's *The Way is Long* (*Der Weg ist Lang*) (1948), written by Israel Becker, about a survivor from the deportations to Auschwitz, were not critical successes. A similar topic also haunted the great actor Fritz Kortner's film *The Call* (*Der Ruf*) (1949). One of the so-called "ruin films," it captured the sense of the powerful presence of fascism and anti-Semitism in the immediate postwar world. A film about the return of Jewish exiles from America, the very question of what German anti-Semitism comes to mean to Jewish thinkers is placed centrally in the context of the Western zones of Germany, where the film is set. But these films were made by Jews and dealt specifically with the fate of the Jews.

In 1963 when Becker returned to Lodz for the first time to begin to research his film script, *Jacob the Liar*, the very act of imagining a Jewish film about the Shoah as conceived by a "victim of fascism" was an undertaking fraught with serious questions. The film was based on an idea created earlier by Becker. The biographical origins of the film are *not* specially Becker's own childhood memories of the Lodz ghetto. He claims that in the 1960s he had few such memories and that only fragmentary ones returned after that. He seems to have been inspired by his father, Max Becker, whose views of his own adult experiences in Lodz and Auschwitz shaped his son's vision. Max wanted Jurek to write of the bravery of the Jews in the ghetto, specifically the tale of a man who hid a radio and was the source of inspiration to his friends. Becker decided to do exactly the opposite. His father's response was: "You can tell the stupid Germans what it was like in the ghetto; you can't tell me, I was there. I was a witness. You cannot tell me silly stories. I know that it was different."[14] For the audience in the GDR (and the rest of the world), Becker's film was an appropriate (read: comic) response to the Shoah, but not necessarily for his father (whose death in 1972 precluded his actually seeing the final film). Indeed, Becker noted, his father did not speak to him for a year after the novel was published.[15]

The initial film based on Becker's script was not made. The script was submitted to the Deputy Minister of Culture Wilfried Maaß by DEFA for approval on February 9, 1966, and approved on February 22, 1966.[16] Given the complexity of the internal politics in the ministries, this was done extremely quickly. The proposal was accompanied by a recommendation from a specialist. It stated that the script was felt to be too "full of a humanistic spirit rather than indicating the specifics of a spirit of socialist humanism" according to Dr. Jahrow, who was the official evaluator of the film.[17] After some negotiation between the head of the studio production and the division of film of the Ministry of Culture, the film was approved, in spite of its emphasis on the "general humanistic, antifascist ideal." The final evaluation stressed that Becker should develop the script in the light of "the specifics of a socialist realistic aesthetic" and stress the importance that the story "gesture toward the forward-looking forces."[18] The little girl and the Soviet soldier who, mute in his bravery, holds her hand, made the film imaginable, even with its emphasis on the Jews of the East. (One must add here that this ending was also seen by the DEFA studio director in charge as needing to be checked for "historical correctness and truth."[19] In other words, with an eye to using history in a specific type of reeducation.)

Becker's initial script, his reworking of this script as a novel, and the second script, which diverges more from the first script than from the novel, gestured toward this in explicitly making the news on the radio the location of the Soviet army as it moved toward the West. But in general, the film worked against all of the expectations of the heroic genre. It stressed the little man rather than the hero. In his 1969 screenplay for the film *My Zero Hour*, the hero, Corporal Hartung, begins as a rather apolitical working-class corporal in the Wehrmacht who is converted to communism and then volunteers to kidnap his former commanding officer. Based on the autobiography of Karl Krug and starring Manfred Krug (no relation), it recounted the adventures of the Russian prisoner of war Corporal Hartung who went behind the German lines on the Eastern Front in 1943 to kidnap his abusive com-

manding officer. The officer, portrayed as vicious and mean, ordered Hartung at the opening of the film to carry off an unex-
ploded bomb that had been dropped close to his headquarters.
When he hears the explosion in the distance, he dismissed Hartung, whom he assumed to have died carrying the bomb, as "not a
good German." Indeed, this was the label for all the other Germans in the film. Hartung, in his collaboration with the humanistic Soviets (and their German political officers) comes to represent
the "good Germans."

Hartung moves from a marginal little man to a hero. Jacob
clearly never can achieve this status because he can never be the
master of his fate. It is not conviction but the press of events that
moves him to action. Heroism is never the quality that the audience ascribes to him. What is comic is precisely the qualities ascribed to the little man *in extremis* who can only act to ameliorate
the suffering about him but cannot act to alter the randomness of
the Shoah.

Beyer's film of *Jacob the Liar* was planned and scheduled. It
was to be filmed in Poland, indeed near Krakow where *Schindler's
List* was filmed decades later At the beginning of July 1966 the
Polish authorities acknowledged that there was free space in their
studios there and that the film could be scheduled.[20] Three weeks
later, the authorities in Poland informed the DEFA producers
that there was suddenly no space available because of the demand
for production space from the Soviet Union. What had happened
in the meantime is that they had seen Becker's script. As Frank
Beyer later commented, a film about Jews in the East, even
though not specifically in Poland, that was sympathetic to the
Jewish perspective simply was inconceivable in communist
Poland which regularly used anti-Semitism in the form of anti-
Zionism against its own citizens.[21] On July 27, 1966, the film was
canceled. Becker was paid for the script but it was struck from the
1966 budget. This was not that unusual, but Becker's need to

have control, especially of this story, was extraordinary. He sat down and did what other writers in the GDR did when their scripts were rejected and they felt they had a story to tell. He sat down and rewrote the film script into his first novel. In the GDR, novels had a different mode of reception. Films were understood as mass culture, the novel as high culture. Becker's novel appeared in 1969 and has since been translated into 20 languages. It created a literary career for Becker, who to that time had been known only as an author of film scripts, and through it he achieved worldwide fame. He was awarded the Heinrich Mann Prize of the GDR's Academy of Art, the Swiss Charles Veillon Prize, and the Literary Prize of the City of Bremen. And in 1974 the DEFA finally decided to let Frank Beyer make a film version of the novel based on a highly revised script by Becker. It was that film that was nominated for an Academy Award.

The novel was a success because of its seemingly realistic representation of the central questions of the Shoah cast into a comic narrative frame. But it is the question of seriousness, which should most concern us here. In state socialism the memory of fascism is serious; the memory of the past is heroic. Here, Max Becker's demand for a tale about a heroic Jew is of importance: first, the desire to tell the story for the Jews, but especially to tell that story within the traditional heroic role that the Jews were rarely if ever cast after the war. Victims were not heroes. And the tales of Jewish heroism, as in the Warsaw ghetto uprising, were only marginally part of the narrative of state socialism. The contrast was somber, heroic, and serious. Nazis, as in the communist writer Bodo Uhse's *Lieutenant Bertram* (1943), one of the classic antifascist novels read in the GDR, could be the stuff of satire in the GDR, but neither the victims nor the defenders of freedom and state socialism could be represented in this manner.

In the culture of the GDR, the Jews as victims of the Shoah were present but in very specific ways. Much as in West Germany (and, indeed, in the United States) the Jewish aspect of the Holocaust was marginalized or folded into the general question of fascism and its horrors immediately after the end of the war. And yet Becker turned the expectations concerning reeducation of the antifascist film against itself. Here, the reeducation was to make the Germans in the GDR see the complexity of a single life destroyed by fascism, rather than being appalled by the horrendous toll of dead and the overwhelming horrors of the camps.

THE FILM

Jacob the Liar is a film about the perils of belief and about the dangers of reeducation cast into the world of the Shoah. Set in an unnamed Eastern European ghetto run by the Germans, both the novel and the film tell the story of Jacob Heym (played by Vlastimil Brodsky), the owner of a small restaurant, who seems to be the classic schlemiel. One evening, seemingly after curfew, he is seized by a German guard. He is ordered to the German police station in the ghetto for his "appropriate punishment." In the police station he overhears by chance a radio broadcast providing information about the location of the Russian front. Rather than being killed, as he expects, Heym is thrown out of the police station. He makes his way home, and the next day, in order to stop one of his fellow workers from an action that would certainly result in his death, he informs him of the location of the front. The young man does not believe that Jacob had heard the news at the police station. Only when Jacob "admits" to having a hidden radio, an item banned in the ghetto, is the truthfulness of his statement accepted. This information, even more than that about the Russian front, is important in creating a sense of hope.

The knowledge of the radio provides a ray of hope in the ghetto, and Jacob becomes the source of this hope in a collapsing world. His is a seemingly constructive opposition, not an angry one. Because of his claim to have a radio, the suicides in the ghetto suddenly stop. The very belief in the possibility of rescue enables individuals to live each day in some sort of hope. Jacob had taken in Lina (Manuela Simon), a child abandoned when her parents are seized by the Nazis and transported to the east. In the pivotal scene in the movie, Heym enacts a radio story hour for her. It is the story of the sick princess who asks for a cloud in order to cure her ailments. A young boy comes to her after all have failed and asks her what clouds are made of ("cotton batting") and how large they are ("as large as my pillow"). He then gives the sick princess a "cloud," and she dances off with him, in her nightclothes marked with a *Judenstern* (yellow star). Laughter is possible in this moment that time is suspended, and the act of listening to the fantasy radio places both characters outside of time and space. Radio is at this moment a source not of news but of comfort. It is the possibility of engendering hope for the moment, without any promise of eventual resolution. The fairy tale is indeed the key to this use of laughter as the momentary respite from horror, rather than its resolution. The audience's laughter that results during this scene is as much generated by Jacob's self-deception in believing that he can trick the child as it is in the juxtaposition between his dreamy memories of the past and the crude present. The seeming worldliness of the child, whom we in the audience assume wants to hear the fairy tale even knowing that there is no radio, stands at the center of our ability to laugh.

Listening to the radio was one of the comforts of life as it had been in Europe before the war, before the ghetto. It had become part of the culture of the day. Portraits of radio listeners such as that of Max Radler in 1930, or of Kurt Günther in 1927, or most extraordinarily the nude "Homo sapiens Listening to the Radio" in Kurt Weinhold's 1929 image captured the centrality of the radio experience for the prewar world. Nazi films, such as Eduard von Borsody's feature film *Request Hour* (*Wunschkonzert*) (1940), which begins at the Berlin Olympics in 1936 and centers on the popular radio program, echoed this fixation after the beginning of the war. But in the ghetto, especially in Litzmannstadt, the German name for the ghetto in Lodz, the radio took on a very special meaning. The Germans forbade Jews from possessing radios, but the radio did not vanish. In 1942, for example, there was suddenly word of potatoes coming into the ghetto. And the word was spread, according to the contemporary documents, by the "radio," the ghetto term for gossip. Over and over in letters and documents buried in 1943 and uncovered after the war are references to this means of communication, as important to the ghetto as the actual radio was to prewar Europe and to Nazi Germany, but for very different reasons. It was the source not so much of information as of hope, as most of the "radio reports" turned out to be false.[22] In the GDR it was television that served this purpose. Television provided the corrective (or the falsity) of Western culture for all but those few unable to receive it. It was the media, such as film, that provided a test for the validity of a system.

In Jacob's world, the children's program he mimics is a solace for the child as is the news for the adults. The Nazis continue to clear the ghetto, and Jacob, the child, and the rest of the inhabitants find themselves on a train headed east toward the death camps. The impossibility of a happy end is clear. The laughter of the child (and the audience) at the fairy tale reveals to the audience that her laughter had been built on a false premise of knowing. The image of the blue sky and the floating clouds seen from the cattle car in which she and Jacob are being transported to the death camps is the movie's final image. In the film, Lina is not actually fooled by Jacob's claim about the nonexistent radio. She looks behind the wall to see whether or not the radio is there. There she sees Jacob acting out all the parts, even humming the parts of the orchestra. And yet, in her knowledge her innocence is preserved. The final sequence in the movie picks up on the theme of the fairy tale told on Jacob's radio—the tale of the sick princess who asks to have a cloud in order to get well. In the cattle car on her way to the camp, Lina asks whether the story of the princess is true, whether one can be cured by cotton batting. Jacob in his adult (and nonschlemiel) voice says that is not the point of the story. For the princess asked for something she could not have, a cloud, and was given something that she could receive, cotton. It is a symbol of hope and belief, according to Jacob. The film concludes with Lina turning to Jacob and asking— "clouds *are* made of cotton? Aren't they?" The innocence of the child is preserved even in the child's knowledge of the realities of the world. And the audience's laughter at the ironic knowledge shown by the child about the realities of the world as reflected in our awareness of her consciousness of Jacob's fraud is suddenly undermined. Not knowing what a radio is, she has taken Jacob's act as the real radio. The realities of the camps, including death, are both within her awareness and beyond it, as they were for everyone to one degree or another. The reality of the adult is in no way the reality of the child, which is preserved even in the most extreme situation. The unstated knowledge of the audience is of the potential for the inevitable outcome. At the conclusion, Lina will certainly die in the camps. Her cotton clouds will not provide any succor from the brutality of the Shoah, in spite of the audience's expectations.

This scene has a double function in reeducation. It provides a critique of the naïve assumption of knowledge, but this assumption is as true of the claims of the media to be the conduits of truth in the West and the East during the cold war. The child—here the ideal viewer or listener—is not deceived by the claims of the medium. She knows that it is Jacob behind the wall creating the truth on the radio. And we acknowledge her realization of that deception. It is clear that Becker's claim is not aimed at the GDR or at the FRG, but at the falsity of the artificial world that it was necessary to construct in the ghetto. But this ghetto surrounded by its wall with its guards is as much the GDR as it is the FRG.

The themes of *Jacob the Liar* began to shape Becker's own life. With the popularity of the book and the subsequent film, he laughed at Walter Ulbricht's claim that there was no press censorship in the GDR. He stopped subscribing to the official party newspaper, *New Germany.* To get news about the world outside and inside, he watched and listened only to Western TV and radio. When his son Nikolaus would come home from school, he included him in watching and listening to the forbidden broadcasts. He told him if he was asked about this in school not to lie. He began to rethink the role of the Berlin Wall as a mark of the isolation of the GDR. The wall about the ghetto signified a certain type of isolation, one that was dangerous to the inhabitants. The wall in this sense was no longer around West Berlin, but around the GDR. The idea that the GDR was a type of huge ghetto in which the need for an actual radio really existed and that you listened to Western broadcasts, including the BBC, in order to find out what was actually happening in your immediate neighborhood became clear to him. If you listened and knew about the world, then you had an obligation not to lie about it. Its language, like the language of the radio that Jacob heard in the commandant's office, seemed to be convincing. You knew the words, but you also knew that they meant something very different if they were spoken in the West, rather than in the East. You were required to be straightforward and admit to listening to it, even if no one believed you.

The medium is the message. In Becker's second novel, *Misleading the Authorities,* his protagonist's father buys at his mother's urging a very expensive television, as they both spend much of their time at home. Unspoken is what program they will watch. When Becker's friend, the "half Jewish" poet Günter Kunert, wanted to mislead the authorities about why he was attracted to a woman living in the West, he claimed it was her radio that attracted him, "a really cool radio, with push buttons and a magic eye."[23] All of the GDR (with the exception of Dresden that could not receive it) watched West German television. This meant that there was also a medium that did, indeed, present an alternative message. And the clash of these two worlds, these two accounts of reality, was nowhere clearer than at 7 P.M. each night when on competing channels in West and East television appeared "The Sandman," a program for children that told fairy stories. The song that accompanied them was known to everyone in West and East alike: "I am the sandman, every child knows me. And when I come, I say: 'into bed quickly!'" ("Ich bin der liebe Sandmann, mich kennt jedes Kind. Und komm' ich, dann sag' ich: 'Ins Bettchen—geschwind!'") Even fairy tales were political during the Cold War. The media competed for the hearts and the minds of the children on each side of the wall. They were assumed to be able to understand the advantages and disadvantages of both systems by simply flipping the channel (albeit in secret). For Becker, this became a family activity and also underlies the complex account of the perception of reality in *Jacob the Liar*.

Suddenly what was a novel of the past becomes a description of the present. While *Jacob the Liar* was finished before the invasion of Czechoslovakia, it came to be read through that experience. What suddenly emerges is a model that provides a reading in 1968 of the frame of the novel, a test case for Becker's post-1968 view of the GDR. That the novel (and the subsequent film) is post-1968 is an historical accident, but as with all accidents, not without meaning.

Becker's final film script provides the basis for a critique of all ideologies that claim a true account of the world by presenting the means of seeing how ideologies deform belief systems and by understating the function of the media in these systems. Here his claim is indeed "universal," as the censor stated, but also "oppositional and critical" as he himself had stated in his earlier film review in 1959. Like Ulrich Plenzdorf, who reverts to German classical literature in the form of Goethe's novel to present an analogous critique, Becker employs the Shoah and the world of the Nazis. While Becker was struggling with the recrafting of the first film script into the novel, Reiner Kunze (1966) wrote his poem on the problem of censorship:

Von der notwendigkeit der zensur	On the necessity of the censor
Retuschierbar ist Alles	One can retouch Everything
Nur das negativ nicht In uns.[24]	Only not the negative In us.

The rewriting of history is for Kunze and Becker not only possible but also likely. They had seen it already happen twice, both under the Nazis and following the fall of Stalin. What seemed to remain, however, was the sense of blame felt by all, the helplessness felt by the artist in the face of an acknowledgement of the deformation of history, and the changing role of the creative artist. Becker attacked this sense of the negative within the artist through a new medium for the GDR, the comic, and specifically the Jewish aspect of the comic.

THE RESISTANCE OF THE COMIC

Becker's choice of a comic approach to the theme of the Shoah was not accidental. He had written a number of feature films for DEFA before, many of them were somewhat lighter fare. For this film, he literally went into the archives. He returned to Lodz for the first time, found his own family's entries in the various ghetto archives, spoke extensively with survivors. He wanted, he wrote, to distinguish between reality and fantasy and to know when he was transgressing that boundary. He wanted to be able to "compose" the variants in the stories himself, rather than falling into simple errors.[25]

The film was finally made by DEFA in 1974 as a joint production with GDR TV, based on a new screenplay version of the novel written by Becker and directed by Frank Beyer. The film was awarded the National Prize Second Class (1975) in the GDR, was the first GDR film shown in the Berlinale, and received the only American Academy Award nomination for a film from the GDR. Becker was also aware that the film and (by extension) the novel were texts of the late 1960s and the early 1970s. In an interview in the GDR weekly *Der Sonntag* (*Sunday*), of April 20, 1975, he commented that such a film would have been seen as impossible five years after the war. "Immediately after the war the observer would have seen such a treatment of this theme as blasphemy. I believe that our tale demands a high degree of knowledge. I can approach people with a tale like this only after they have been bombarded with information about that time for twenty or thirty years. In other words, for someone who knows nothing about what had happened then, this is an inappropriate text." Becker's sense of the film in 1975 is that it does constitute some type of "reaction formation" to his earlier experiences. The interviewer notes this reaction formation is found, according to Becker, in the ironic voice and is the key to what made the novel and the film different from the wide range of socialist films dealing with fascism. Indeed in April and May 1975, the GDR held a film festival of "anti-imperialist films," among them *Jacob the Liar* (*Jakob der Lügner*), throughout the entire country. The only film with any sense of irony and self-reflection was Becker's.

Why did Becker choose the comic as his mode of representing the Shoah? Certainly one biographical reason is as a response to the silencing in the GDR of the voices representing the Jewish component in Nazi atrocities. Jews were often listed in terms of their national identity (as Russians, or Poles, or Germans), and the specific Jewish (anti-Semitic) aspect of the Shoah was repressed. This silencing forced Becker to create a "talking Jew," the narrator who is in no way comic, who tells the life of Jacob. Then the comic moments become the problem of classic comedy: the misperception, purposeful or not, of the world. The rumors about the radio and the lies that a single truth heard on a radio cause Jacob to make are part of this misperception. The narrator, trying to string together a story in which he knows that truths and lies are hopelessly confused, is serious, even tragic in his narration. In the culture of the GDR, the Jews as victims of the Shoah were present, but in very specific ways. Even more than in West Germany (and, indeed, in the United States) before the early 1960s, the Jewish aspect of the Holocaust was marginalized or folded into the general question of fascism and its horrors immediately after the end of the war. Becker uses humor as a means of grabbing his audience's attention and lowering their guard for something new. He claimed that it was a means of overcoming the defensiveness of his viewers in the GDR who expected only certain types of tales about German fascism, and those tales told in a very specific way. Humor was unexpected in this context. Also, Becker needed to deal with this expectation as he began to think of himself as a writer, but at first at least a writer for the movies. He attacked this sense of the split consciousness within the artist through the medium of the comic. The comic was always an acceptable weapon for the weak, but it was also a means of control by the strong.

There is a second, contemporary cause for Becker's sense of outrage at breaking the taboo on telling such a tale. For Becker, the Prague Spring and its destruction by Warsaw Pact troops on August 21, 1968, presented a context for a reading of the novel and the planned film. From January 5, 1968, to April 17, 1969, Alexander Dubcek, the first secretary of the Communist Party of Czechoslovakia, had led a reform movement that was characterized by an opening of cultural freedom unparalleled in the Eastern block after World War II. It was especially marked during the early months of 1968 by a greater freedom of expression given to the Czechoslovakian media. Indeed, it was this cultural freedom that started Becker rethinking his relationship to "real existing socialism" in the GDR. The troops of the GDR seemed most prominent, given the memories of the Nazi invasion of Czechoslovakia. This was the moment of Becker's "break in his relationship with the GDR."[26] He was no longer simply a loyal citizen of the GDR, the film writer employed by the state to write amusing, time-killing tripe. He suddenly saw himself as an outsider and the socialist state—a state that promised him a strong identity as a GDR citizen, rather than as a Jew—as the father that failed. Retrospectively, the GDR became a problem for him rather than a solution.

A report of August 26, 1968, to the Stasi noted that on August 23 Becker and his wife discussed the situation in Prague with an "unofficial source" who reported it in detail.[27] The source was quite surprised about the vehemence that the turn in Becker's politics had taken as "Becker's political view appeared surprisingly quickly, because he had always spoken correctly before." His views were clearly expressed in the report and certainly parallel his own later accounts. He stated to anyone that would listen that the invasion of Czechoslovakia marked the beginning of the end for the Warsaw Pact as Rumania, he believed, would leave the Warsaw Pact because of it. More than just destroying an alliance of progressive states, the USSR destroyed with this act the worldwide communist movement. Richard Nixon rode the wave of anti-communism to win the U.S. presidential election that year. Becker believed that the invasion violated the ability of the people to determine their own political direction. The people stood behind Alexander Dubcek, unlike, it is implied, the citizens of the GDR behind Ulbricht (who, one might add, met with Dubcek shortly before the invasion).

Even more important is how this discussion shaped Becker's sense of his own identity. Following the anti-Zionist rhetoric of the GDR, he started to question how one could judge Israel and Vietnam when one undertakes aggression oneself. Israel is really no different in its relationship to the Palestinians than the GDR is to the Prague Spring. He saw himself as a citizen of the GDR, but now this identity was drawn into question. As citizens of the GDR "we" have to have another identity when we travel to Czechoslovakia. All through his attack, Becker spoke of the "Russians," not the Soviet Union. It was the Russians who invaded Czechoslovakia as the Germans had decades before. And he called the Russians SS men. Retrospectively, the GDR becomes a problem rather than a solution.

EXPECTATIONS

The socialist hero is never a comic figure. The notion of the Jew in this role is an older one in German culture, both philo- and anti-Semitic. The Jew as the marginal little man, whose qualities do not include heroism and who is tossed by fate, is a standard trope; it is the image of the schlimazel in Jewish folklore. Becker uses this figure to soften the demarcations between the victims, passive like the Jewish baby in Buchenwald who figured centrally in Frank Beyer's *Naked Among Wolves* (*Nackt unter Wölfen*) (1963), and the brave antifascist (who is rarely if ever self-consciously identified as a Jew in the DEFA films). For Becker, the Shoah was the world devoid of directed meaning. It was a world in which randomness dominated the potential of any meaningful action. Laughter was a sign of the ability for the individual to act and to effect only the most minor of changes, changes which, however, enable individuals, if only for a moment, to survive as human beings. Even the comic figure of the Jew, as appropriated by Becker, can be recast in this mold.

The persuasive power of the initial script of *Jacob the Liar* rested on the simple fact that Becker was a Jewish survivor of the Shoah. His status was that of a victim of fascism (as opposed to an opponent of fascism). Certainly the early reviews of the novel and the "selling" of the actual film stressed the personality of the writer. Even the name Jurek (a Polish diminutive) pointed to the East and to the world of the survivor. Becker's presence gave the film its claim to authenticity. He felt this too. For this film, he could not rely on his own repressed sense of the past. He claimed in the 1960s (and well into the 1980s) that he had forgotten everything about his own experience of the past. In returning to Lodz, in going into the archives, he needed to provide his own sense of this authenticity, which would enable his audience to laugh. If the survivor-author could evoke laughter, then we, too, are permitted to laugh.

For the audience in the GDR, the laughter evoked was two-pronged. It was a response to the notion of the Jewish (here read: Yiddish) writer of the comic. In 1970 Walter Felsenstein produced Jerry Bock, Sheldon Harnick, and Joseph Stein's 1964 American musical *Fiddler on the Roof* at the Comic Opera in Berlin.[28] The unprecedented success of this event in presenting what passed in East Berlin (as well as New York City) as "live Jews in their authentic Eastern context" set the stage for the reception of Becker's second attempt to bring *Jacob the Liar* to the screen. The film of *Fiddler on the Roof* appeared in 1971. It was necessary to have the object, the theme of Jews and the Shoah, and the Jewish novelist-filmmaker writing in a Jewish (read: Eastern European Jewish) mode for the film to be acceptable to the GDR audience. The readers of the novel immediately associated its narrative stance with Sholem Aleichem, the Yiddish author of the tales on which

Fiddler on the Roof was based. Becker denied knowing this tradition. What he did know and use was the GDR tradition of representing Jewish narrative as imagined by non-Jews such as novelist Johannes Bobrowski, but turned it from a tragic to a comic mode. What gave the novel and the subsequent film its claim to authenticity was the comic voice of its author as a Jew and as a survivor.

For Becker, the theme was the reeducation of the audience about the Shoah, but also equally about the problem of belief in systems that may or may not be congruent with the expectations of its believers. Becker uses the expectations of the audience about what should happen under such circumstances to destroy their certainty. Thus, the film is certainly about the Shoah, but it is even more so about belief systems and the expectations of life in extreme circumstances. What makes this double level of viewing possible is the use of the comic in the film. This is not satire. Satire would have to be aimed at one system or the other (as in Swift's little- and big-enders). Instead the film addresses a metatheoretical problem, where one level of viewing is just as true about people in the GDR "believing" what they see on television from the West as it is about the Western presuppositions regarding cultural life in the GDR. By using humor and by placing this question in the collective past of the Germans, Becker is able to present a model of reeducation that seems to work for him and his audience in the early 1970s. By 1975, it is clear that it no longer works for Becker. This disillusionment is indeed the theme of his next novel, *Misleading the Authorities* (1973), which received literary prizes in both West and East Germany. In this novel, the compulsive watching of films comes to be a refuge for the protagonist. The slide toward a critical opposition had already begun.

Becker gave his rather notorious radio talk about what it means to be Jewish in 1977, immediately after leaving the GDR for the West following the expulsion of his close friend, Wolf Biermann. He was asked by the interviewer how one made a Jew; he understood that when two human beings reproduced, they made another human being. How did one make a Jew? His secular identity, formed in the GDR after 1949, was the natural extension of his father's Polish Jewish secular identity of the prewar years. The experience of the Shoah, his survival of the Lodz ghetto and the Ravensbrück concentration camp, seemed to have been bracketed. The Enlightenment roots of Becker's notion that Jews, too, are simply human beings were clear— all human beings are equal. However, history made that an impossible promise for Jurek Becker, and his struggle with that promise of his own personal autonomy as a human being, rather than as a Jew, and then as a human being who was a Jew marked his creative life. However, it was, of course, as a Jewish filmmaker and a Jewish writer about the Jewish theme, the Shoah, that Becker is established in the consciousness of the West and the East. Thus, Becker, alone of those who leave the GDR following the Biermann affair, is given a decade-long visa, one that actually in its final form outlasted the state that gave it to him. One simply did not exile those seen in the public sphere as Jewish survivors from the peasants' and workers' state.

Immediately after he moved to the West in 1977, Becker authored two further screenplays about the Shoah, both serious treatments of the subject. The first West German film about the Shoah in West Germany undertaken by a Jewish writer and director, Peter Lilienthal's *David* (1979) had its initial script penned by Becker. This was a disaster, from Becker's point of view, and he emphatically wrote on the final draft of the film script that he had had nothing to do with this version at all! A later film about the Shoah and its repercussions, written with his fellow GDR-expellee Thomas Brasch, himself half-Jewish, was *Der Passagier—Welcome to Germany* (1988) starring Tony Curtis. Neither of these films were "comic," nor were they successful.

The resonance of Becker's image of the Jew in the Shoah is both that Jacob is everyman but that he is a particularly Jewish everyman. Becker's world is the world, not of such cultural invisibility, but of the inherent visibility of the antihero, who is labeled as Jewish from the opening moment of the film. The flashbacks to the prewar world of Jacob Heym as the owner of a small restaurant, with a love life, and a place in the society, provides a continuity to the Jacob of the camps. Viewers and readers understand Jurek Becker's world as authentic because of his biography: it is the world of the Jew in the Shoah. This world is defined as a discontinuous world, one that had been ruptured by the Shoah. There is no real possibility of there being any sort of continuity that extends past the death camps.

Becker works self-consciously against type in this film. He avoids the pious clichés of the socialist-realist representation of victim or hero, of antifascism as an ideology. What he does use are the assumptions about Jewish difference that dominate German (and Western) culture and he turns them on their head. These turn out to be qualities ascribed to the "stage" Jew, the schlemiel, which run counter to the heroic. The character of Jacob Heym becomes a positive figure in his status as a little man. He is the schlemiel who cannot avoid the randomness of the world in which he exists, but can, through simple actions, attempt to ameliorate its suffering.

In the Shoah, individual action could not guarantee the salvation of any individual. The famed German Jewish sociologist Theodor Adorno tells of overhearing two women leaving a production of *The Diary of Anne Frank* in Frankfurt in the 1960s. One turns to the other and says: "Yes, but that girl at least should have been allowed to live"[29] Becker's deep pessimism knows that at the end those who are spared, like the narrator of *Jacob*, are spared accidentally, and have the obligation to tell their stories. That these stories are comic is the result of the pattern of accident. Here A. C. Bradley, the great Shakespearean scholar of the early twentieth century, was right about the relationship between laughter and accident.[30] Accident is the wellspring of comedy and laughter, not because it is the opposite of tragedy, but because it is the substantiation of the random in life over which one can only laugh or weep. In *Jacob*, Becker provides the ability to do both and made it possible to use the elicitation of laughter as a means of representing the unrepresentable—not only the Shoah but the randomness of life.

Becker's film script (and his novel) entered into the world in which the struggle against fascism, the Shoah, and the survivor were all constituent parts of both the experience and the ideology of that experience. Whether acknowledged or repressed, the murder of the Jews was a fact in the lives of the survivors (like Max Becker and his son) as well as of the Germany they chose to live in. This would have been true in different ways in West Germany or Poland in the 1950s and 1960s.

The heroic, as in Steven Spielberg's complex and contradictory image of Oscar Schindler, can now be an acceptable part of the telling of the Shoah's *history*. Oscar Schindler's tale makes sense as a 1990s narrative of the Shoah because it recounts his success in rescuing Jews. His is a world of the survivor, not the world of the victim. Purposeful action can change the world. It can avert the accidents of history. The world historical personality can change the shape of history.

The movement of the Shoah into history means that the claims for authenticity, which made a film such as *Jacob the Liar* even conceivable for the general audience (if not for the survivor such as Max Becker), are no longer needed. The Shoah is becoming (has become?) a factor of general historical experience of the West rather than of the experience only of those who were or were imagined to be the primary victims. In this case, the topic of the Shoah is also analogous to the earliest comic films in which anti-Semitism was seen as a sign of the general inhumanity of fascism rather than as its most evil and salient feature. On the frontier that was East Germany this was as "Jewish" as one identified as a survivor and thus a Jew, such as Jurek Becker, could be.

CHAPTER TWO

IS LIFE BEAUTIFUL?
CAN THE SHOAH BE FUNNY?

On the Frontier between Acceptable
and Unacceptable Representations
of the Holocaust in Some Newer and Older Films

LAUGHTER AND THE SHOAH

JUREK BECKER'S COMIC FILM WAS A PRODUCT OF HIS LIFE
on the frontier that was Germany after the Shoah. It illustrated
the complex nature of being Jewish on that frontier with all of its
contradictions and confrontations. The path-breaking work that
he undertook in the 1960s and thereafter led to a strange sort of
debate in the subsequent decades. In the years after he wrote *Jacob
the Liar*, there was much public speculation about the impossibility
of imagining the appropriate way of representing the Shoah.
Humor or the comic rarely figured in this discussion in the 1960s
and 1970s even after the success of Becker's novel and film. They
were somehow considered beyond the bounds of propriety. Even
if the Shoah could be represented (and this was contested), how it
should be represented seemed not at all in question: it should be

serious and sober. Even the appropriation of forms such as the commix (the graphic novel), by artists and authors such as Art Spiegelman in his *Maus: A Survivor's Tale* (1986), self-consciously stripped these forms of any comic, humorous, or witty content or intent.[1] Indeed, Spiegelman's text works against the popular American assumption that serious themes cannot be dealt with in the graphic novel form. In Israel such appropriations even in the form of the commix seem not to have been imaginable at all.[2] In Japan, on the other hand, one of the most powerful series of Osamu Tezuka's *manga* [commix], *Also Tell Adolph* (*Adolph ni Tsugu*) (1983), which received the Kodansha Manga Award in 1986, chronicles the Shoah as seen from the viewpoint of the Japanese.[3] Neither Spiegelman's nor Tezuka's commix is comic.[4]

If even commix have avoided the comic in representing the Shoah, let us pause for a moment and ask one of our title questions again: "Can the Shoah be funny?" Can horror be understood through laughter? Who laughs? (*Quid rides?*) was the ancient's question. The audience, the victim, the perpetrators? Is laughter the intention of the creator of a work of art or the response of an audience? Is laughter intentional or, as in the case of the high school students at Castlemont High School in Oakland in April 1994 who laughed at a screening of *Schindler's List* at a school assembly, situational?[5] (Anything and everything at a school assembly is understood by high school students as potentially the source of laughter.) Even more basic to our question: what is the Shoah? Is the Shoah a specific moment in time, a specific set of horrors or is it a metaphor for all genocides, past, present, and future? Is it European history or is it an American "problem"? as Peter Novick asks.[6] Clearly it is the attempt to murder all of Europe's Jews, an attempt that succeeded in murdering millions of Jews along with millions of others. But any understanding of the Shoah must acknowledge that its meaning and function has changed over the fifty years since it occurred. The murder of the Jews moved over half a century from being one aspect of the crimes of the Nazis to being the central, defining aspect of the Third Reich. Over the past decade or so, it has evolved from a specific historical moment to the metaphor for horror itself. Can the Shoah be funny? This is a question, which must be framed in both its historical and its ethical dimensions.[7]

Central to any discussion of humor in the Shoah is an understanding of what concept of humor is evoked. Virtually all of the theoretical views of the comic in the West are ways of speaking about narratives: the stories that are told that encapsulate humor. If you begin with Thomas Hobbes's notion that humor is in complex ways wedded to notions of power or the illusion of power, then humor is a weapon aimed at those perceived as weaker or stronger than oneself. Yet if Sigmund Freud's image of humor (*Witz*) is employed, then the tendentious laughter that results is a sign of an attack on the object of the joke, an attack shared with the listener, reader, or viewer. Mikhail Bakhtin saw the comic, at least in the world of carnival, as part of a permitted reversal of all values in which the world is turned on its head, but within acceptable limits. What are these limits in regard to the Shoah? Is humor a gratification of the forbidden or unspeakable desires which Hobbes's notion of humor places in the public sphere? Henri Bergson saw in humor the desire to humiliate and to correct those who are perceived as different in a public manner. These are quite contradictory models of humor and yet they all rely on one marker—the physiological production of laughter—for the clear distinction of what is humorous.[8] Laughter is, of course, the prime marker of the comic whatever the theoretical explanation of why we laugh.[9] Can we imagine laughing at representations of the Shoah? Is there an earned laughter that teaches and a false laughter that obfuscates?

The late Terrence Des Pres, writing shortly after Art Spiegelman's *Maus* was first collected in book form, wrote of the clear proscription against laughter in representations of the Shoah.[10] He saw a form of "Holocaust etiquette," which "dictates that anything pertaining to the Holocaust must be serious, must be reverential in a manner that acknowledges (and supports) the sacredness of its occasion" (278). Yet, he argued that laughter, humor, and the comic mode are helpful as coping mechanisms. Tragedy is rooted, according to Des Pres, in an unmediated claim of realism; the comic makes no claim on realistic representation. The comic, countering the Shakespearean critic A. C. Bradley, is more than a world of drama divided between the tragedies that dealt with the permanents of life and the comedies with the accidents.[11] In refusing to accept mimesis as possible, the comic could potentially reject the idea that the Shoah is historically bounded. The comic allows for distance, self-possession, evaluation, and protest in regard to the finality of the "final solution to the Jewish Question." Des Pres, in his essay on "Holocaust Laughter," wrote: "In the realm of art, a comic response is more resilient, more effectively in revolt against terror and the sources of terror than a response that is solemn or tragic. . . . Comic art resists that which has come to pass." "Holocaust laughter," he says, is "life-reclaiming" (281).

It is clear, in spite of Des Pres's title, that no one ever actually *laughed* while reading *Maus*. It was never received as the equivalent to Roadrunner or to the Itchy and Scratchy Show. And that is certainly even more the case with Osamu Tezuka's work, which does not replace human figures with animal analogies. Graphic novels need not be comic at all. What is striking is that even when humorous modes of expression are used in representing the Shoah, laughter is rarely the desired reaction. Certainly there are some contexts in which laughter is desired, but these have been clearly circumscribed. That there are tasteless jokes about the Shoah there is no doubt. And people are supposed to laugh at them (or perhaps at their tastelessness)! Allen Dundes and his colleagues in the United States and in (then) West Germany collected sets of Auschwitz jokes, which, by their very nature are understood as the perpetrators "laughing" at the victims.[12] Their tone is similar to the "little moron" jokes of the 1950s while their content often verges on the obscene or the anti-Semitic. They are read as comic because their narrative voice seems to be neutral, that is, they are understood as being told "about" Jews rather than "by" Jews. The Jew in these jokes is the object and there is no sense of identification with the Jew. Thus, laughter can occur in a joke about the Shoah only when the Jew is literally moved to the margins of the joke. The jokes become, at least in Dundes's reading, a means of distancing the teller and the listener from the horrors of the Shoah.

But with the exception of such jokes, none of the comic representations of the Shoah are intended to evoke laughter. All assume that the author and the reader (the teller and the listener now as disembodied entities) will not laugh, even at the comic turns of the fiction. Serious fiction dealing with the Shoah—with few exceptions such as Edgar Hilsenrath's *The Nazi and the Barber* (1973) or Leslie Epstein's *King of the Jews* (1979)—has avoided the very use of the comic as a narrative device.[13] But even in those cases, it is black comedy, framed by a satirical narrative voice to guide the reader, who rarely or ever actually laughs at the bleak vision of the Shoah. Much like the work of Art Spiegelman, himself the child of a survivor, there is a need to bend the form to the topic rather than the other way around. Such works can generate no laughter.[14]

But more than this seems to be necessary for such works to be accepted. To have been accepted into high culture as an adequate representation of the Shoah, such texts have to be seen as stemming from the pen of Jews. And, one should note at this point, that the authors of such texts are more often than not clearly self-identified as Jews. Spiegelman and Epstein have this declared on the jackets of their books. Hilsenrath has been paraded by his publishers as a survivor of the Nazi ghettos in Transnistria. His persona was key to the reception of *The Nazi and the Barber* in both

the United States and Germany. One should note that Hilsenrath's novel was first published in the United States in an English
translation in 1973; it had to wait four years before it found a German publisher. When it was finally published in German, it was in
a version expurgated by its author of its most critical, satirical conclusion. When asked why he had cut the conclusion that condemned God for being passive while the Jews were being
slaughtered, he noted that such a text could be read by Americans
but would be misunderstood by Germans. They would read it, he
noted, as a statement exculpating them and blaming God![15] Being
heard as a comic Jewish voice in Germany in the 1970s was something quite different, at least in regard to the meaning of the
Shoah, than being heard as a comic Jewish voice in America. Such
a comic voice is of course not the voice that evoked laughter but
rather nostalgia. There is no intention for the reader of either version of the novel to laugh.

The evocation of identity and life experience as a means of
even permitting the use of the comic in a limited sense to represent the Shoah seems vital. Certainly, even in the historical and
autobiographical accounts of life in the Third Reich and among
Jews during the Shoah, there are glimmers of discussions of
humor.[16] Recently a few of the videotaped memoirs of survivors
of the Nazi camps and ghettos stressed the pragmatic function of
humor as a means of coping or even of survival.[17] Such laughter
is a response to the reality of the Shoah as individual experience.
It seems to be, at least in the survivors' accounts, a rather surprising means of keeping one's sense of control in a situation
where no control was possible. Laughter on the part of the interviewer or on the part of the viewer of such videotapes, however,
is missing.

Laughter, however, does not moderate the representation of
the Shoah. Art Spiegelman can never truly understand his father's
life; jokes and humor in the camps seem virtually foolish in their

inadequacy. No one can laugh at or even with his figures. Their laughter (if it occurs) seems inexplicable, while the laughter in the accounts of the actual survivors seems comprehensible. And for those who have had no exposure to the events except through the cultural representations of the Shoah, comedy seems to have been simply more problematic than the tragic: laughter cannot ever be evoked. Why is it that if humor does have a function in ameliorating the effects of the Shoah, we are so very uncomfortable imagining laughter in the context of the Shoah? Indeed, can there be anything funny about representing the Shoah?

One might say that laughter in regard to the notion of a Shoah is especially marginalized since there remains in today's world the strong image of a Jewish comic voice evoking laughter.[18] The great comic tradition of modern Jewish letters is seen to run from Sholem Aleichem to Josef Roth to Philip Roth to Woody Allen to Simon Louvish. (Never mind from Eddie Cantor to Lenny Bruce to Jerry Seinfeld.) The Jewish voice seems to be one in which the comic and humor dominates. (Of course, there is another voice, that of deep pessimism, which runs from Shalom Asch to I. J. Singer to Aaron Appelfeld, but let us bracket that for the moment.) Jewish voices can be—indeed are often—understood today as comic voices *evoking laughter.* This was clearly part of the powerful reception of Jurek Becker's work. Yet in regard to the Shoah, this comic voice is marginalized if not suppressed.

Is it appropriate to use the comic (and its physiological response, laughter) in representing events of transcendental horror? How much does the redefinition of the horrors of World War II (after 1945) into the central position of the Shoah (by the 1970s) preclude or enable laughter to be imagined as a possible mode of representation? And how much does the presupposition of the image of the Jew as the comic and as the victim enable or preclude Jewish or non-Jewish uses of laughter in making representations of the Shoah publicly acceptable?

FUNNY FILMS

It is only in the cinema after Jurek Becker's filming of *Jacob the Liar* (1974) that the comic and its corollary, laughter, seem to have a role in an adequate representation of the Shoah. (One might note that the comic in the cinema from its very origin is coupled with laughter; from the silent screen on, film comedies intend for their audiences to laugh in the anonymity of the darkened theater. Our sense of distance is much greater than when we are told a joke or when we read a novel.) Certainly in most films on the Shoah, from Alain Resnais's *Night and Fog* (1956) to Claude Lanzmann's *Shoah* (1985) to Steven Spielberg's *Schindler's List* (1993), laughter is not only missing but also inconceivable.[19] These films also provide a trajectory. They move from the image of the Shoah in which the victims are literally missing or present only as photographs from the liberation of the camps to accounts in which living survivors provide narratives of the past (and in the case of Spielberg's film, accounts of their meaningful survival). And yet there are films in which the comic seems to be appropriate—at least to some viewers and critics.[20]

The comic is possible when imagining the Third Reich and the Nazis as the enemy. It is a means of assuring the viewer that the victim is smarter and more resilient than the aggressor. The victim must be in a position to win or at least to survive the world of the Nazis. Not all film evocations of the Third Reich seem to need to (or want to) evoke the Shoah. Partially this has to do with when the work was made and the meanings attached to the Shoah at the time. But it is possible to write a comedy about the Third Reich two decades after the 1940s, such as the long-running TV series *Hogan's Heroes* (1965–1971), without evoking the Shoah. Indeed, such representations are possible only if the survival of the victims, here the Allied prisoners-of-war, is never drawn into question. Like its model, the German Jewish director Billy

Wilder's *Stalag 17* (1951), a murder mystery set in a prisoner-of-war camp, the central problem of the television series is the necessary preservation of the prisoners' lives. The laugh track on this series was possible only if the idea of the Shoah and its horrors were eliminated from the audience's consideration. No randomness is permitted, and thus the inherent randomness of the Shoah must be eliminated in such representations.

The earliest comic films dealing with the Third Reich and its treatment of the Jews were made before or at the very beginning of the murder of Europe's Jews.[21] No reference to the Shoah is possible in such films, a fact not lost on their makers. The Anglo Jewish actor Charlie Chaplin's Jewish barber in *The Great Dictator* (1940) (with Paulette Goddard as his Jewish wife) presents a critique of fascist racism that historically prefigures the Shoah. (One can also mention the Three Stooges short *You Natzi* [*sic*] *Spy* of 1940 as another example of such pre-Shoah parodies of the Nazis.) Chaplin himself commented well after the war that "had I known of the actual horrors of the German concentration camps, I could not have made *The Great Dictator*; I could not have made fun of the homicidal insanity of the Nazis."[22] Nor could his audience have laughed. Yet the evocation of laughter by this film is possible *today* because the film's treatment of anti-Semitism makes it seem relatively harmless in retrospect.

Indeed, the German Jewish director Ernst Lubitsch's *To Be or Not to Be* (1942) was a film intended to evoke laughter. It starred the Jewish vaudeville and radio comedian Jack Benny as the actor Joseph Tura, about whom it is said by a Nazi officer: "What he did to Shakespeare we are now doing to Poland."[23] In the film there is no intimation of the persecution of the Jews. The response of at least one critic was to wonder why audiences should "laugh at some broad anti-Nazi satire while we are weeping over the sad fate of Poland."[24] For Lubitsch the answer was clear: "American audiences don't laugh at those Nazis because they underestimate their menace, but because they are happy to see this new order and its ideology being ridiculed."[25] Even though Chaplin and Benny were Jewish (as were Jerome Lester Horwitz a.k.a. Curly Howard, Louis Fienberg a.k.a. Larry Fine, and Moses Horwitz a.k.a. Moe Howard), the reference for the film in the 1940s was anti-Semitism, not the potential or actual destruction of European Jewry. Such films seem today to be relatively harmless period pieces in their evocation of laughter. And we do laugh at them now as they were laughed at in the 1940s.

In his remake of *To Be or Not to Be* (1983), Mel Brooks could not avoid the omnipresence of the Shoah in the American audience's mind.[26] In this film Brooks played a triple role: the actor-protagonist, Hamlet, and Hitler. The strained nature of the remake was to no small degree the result of that oppressive if unspoken presence of the Shoah in the audience's awareness. That Mel Brooks was Jewish did not ameliorate this sense of unease, but it did give the film a level of public acceptability. Comedy in this context was only possible by bracketing the Final Solution. And such a bracketing was impossible, at least in America, once the Shoah became the stuff of mass culture following the showing of the NBC-TV series *Holocaust: A Story of Two Families* on April 16, 1978. This series was even more widely viewed than the 1977 TV miniseries on the African American experience, *Roots!*

Brooks's most successful use of an anti-Nazi satire was the musical-within-the-film "Springtime for Hitler" in his first film, *The Producers* (1967). This satire worked only because it was *not* supposed to work. But it also worked because in 1967 the audience was still at a moment in time when the name Hitler was not solely identified with the Shoah. The musical in the film was to be the ultimate bad-taste flop for the producer Max Bialystok (played by Zero Mostel) but it almost destroys him because it becomes a popular success. After the 1980s such images of the Nazis could be made only with the implicit evocation of the Shoah. In Brooks's popular remake of his 1967 film into a Broadway musical in 2001, he again worked against the seriousness of the world of the Nazis by avoiding any mention of the Shoah in his transformation of Hitler into a comic musical character. Yet, while he avoided any reference to the Shoah, Brooks was attacked for his use of the figure of Hitler, which by this time had become completely identified with the image of the Shoah. He responded: "Hitler was part of this incredible idea that you could put Jews in concentration camps and kill them. . . . How do you get even with the man? You have to bring him down with ridicule, because if you stand on a soapbox, you're just as bad as he is, but if you can make people laugh at him, then you're one up on him. It's been one of my life-long jobs—to make the world laugh at Adolph Hilter."[27] By 2001, the public had returned to the power of humor to define its relationship to the Shoah, as Ernst Lubitsch had done with his image of the Nazis in 1942.

Similar to Brooks's remaking the pre-Shoah Lubitsch film, the American playwright S. N. Behrman reworked Franz Werfel's "comedy after a tragedy" *Jacobowsky and the Colonel* after 1945. Originally written in 1941–42 and published at the end of the war, Werfel's sad comedy was turned into a preachy and rather heavy-handed Broadway comedy of manners with some reflection on the global nature of prejudice. (It became a sort of comedic *South Pacific*.) When the Jewish comic Danny Kaye redid Behrman's text as the film *Me and the Colonel* (1957), there seemed to be no trace of the ultimate future of such Polish Jews as the central characters in the Shoah. All is reduced to a cat-and-mouse game to be won eventually by the pursued not the pursuers. The comic here, as in *To Be or Not to Be*, is employed as a means of avoiding any representation of the Shoah. Laughter can exist because the Shoah is unmentioned (and unmentionable).

More recently there have been a number of films by self-identified Jewish authors and directors that use the comic as a means of representing the Shoah. The Australian Jewish director of operas Elijah Moshinsky created his black comedy *Genghis Cohn* (1992) for BBC-TV. Starring Robert Lindsay, Diana Rigg, and the South African Jewish actor Anthony Sher as the title character, it was adapted by Stanley Price from the Franco Jewish author Romain Gary's novel *The Dance of Genghis Cohn* (*La Danse de Genghis Cohn*) (1967). Moshinsky's film is an account of a former Nazi camp commander at Dachau, living incognito in a quiet village after the war, who finds his sins coming back to haunt him as the ghost of a Jewish comedian he put to death lures him into becoming a Jew. Laughter results in this film from the audience's identification with the ghost, who, as a convention in the film, marks not the dead of the Shoah but their continued existence (as memory) in the present. Since the murder of Cohn did not result in his obliteration but in his continued existence, laughter can result.

Moshinsky's film uses the Hollywood convention of the feature film that employs ghosts as living beings to comment on and interact with the world (as in *The Ghost and Mrs. Muir* [1947]). The Canadian film *Punch Me in the Stomach* (1994), from a screenplay by the performance artist Deb Filler and Francine Zuckerman, and starring Deb Filler, uses the convention of the monologue film (such as Jonathan Demme's film of Spalding Grey's *Swimming to Cambodia* [1986]) to evoke laughter. The monologue is the autobiographical adaptation of comedienne Filler's one-woman stage show, in which she plays the role of 36 different characters from her extended family. She is self-identified in the film as the daughter of a Shoah survivor. She presents an account of how her father requested her to accompany him on a tour of the concentration and death camps he had been in. She narrates this experience but only after framing this with other stories about her own family and upbringing.

Many of her stories are invented, as she tells her audience toward the end of the show, such as the one about her father as a survivor-as-television-star. Her father did indeed become famous in Australia because he was a survivor and because of his daughter's stage work, but that was life imitating art, not vice versa. During the television scene, the schematic course of her father's testimony suddenly gets interrupted when he says: " . . . and also, sounds funny I know, but you had to keep your sense of humor." Then he tells the story about his first night in the barracks. There was not enough space. He and his fellow inmates were crammed so tightly into a bed that they could turn over only together and on command. "We laughed, we had to," he says. "What else could you do? We laughed the whole first night in Auschwitz." Laughter is, in the memory of the survivor, a coping mechanism. When he travels to Theresienstadt decades later with his daughter, the visit ends too, in Filler's enactment of it, with a powerful comic twist. Returning from the run-down toilets of the museum and holding in her hand a broken toilet chain, she and her father burst into laughter. "We were laughing so hard we couldn't stop." The laughter, however, is the laughter of the participants, not of the audience. Indeed, the viewers' reaction is dumfoundedness as the daughter narrates her father's laughter.

One can mention the extraordinary, supposedly autobiographical German-language film by the Hungarian Jewish playwright and theater director George Tabori, *My Mother's Courage* (1996), directed by the Dutch filmmaker Michael Verhoeven, who was also responsible for one of the best films about the German response to the Shoah, *The Nasty Girl* (1990).[28] Using the putative account of his mother's one-day round trip from Auschwitz to Budapest, Tabori notes the often arbitrary nature of personal survival and destiny. "Where were you? Why were you out so long without letting us know?" her family demands in the film when she returns after her day at Auschwitz. The cultured and soft-spoken Mrs. Tabori, played by British actress Pauline Collins, is an unlikely match for her captors. Yet, she quietly sizes up her ill-bred fascist jailers and determines a courageous way out by claiming loudly that she has papers at home that protect her. As she manages her escape, we are well aware that she is the sole passenger on that crowded transport who does. The comic in Tabori's account lies in the contrast between the audacious nature of his mother's actions and the accident of her survival. Laughter from the audience results because of the seeming implausibility of both the actions and the attitudes. The comic is the result of different readings of Jewish chutzpa and German obduracy.

The comic in all of the films results from a double presence: the speaking daughter of the survivor on stage; the 80-year-old Tabori in Verhoeven's film framing his mother's life; and the dead comic, as a ghostly presence in the present, manipulating the world of the Nazi by forcing him to convert to Judaism. Laughter haunts *Genghis Cohn* not only because of the ghostly presence of the past throughout, but more importantly a past that exists in living form in the present. As with the dramatization of the diary of Anne Frank, the dead are brought back to life, if only for a moment.[29] This coupled with the claim of the authenticity of a living Jewish voice provides the potential for the audience's laughter.

Filler, Verhoeven, and Moshinsky use the comic and its power to evoke laughter in different ways to translate the Shoah for the viewer of the 1990s. All three films, however, had very limited release and very limited critical response. (Here one should mention the unreleased 1972 Jerry Lewis film *The Day the Clown Cried*, about Helmut Drook, a clown who is forced to entertain children on their way to the gas chambers to keep them quiet.) They were unsuccessful as generally accepted representations of the Shoah because they used humor as their central narrative strategy. And as self-conscious products of Jewish directors, they made a claim on the comic voice of the Jew. However, in the context of the world of *Schindler's List*, the general public did not accept any such comic voice.

BENIGNI'S *LIFE IS BEAUTIFUL*

There is no doubt about the success of Roberto Benigni's tragi-comedy *Life Is Beautiful* (*La Vita e Bella*) (1998) released by Miramax. The Italian film opened its American run on October 22, 1998, in New York and Los Angeles, having won the Cannes Grand Jury Prize as well as the Jerusalem Film Festival Award. The following March, the film was awarded Oscars for the best foreign film and original dramatic score, and Benigni won an Oscar as well for best male actor. This triple win indicates some level of commercial and critical acceptance in the United States. Part of this is attributable to Roberto Benigni's international reputation as a contemporary Jerry Lewis or Jacques Tati or Cantinflas, a comic actor whose presence evokes specific comic turns well beyond the national culture in which he was initially best known. In Jim Jarmusch's *Down by Law* (1986) and *Night on Earth* (1991), Benigni presented his physical comedy (similar to Robin Williams or Jim Carrey) to a "high art" audience—which loved it. Of course, Benigni also replaced the late Peter Sellers in Blake Edwards's sequel *Son of the Pink Panther* (1993), which was a critical as well as a commercial disaster. In all of these humorous films, laughter was the intended (if sometimes missed) goal.

Life Is Beautiful opens as a rather standard love story concerning a marginal figure, Guido (Roberto Benigni) who moves to a small town in the Tuscan countryside to begin work as a waiter under the tutelage of his eccentric uncle. Upon his arrival, the schoolteacher Dora (Nicoletta Braschi) literally falls into his arms when he rescues her from a bee and then again when he runs into her with his bicycle. She is clearly socially a class above him. He begins a romantic pursuit of the schoolteacher despite her engagement to another man, a fascist officer. Historically it is set in Mussolini's Italy, but it is an idealized world, a world before the Germans come and ruin Benigni's pure memory of childhood.[30]

A series of comic exchanges follow in Guido's pursuit of Dora. One foreshadows the turn at the core of the film when Guido takes over the role of a fascist school inspector and presents a lecture about pure and beautiful racial types, with himself as the primary example, to Dora's students and colleagues. The sole intent in this scene is to create a double world of laughter. The teachers (at least Dora) and the students break into laughter at Guido's exaggeration; the audience does also but at the "secret" that the audience shares with Guido. For Guido is Jewish, a point made in his exchange with his waiter-uncle who has been harassed by fascist toughs.

Eventually Guido captures the heart of Dora from her fascist fiancé and they elope. Flashing forward to several years later, Guido and Dora are seemingly happily married and have a small son Giosue (Giorgio Cantarini). The underlying tensions in this world are revealed when it is clear that Dora's upper-class mother had cut her daughter off from the family for marrying a Jew. Yet when she meets Giosue in his father's shop, she is overwhelmed and agrees to join the family for dinner for the first time. While fascism is a bother to the young family and while it has some anti-Semitic overtones in the film, it is only the arrival of the Germans that destroys their idyll. This happens in literally the same moment as the mother-in-law's first visit. She arrives with her daughter to an empty house, Guido and Giosue having been seized and sent to a concentration camp. After the SS comes to deport Guido and his Jewish son, Guido invents a game as an excuse for their being ripped from their home as well as from their wife and mother. The game is simple: father and son are in an elaborate competition with the others in the camp to see who can collect the most points by undertaking a series of "games": who can stay still longest in the barracks, who cannot cry for his mother, who can go without much food, etc. The daily experiences of rescuing the child have been made into a contest.

Shifting in tone from the fairy tale romance, *Life Is Beautiful* follows the events experienced by Guido and Giosue at a concentration camp, which bears all of the hallmarks of the Auschwitz scene in *Schindler's List*. To preserve the idea that this is all a game for his son, Benigni offers to translate for the Nazi officer by pretending to speak German. As the officer barks out the camp's rules and regulations, Benigni translates them as the rules of a game for his young son. The grand prize of a tank awaits the little boy who does not whine that he misses his mother and who plays hide-and-seek all day from the guards. The comic moment is the misapprehension of the guard that his brutal rules are being understood. The quizzical look on the face of those inmates who understand Guido's Italian "translation" creates laughter on the part of the viewer.

As the days of the supposed game drag on into weeks, Guido finds it more and more of an effort to keep up the facade. Desperation seeps in during his moments alone, but he always keeps a positive face for his young son. When he discovers his wife, Dora, has volunteered to enter the concentration camp even though she is not herself Jewish, Benigni finds one more reason to stretch out the game. When the camp is being emptied upon the arrival of the Americans, Guido is almost randomly taken out and shot, having first concealed his son. This moment comes when the boy had amassed sufficient points to win the fantasy game that the father had created to keep his son from the realities of the camp. The boy is rescued by an American tank (the promised reward for winning the competition) which bears him along a column of prisoners who have walked out of the camp. The tank and its crew are the real *deus ex machina*, for through them he finds his mother. Child and mother are reunited. Happy end.

Throughout the film, indeed up to the very end, Roberto Benigni's physical comedy underlines the childlike nature of the actor and the necessity of representing the image of innocence.

This is his image in the international cinema. It is not a Jewish image as Benigni is neither Jewish himself nor has he self-consciously played Jewish characters in the past. Indeed, his selection of the theme and setting seems to have had more (at least according to his own account) to do with his desire to play a figure *in extremis*, rather than with a figure in a movie about the Shoah. He noted that the germ of the film took shape in a conversation with his coauthor Vincenzo Cerami in 1995 with the "idea of a man in the most extreme circumstances who tries to convince himself he's not there."[31] What better setting than the Shoah for such testing of character and actor alike.[32] The idea of doing a comic film about the Shoah was first dismissed by Benigni, who imagined it might appear as "Donald Duck in an extermination camp."[33] And yet when working on the film with Cerami, he began to emphasize his own identity as the "child of a survivor." His father had been fighting as a member of the Italian army until Italy was forced to switch sides in 1943. He was then rounded up and sent to work as a laborer in Germany. Benigni reads his father's account as follows: "He was an antifascist, but he was not political. . . . So he was suddenly captured by the Nazis and put in a work camp in Germany for two years. He came back a skeleton, covered with insects. . . . And when he came back he told stories about what a nightmare it was, like Primo Levi did in his book."[34] The work camps, no matter what their horrors, were, of course, not Auschwitz. In order retrospectively to give him the moral authority to make this film, Benigni reconsiders his history so as not to appear merely like "Donald Duck in an extermination camp." In doing so, he created a quasi-autobiographical film about the Shoah.

Needless to say, *Life Is Beautiful* did not have a uniformly positive reception. Many critics actively loathed it. In its reception and its structure, Roberto Benigni's film in a strange way picks up the theme and the tone of the concentration camp as a site for the grotesque and the unreal that began in Italian film with Lina

Wertmuller, the first woman director to receive an Oscar nomination, especially with her film *Seven Beauties* (1976).[35] There slapstick humor was used to frame a concentration camp experience of a small time-Casanova, a non-Jew, Pasqualino Settebellezze (played by Giancarlo Giannini). Like that film, Benigni's has been the subject of both praise and attack. During a press conference at the Cannes festival, one French journalist stood up to accuse Benigni of mocking the victims of the Shoah, declaring that he was "scandalized" by the picture. A reporter from the *International Herald Tribune* stated the she "loathed this film," and London's *Guardian* wrote that it is "a hopelessly inadequate memorial to the vile events of the Holocaust."[36] The Israeli humorist Ephraim Kishon, perhaps the best-known Jewish writer in today's Germany and himself a Hungarian survivor of the death camps, observed that the film violates all the realities of the camps. No child, he noted, could be so hidden without being discovered and killed. It is a film "made for Hollywood and not for those who have experienced the Holocaust. One can speak with humor about the Holocaust, only when one completely falsifies it."[37] The notion that any fiction about the camp that uses humor is immediately both "Hollywood"—that is, an American fantasy about the past—and a falsification was heard from many survivors.

There was even some discussion as to whether Benigni "appropriated" bits of a French Rumanian director's comic fable of the Shoah, Radu Mihaileanu's *Train of Life* (*Train de Vie*) (1998).[38] In this film, starring Lionel Abelanski as Shlomo, the town idiot, Shlomo masquerades as a German officer to commandeer a train and rescue the inhabitants of a *shtetl*. Unlike the Italian film, the end of this film is tragic. All of the comic turns still do not give the Jews any real control over their lives. Death seems the one option that in the end does triumph.

In a symposium of the U.S. Comedy Arts Festival in Aspen, film director James L. Brooks called *Life Is Beautiful* "a movie about the comic spirit." He noted that "he was dumfounded by criticism from people offended by what they have perceived to be its lighthearted treatment of the Holocaust." One of the other speakers, the comedian Janeane Garofalo, noted that she had a friend who "felt that as a subject [the Shoah] there was no way to put a positive spin on it."[39] While the Italian press was generally ecstatic by Benigni's winning the Oscar, *Il Corriere della Sera* (March 23, 1999) asked on its front page whether the comic was the best possible way for Italian culture to be judged abroad. It answered the question by having Dario Fo note in an op-ed piece on page 9 that 1999 was the year that he, a comic writer, won the Nobel Prize for Literature. It was also the same year that Benigni won the Oscar. For the Italian commentators, there was no question about the substance of the film, only its Italian provenance. We must ask along with the doubters, what would be an adequate cinematic representation if Roberto Benigni's comic spin were not?

What is clearly the case is that Benigni's figure is Jewish only within the Italian model of the hidden Jew. The Italian model was that Jews were literally invisible within Italian culture and that it was only German bestiality that differentiated them from their non-Jewish Italian neighbors. Certainly the notion in the film is that the viewer sees Guido as a Jew only when his uncle complains that he has been made the brunt of anti-Semitic attacks. Only then does the marginal figure that we see on the road become a version of the wandering Jew. While Italian fascist anti-Semitism is evoked, it is of a rather comic type, such as the painting of anti-Semitic slogans on the side of a horse. This myth is perpetuated in the film, even though there are clearly socially isolating moments stressed, such as the response of Dora's mother who is alienated from her daughter because of her marriage to a Jew up to the day when the Germans seize her husband and child. This juxtaposition again stresses the "good Italians" and their relationship to "their Jews" as opposed to the bad, murderous Germans of the camps.

Benigni's character is not seen at the beginning of the film as a Jew. From the standpoint of the non-Italian viewer, his character is not Jewish in terms of the cultural semiotics of this category. Rather, he fulfills the stereotypes and self-image of the Italian Jew as held by Jewish survivors such as Primo Levi, that they were well integrated into Italian prewar society and no different than other Italians. In contrast, Jurek Becker's world in *Jacob the Liar* is a world not of such cultural invisibility but of the inherent visibility of the antihero, labeled as Jewish from the film's start. Benigni's non-Jewish world is a world that promises continuities between the past, the Shoah, and the future.

Benigni too attempts to use the Shoah's victims, but unlike Jurek Becker who self-consciously uses this vocabulary as an antidote to the heroic, Begnini simply uses them for their own worth, for their own value. The fairy tale sequence in *Jacob* is different in kind than the game in *Life Is Beautiful.* While both center on acknowledging the fantasy world of the child, in preserving it, in focusing on the difference between the expectations of adults and those of children, Jurek Becker's goal is the momentary suspension of anxiety, which seems to be the purpose of his film. Roberto Benigni's goal within the plot is the physical rescue of the child. In this way, Benigni makes a claim for the true heroism of the father who puts his son's life ahead of his own and *succeeds* in rescuing him. This is the promise of laughter in comic representations of the Third Reich from *The Great Dictator* to *Hogan's Heroes.* When we laugh at the protagonist in his attempts both to ameliorate the life of his son under fascism and finally to save his life in the death camp, we acknowledge the fact that these attempts must be successful. Laughter as evoked by the comic turns in this film is our guarantee of the happy end, the rescue of the child.

However, it is a rather complicated happy end. Not only have all of Guido's actions resulted in his son's rescue, but the reunion of mother and son provides the perfect resolution to

Guido's disruption of Dora's Catholic world. The son, who by Nazi law was Jewish but by Orthodox Jewish law is not Jewish, and the non-Jewish mother are seen in the final shot as a Madonna and child, a restored Italian family with its divisive Jewish aspect missing. This seems to be a perfect happy end for a film about the ability of any individual to shape history. The rescue of mother and child reconstitutes the Italian utopia that existed before Guido interrupted it by his conquest of Dora. The promised future, impossible in Jurek Becker's world, is guaranteed by the selfless act of sacrifice of the father. Laughter is the key in our understanding both these films. Becker's laughter is undermined. We laugh because we are confronted with our own assumptions about the rules by which the world of the camps functioned. Benigni's laughter is proof that whatever else will happen, the rescue of the child must take place. Our expectations are fulfilled and we feel good about our laughter.

ANOTHER *JACOB THE LIAR*

The central difference between Jurek Becker and Roberto Benigni, however, lies in the movement of time and the permanence of the cultural record. By the 1990s, the Shoah had become history rather than memory. Chaplin's and Lubitsch's images of fascism are as much a part of the visual history of our time as are Resnais's and Spielberg's. By the 1990s as the Shoah became part of history in film, its representations became tied to the figures of the survivors and became heroic. Roberto Benigni could select a mode of evoking laughter as long as he tied it to the heroic. And the heroic, in this case, must be a success. No laughter could result if, by the conclusion of the film, not only the father but also the child (and his mother) were dead.

Laughter is again possible in the 1990s as it was in the early 1940s. But it is also possible by a filmmaker who is self-consciously understood as not being Jewish, as not needing the authenticity that a Jewish public identity would bring to the telling of the tale. This is, of course, also analogous to the cases of Chaplin and Lubitsch. While the Nazis labeled both as Jewish, in neither case was this an aspect of their public persona in the early 1940s. In Jurek Becker's world, a world defined by the Jewishness (that is, the victim status) of the author, laughter was possible only with the suspension of the knowledge of the eventual (and seemingly random) death of all of the protagonists. These two traditions now live side-by-side rather than historically succeeding one another. The cinema, like all art forms, levels the moment of its own origin and becomes part and parcel of the viewer's own time.

On September 24, 1999, the remake of Jurek Becker's *Jacob the Liar* was released, altering Becker and Beyer's texts for a post-*Schindler's List* sensibility. The new version of this film so transformed its inner structure as to make it a clear barometer of how the comic can now be used in representing the Shoah at the close of the millennium. The TriStar Pictures-Blue Wolf production, directed by the Hungarian-born, Francophone director Peter Kassovitz, stars Robin Williams as Jacob Heym with Alan Arkin as the actor Frankfurter and Armin Müller-Stahl as Dr. Kirschbaum in major supporting roles. (Armin Müller-Stahl is the only actor from Frank Beyer's film to reappear in the new version.) The new script was written by Kassovitz and the French writer Didier Decoin, based on the French translation of the novel. Kassovitz initially developed the idea for a revision of the material with the French producer Gouze Renal in 1990, before Becker's death. Becker read the early draft of the script; however, it was only in October 1997 that Williams's Blue Wolf Productions began filming. Marsha Williams, the company's president, had been instrumental in furthering the film as a serious vehicle for her husband. Its producer was Steven Haft, who had worked with Robin Williams on *Dead Poets Society*.

With few changes, this version follows the path of the novel as well as Beyer's film up to the moment when Lina (played by Hannah Taylor Gordon) is allowed to listen to Jacob's radio from behind a screen. The seemingly small changes early in the film are, however, important in framing the odd twist that Kassovitz gives it. The scene in which Jacob accidentally overhears the news on the radio in the German officer's room is an extraordinary moment of Chaplinesque slapstick in Beyer's film.[40] Jacob gets his coattails trapped in the door and cannot escape. This is cut in Kassovitz's version. In this role, Robin Williams is unexpectedly understated. His acting has few flights of fancy, little extemporization. His Jacob is the little man trapped in a tragic world.

The other change early in the film is the audience's introduction to Lina, who is rescued from a train that had slowed near the ghetto on its way to the death camp, when her mother drops her through a hole in the floor of the car. She joins with Jacob, just released by the German officer, on his flight back into the ghetto. Jacob hides her in his attic and she becomes the focus of his life. When she becomes ill, he promises her that she can listen to the radio if she wishes herself well. When she does, he enacts the radio for her. He imitates Winston Churchill. He then puts on a dance record on his record player and dances with her. Here the illusion of Jacob creating the radio is broken. Both the record player and the music it plays exist in the world. Unlike in the Beyer film—where the dancing and the music exist only in Jacob's memory (and the audience's but not the child's view)— here reality dominates. And because of this there is no ironic break. The child never looks behind the screen. She is too busy dancing with Jacob. There is no seeming shared sense of the positive duplicity of the adult between the child and the audience. The moment that the record player is introduced, foreshadowed in the revised scene in which her mother drops Lina from the train, establishes the new theme of the film. The child, who must be rescued in this film, is innocence itself and innocence must survive.

In order to accomplish this, Kassovitz's major change is to make Jacob and Dr. Kirschbaum (Müller-Stahl) into heroes. The radio comes to represent not only the ability to introduce some modicum of hope into the ghetto but, since this is now a heroic film, it becomes the focus for a planned insurrection against the Germans. Jacob, much against his will, becomes the ringleader of this planned uprising. Kirschbaum turns out to be a world famous cardiologist who is called on to treat a vicious German general (also introduced into this version) who suffers from (what else?) a bad heart. Kirschbaum commits suicide in the general's office rather than reveal who has or does not have the radio. This marks the first true break with the spirit of Becker's novel. The doctor's suicide is the first sign that Jurek Becker's father's desire—to have his son write a novel about the heroic aspects of the ghetto—will dominate this version. Jacob begins to spin more and more elaborate tales about the advances of the Russian troops based on what his audience imagines he has heard on his nonexistent radio. One has American tanks arriving on the Russian front accompanied by a jazz band that he can hear in the background on his radio. It also foregrounds precisely those figures whom Jurek Becker consciously and deliberately put into the background. In Becker's conception of the work, the Germans are peripheral figures. They dominate life in the ghetto but from its edges. They are a felt rather than a seen force. Peter Kassovitz changes this substantially. Not only are the Germans present, they have contours and faces, such as the sadistic German general with the bad heart, which are clearly indebted to figures such as Amon Goeth in *Schindler's List*.

After the doctor's suicide, the Germans take hostages in order to flush out the owner of the radio and stop the planned uprising. Jacob is forced to give himself (and his radio) up to rescue them. He enters the German command and it is clear that, as in the final scene in *Life Is Beautiful*, the Germans are preparing to flee. This is a clear sign that rescue is at hand, that Jacob was right all along, and that the Germans must lose historically. This is quite different from the mood in Jurek Becker's novel in which at no point can the audience be sure of the outcome of events. Even with defeat imminent, the Germans are still afraid of a potential insurrection that might inhibit their withdrawal. A torture scene is introduced in which Jacob is forced to admit that he has had no radio. Then Jacob is taken before the entire ghetto to announce that he had no radio and that the insurrection against the Germans that had been planned would be a failure. On the scaffold, Jacob says nothing. This infuriates the evil general who shoots him. A voice over a shot of Jacob's dead body observes that he had prepared a brave speech that he could not deliver. His silence is brave enough.

The ghetto is cleared. The inhabitants, including the little girl, are loaded on a train for the death camps. And then Kassovitz reintroduces the double ending from the novel. Do they all die or do the Russian troops stop the train and free them? While both are stated, the latter is clearly the case as we begin to see the world through the child's eyes. First she sees the Russian soldiers and their tanks. Then she sees two Russian musicians accompanying the troops, and finally she sees the American jazz band (with the Andrews Sisters singing) that had peopled Jacob's account of what he had heard on the radio.

The similarity to the conclusion of *Life Is Beautiful* (which had not been released when Kassovitz's film went into postproduction) is striking. The child is rescued and the rescuer dies. The *deus ex machina* of the American and Russian tanks marks the end of the Shoah. Jacob may have died (even though his voice seems to exist in the film after his physical death). Yet he is still very much alive in the mind of Lina, whose final word, mouthed as she sees the vision of the American jazz band, is "Jacob."

In an interview Robin Williams noted that "How you go on in the face of that is with anything you have, everything at your power, and humor is part of it. It's weird to think of people still having a sense of humor in the face of that, but they did. Amid people committing suicide and getting shot if they went near the gate." It is "art" that transcends the horror; as Williams continues, "they would still have concerts and productions, all these different things. They were still trying to maintain that." In this film art is trapped between the comic and the tragic. "[The film] went back and forth between being very funny and very tragic and very brutal within moments. Most of the scenes were about everyday life— this interaction in the face of something quite horrific." Kassovitz seeks the amelioration of this tension through the introduction of the heroic.

The tension between the comic and the tragic is one that is perceived in this film not as Jewish but as human, a dichotomy that underlies many of the recent films about the Shoah. "Jacob says, 'I'm not [Jewish]. I don't light the candles at Shabbat,'" says Williams. "But to the Gestapo, he's the biggest Jew there ever was. He thought of himself always as Polish, and then he's forced to be here, and then in a weird way he finds out how Jewish he is—first by force, but also by connection to the situation." His juxtaposition of the comic and the tragic produces, according to Williams, the human that is understood as the universal aspect of the Shoah, as opposed to the particular Jewish aspect framed by Jurek Becker. "The purpose of this," says Williams, "is to look at these people as human beings. Not as a statistic, a number."[41]

The universal heroic in art comes to be the pattern for the comic representation of the Shoah at the end of the millennium. Jurek Becker's great novel of action in the face of the vagaries of fate has become part of a rereading of the Shoah as the place of heroic action. On the new frontier, the very idea of a humanistic but nonheroic image of the Shoah becomes difficult to maintain.

The comic reinforces the heroic so that the audience can only laugh if it can simultaneously admire the protagonist. This compromise shows how the very idea of the Shoah has come to be incorporated in greater models of Western cinematic culture, rather than as with Jurek Becker, having its roots in a Soviet antifascism crafted on the frontier of the cold war.

PART II

DISEASES AND BOUNDARIES

CHAPTER THREE

SMOKING JEWS ON THE FRONTIER

JEWS AND TOBACCO

THE MYTH SEEMS TO BEGIN AT THE VERY START OF EURO-
pean exploration of the frontier in the New World. On November
2, 1492, Christopher Columbus, having landed on what will later be
called Cuba, sent two of his crew to spy out the land. They returned
to him on November 6, 1492, announcing that they had found a village of people who "drank smoke." They "light one end of the
tabuco [*sic*] and by the other suck, . . . by which they become be-
numbed and almost drunk." One of the two men was Luis de Torres, Columbus's interpreter, who "knew how to speak Hebrew and
Chaldean (Aramaic) and even some Arabic."[1] It was Luis de Torres
who, according to the myth, introduces tobacco and smoking into
modern Europe.[2] De Torres, modern scholars assume, was one of
the hidden Jews who remained in Spain after the expulsion of the
Jews and Moors that very year. The account quoted here, written by
Columbus's later companion, the priest Bartolomé de Las Casas, as
a commentary on Columbus's widely circulated diaries, was published only in 1825 and Las Casas's magisterial *History of the Indies*
appeared only in 1875. Their actual publication places this "legend"
very much within the nineteenth-century debates about Jews and
tobacco. That late nineteenth-century scholars quickly associated

de Torres with the expulsion of the Jews at the moment of the East European pogroms, and that they made a strong, negative association of the Jews with tobacco should not be astonishing.[3]

Smoking (in all of its forms and in all of its products) is a cultural phenomenon of human societies from the ancient world to modern times. Every culture in recorded history has had something that it smoked, whether as a cure or for pleasure, whether as ritual or as part of popular culture. At different times we have smoked tobacco, opium, scented cigarettes, or marijuana throughout the world. Yet, there is a strange but powerful association of Jews in Europe and beyond with smoking tobacco. This association is so powerful, it forms a means of describing the modernization of Jewish identity from the eighteenth century to the present. Some of this association rests on the actual role that individual Jews played in the evolution of the European tobacco industry from the early modern period on.[4] But though Jews played a substantial role in the tobacco industry (as did many other ethnic and religious groups), their association with it also reflected the changing meaning of smoking from the Enlightenment to the present. Being stereotyped as smokers was a means of labeling the essential nature of the Jew both within and beyond the Jewish community. The association of Jews and tobacco thus had a part in shaping how Jews in Europe were imagined as a group and, indeed, how they imagined themselves and the meaning given to the social act of smoking in Jewish culture.

The association between Jews and smoking was never merely a symbolic one. As early as 1612 the city council of Hamburg permitted Sephardi Jews from Portugal to be residents in Hamburg; while not permitted to live in the inner city, they were also not required to live in ghettos. They were tradespeople who specialized in the wholesale trade of exotic wares such as tobacco, sugar, coffee, cocoa, calico, and spices. Sephardi Jews also settled in the Dutch province of Groningen in 1683, again as tobacco merchants. As "exotics" in Northern Europe and given their role in trade with the New World, especially with Brazil, the Jews of the Sephardi diaspora generally became associated with the positive aspects of tobacco as a luxury product.

As tobacco became a major European staple during the sixteenth and seventeenth centuries, Jews in Northern Europe were also involved in its cultivation, treatment, and processing. In areas outside the traditional Jewish urban settlements of Amsterdam or Hamburg, Jews were primarily engaged in rural occupations or lived and worked in small towns. In states such as Baden in Southwest Germany, an area that was the center of German tobacco production during the early nineteenth century, Jews grew, processed, and traded the plant. They assumed an increasing role as middlemen, buying, curing, and manufacturing cigars and pipe tobacco. Indeed, by the beginning of the twentieth century Jews owned about 40 percent of all of the tobacco-related companies in the city of Mannheim and represented about 4 percent of its population.[5]

In Iceland, where there were de facto no Jews before the twentieth century, the Icelanders strongly linked one imported product with Jews: *Jú<eth>atóbaki<eth>* (Jewish tobacco) that Danish Jews had exported to Iceland since the early eighteenth century.[6] This social fact was read as part of the mythology of Jewish difference that grew up around Jews and tobacco in the course of the nineteenth century.

In Central Europe in the Hapsburg empire, it was only after civil emancipation of the Jews at the close of the eighteenth century that they were permitted to engage in the tobacco trade. Diego d'Aguilar held the tobacco monopoly in Austria using Christian nobles as middlemen from 1743 to 1748, and Israel Hönig established the State Tobacco Monopoly in 1788.[7] From the nineteenth century on, Jews were seen as the face of the tobacco trade in Central Europe as well as in the United States. European Jews had been the work force of American tobacco processing since the seventeenth century. At that point, Jewish merchants, such as the firm of Asher and Solomon, dominated the snuff trade. The Jewish firm of Keeney Brothers, whose brand of cigarettes, Sweet Caporals, was the best-selling brand of the nineteenth century, employed 2,000 Jewish workers. The trade union movement began with Samuel Gompers organizing the cigar makers in the 1870s and 1880s. Jews also became identified with tobacco retailing. Companies such as Loeser and Wolf in Berlin became hallmarks of the tobacco trade. In partitioned Poland, Leopold Kronenberg produced 25 percent of the cigars and cigarettes manufactured in 1867.[8]

In more rural areas of the Russian empire, Caucasian Mountain Jews (also known as Tats and Dagchufuts) were first permitted to own and till land in the course of the nineteenth century. While their oldest occupation was growing rice, they also grew tobacco and became associated with the tobacco trade. The association of Jews and tobacco was thus reinforced as Jews were emancipated or at least permitted to move from purely trading occupations to agriculture.

After World War I, Polish Jews were actually forbidden employment in the state tobacco monopoly. By the early 1930s, before the Nazi seizure of power in Germany in 1933, the Nazi bullyboys in the SA accused one of the major producers of cigarettes of making "Jewish cigarettes" because a member of the board of directors was a Jew.[9] Jewish participation in the tobacco industry by this point was often read through the lens of anti-Semitic rhetoric.

JEWISH SMOKE

Jews themselves had to confront both the simple fact that Jews smoked and the meaning ascribed to smoking in the worlds that they inhabited. The traditional rabbis throughout Europe had already been debating what function smoking was permitted to have within the more or less rigid rules for Jewish daily life. Could one smoke on festivals and the Sabbath when lighting a fire was prohibited? Could one smoke in synagogue or while studying? Smoking had become a fixed part of Jewish life on the frontier as it was with all peoples among whom the Jews dwelt. In Turkey, both Jewish men and women smoked. While the rabbis banned this on festivals and the Sabbath, many were so addicted, according to Rabbi Hayyim Benveniste writing in the mid-seventeenth century, that they would fill a water pipe with smoke on Friday and inhale it on the Sabbath.[10]

Anti-Semites, who saw tobacco as weakening the social fabric, laid its very origin at the feet of the Jews. (There is a strong association between health reform and anti-Semitism in Central Europe from the nineteenth century through to the twentieth century.) This view is documented in the Christian anti-Semitic literature of the nineteenth-century German Romantic poets, such as a contribution of the poet Clemens Brentano to the German-Christian Table Society created in 1811. For him it was the Jews who

> in the year 1696 planted the first tobacco in the Mark Brandenburg. Thus they hindered the development of our countrymen and generated the many sinful and confused thoughts that arose in the devilish steam bath of this plant that already stank while it was growing. Indeed one can survey all of the destruction that this horrid herb generated. One sees in the fall the tall, leafless stems that dominate the poverty-stricken land like gallows. At that moment, one can believe the old Jewish myth that Christ admonished all trees not to bear his body, so that every cross that was made collapsed. Then a Jew bound such plant stems out of the devil's garden together to a great height until he was crucified.[11]

The Jews themselves are so addicted to this narcotic, states Brentano, that they even subvert their own laws prohibiting smoking on the Sabbath to avoid the restriction on lighting fire on the Sabbath. Brentano goes on to associate these apparent character flaws with the "remarkable inherited diseases" of the Jews, diseases that Brentano attributes to the Jews as a punishment for their denial of Christ. Tobacco consumption comes to be a means of describing yet another sign of the innate physical and psychological difference of the Jews.

It was not only among anti-Semites that smoking came to characterize the difference of the Jews. The tradition of smoking came to be one of the major attributes in the biographies of the mid-eighteenth-century founder of modern Jewish mysticism, the Baal Shem Tov, the Master of the Sacred Name. There we find accounts of the *lulke*, the long-stemmed pipe, that he, regularly smoked. The Hasidic tradition imagined that when the Baal Shem Tov "wished to proceed to the upper worlds he would inhale tobacco and at each puff he would proceed from world to world."[12] Smoking and mystic beliefs were associated with the East. Western Jews were thus able to distance themselves from the perceived irrationalism of the competing Hasidic tradition by seeing the addiction to tobacco as a sign of the irrationalism of the Eastern Jew. Modern scholarship has continued this argument as it surmises that the source for the master's mystical visions and the power of his message was that his pipe was filled with substances other than tobacco![13]

Among Jews in Germany in the eighteenth century there was a strong association of smoking as a sign of Jewish difference. The new middle-class Jews of the Berlin Haskalah, the Jewish Enlightenment, attributed an unhealthy addiction to tobacco to the Eastern Jews of Poland and Russia. At the close of the eighteenth century, modern Judaism in the shape of the religious reforms advocated by the Berlin Enlightenment Jew Moses Mendelssohn competed with the mystical reforms advocated by the Baal Shem Tov at more or less the same moment. Mendelssohn's view of Judaism was as an inherently rational religion in which all of the rules for a healthy life were present. His followers saw the Eastern Jewish mystical tradition as the source of illness and corruption. In fact, both confronted what they saw as moribund orthodoxy and saw themselves as competitors to reform Judaism. The quintessential autobiography of such an Enlightenment Jew, the Polish Solomon Maimon (1793), provides the reader with an account of how he moved from the irrationalism of Jewish mysticism to Kantian rationalism and thus became a modern Jew.

Maimon describes his visit as a young man to the Hasidic court of the miracle rabbi, Dov Ber of Mezhirech. There he sees "simple men of this sect, who saunter about idly the entire day, pipe in mouth, when asked what they are thinking about, replied, 'We are thinking about God.'"[14] Enlightened Jews such as Maimon condemned the smoking by the mystics as a sign of their irrationalism and weak character. The mystics believed, Maimon sarcastically implied, that they could reach God through tobacco! He knew better: "as their knowledge of nature was extremely limited; and consequently the condition, in which they concentrated their activity upon an object which, in respect of their capacity, was unfruitful, became of necessity unnatural." When Eastern European Jews smoked it was a sign of naïve irrationality, in contrast to the Western Jew who smoked.

Tobacco smoking had been a sign of the acculturation of Jews into European society in the seventeenth century but now came to be read as an unnatural barrier to Eastern Jews becoming truly modern.[15] In another anti-Hasidic polemic written in 1772, the Hasidim are condemned for postponing morning prayers so that they "can place incense in their nostrils."[16] This insult is actually a paraphrase of Deuteronomy 33:10 where the incense used in the Temple before prayer is mentioned. In at least one mystical tradition "the weed known as tobacco is considered by the *tsadikim* (pious) to be like incense."[17] Thus some of these mystics associated the act of smoking with the divine sparks that exist in all matter. They could only be released from tobacco through the act of smoking.[18] Smoking is thus a form of mystical prayer and was therefore also seen as a form of *segulah*, the magical means of healing.[19] By the end of the nineteenth century, those who had advocated that one could use tobacco on holy days and fast days had won their argument, but smoking was still generally banned on the Sabbath and Yom Kippur. Modern writers in the East could ironically critique this seeming hypocrisy as Raphael Kohen did in Russia in a modern Hebrew satire when he stated that cigar smoking must be permitted on the Sabbath as it is one of the Sabbath's pleasures ("oneg shabbat").[20] Jews smoked and other Jews gave this smoking meaning.

SMOKING AND JEWISH DISEASE

The debate about smoking and the Jews reappears in the science of the late nineteenth century in the context of horrid and unmentionable diseases attributed to the Jews by writers such as Clemens Brentano. The French neurologist Jean Martin Charcot in 1858 described "Claudication intermittente" for the first time as a medical diagnosis.[21] He defined it as the chronic reoccurrence of pain and tension in the lower leg, a growing sense of stiffness, and finally a total inability to move the leg, which causes a marked and noticeable inhibition of gait. This occurs between a few minutes and a half hour after beginning a period of activity, such as walking. It spontaneously vanishes only to be repeated at regular intervals.

Charcot's diagnostic category, intermittent claudication, became part of the description of the pathological difference of the Jew and one of the specific diseases associated with Eastern European Jews. H. Higier in Warsaw published a long paper in 1901 that summarized the state of knowledge about intermittent claudication as a sign of the racial makeup of the Jew.[22] The majority of the 23 patients he examined were Jews, and he found that the etiology of the disease was "the primary role of the neuropathic disposition [of the patients] and the inborn weakness of their peripheral circulatory system." By the time Higier published his paper at the turn of the century, this was a given in the neurological literature. Such illnesses were to be found among the male Jews from the East, from the provinces. Heinrich Singer saw intermittent claudication as proof of the "general nervous encumbrance born by the Jewish race."[23] This is a restatement of the Haskalah's view that the Eastern Jews were diseased because of their form of religious practice as well as their "2000" years in the ghetto. Jewish reformers saw the only way to transform the diseased Jewish body was to liberate the Eastern Jew from his social bondage.

The earlier debate between Enlightened Jews and the Hasidic masters about the meaning of smoking for Jews suddenly became part of the science of the nineteenth century as it sought to explain disease through a model of racial degeneracy. One of the attempts to move this intermittent claudication classification away from a sign of the general weakness of the modern Jew's body was taken up by Samuel Goldflam in Warsaw.[24] Goldflam was one of the most notable neurologists of the first half of the century.[25] What was noteworthy in Goldflam's analysis of his patients with intermittent claudication was not that they were all Eastern Jews, but that they were almost all very heavy smokers. Thus, it is not the ill Jewish body that bears the stigma of nervous disease but rather tobacco intoxication.[26]

In a major review essay on the "nervous diseases of the Jews," Toby Cohn, a noted Jewish neurologist, included intermittent claudication as one of his categories of neurological deficits.[27] While commenting on the anecdotal nature of the evidence and calling on a review essay by the Jewish neurologist Kurt Mendel

(who does not discuss the question of "race" at all[28]), he accepted
the specific nature of the Jewish risk for this syndrome while leaving the etiology open. Two radically different etiologies had been
proposed: the first reflected on the neuropathic qualities of the
Jewish body, especially in regard to diseases of the circulatory system. The other potential etiology noted by Goldflam and Cohn
did not reflect on the inherent qualities of the Jewish foot, leg, and
body, but on the misuse of tobacco and the resulting occlusion of
the circulatory system in the extremities. It is tobacco that, according to Wilhelm Erb, played a major role in the etiology of intermittent claudication.[29] In a somewhat later study of 45 cases of
the syndrome, Erb found, to his own surprise, that at least 35 of
his patients showed an excessive use of tobacco (defined as the
consumption of 40 to 60 cigarettes or 10 to 15 cigars a day).[30] Indeed, the moral dimension that the latter provide in their discussion of the evils of tobacco misuse is an answer to the image of the
neurological predisposition of the Jew's body to avoid military ser-
vice.[31] According to the medical literature, the misuse of tobacco
is a sign of the Eastern Jew, not of the Western Jew. Goldflam's patients were all seen in Warsaw. The noted Berlin neurologist Hermann Oppenheim observed that, of the cases of intermittent
claudication in his practice (48 cases over five years), the overwhelming majority, between 35 and 38, were Russian Jews.[32] The
Eastern Jew's mind is that of a social misfit and his body reifies this
role, but this is not a problem of Western Jewry except by extension.

One must note, however, that the desire to locate the etiology
of intermittent claudication in the heavy use of tobacco by Jews
played directly into the racial theory of the day. What had been a
sign of the irrationalism of the Eastern Jew during the Haskalah
came to be understood as the cause of their pathological difference
from "healthy" non-Jews. By the close of the nineteenth century
Jews were already labeled as a "race" with a particular susceptibil-

ity to tobacco poisoning. In the classic literature of that period on the pathology of tobacco, such as the work of L. von Frankl-Hochwart, Jews were tagged as susceptible because of the presence of intermittent claudication as well as of certain types of cerebral events, such as aphasia.[33] The latter was seen as a disease of Western Jews. He claims that Orientals since they smoke in the open in their "natural" space are less susceptible to tobacco-related diseases.[34] It is the practice of smoking in society, in closed spaces, that causes illness among these same Orientals now displaced into a hostile, modern environment. In this view Jews were Orientals out of their appropriate place (and practices) in the Middle East. This view continues in complicated ways through the late 1930s.

Fritz Lickint, whose work on tobacco reaches back to before World War I, repeats the claim that it is intermittent claudication that marks the major effect of tobacco on the Jewish body. He goes further to state that the overuse of tobacco among the Jews has a religious cause since it is the result of a religious prohibition against the use of alcohol.[35] (Lickint's claim is based on a common medical and popular belief that Jews consumed less alcohol than other groups. It had no basis in ritual prohibition.[36]) Although he came to be an authority on smoking in the Third Reich, Lickint was not a follower of racial theory. Indeed, his model was one of bodily types, following Ernst Kretchmer, with some bodily types being more susceptible to the diseases of tobacco. His work was used by the Third Reich in its campaign against smoking. Hitler was personally opposed to the use of tobacco. The Nazi "war" against tobacco, so well documented by Robert Proctor, relied on older notions that would have appealed to Clemens Brentano more than a century before. In 1941, at the opening of the Institute for Tobacco Hazards Research in Jena, the editor Johann von Leers argued that the Jews were responsible for introducing tobacco into Europe and that they continued to use the tobacco trade as a means of destroying Aryan culture.[37] Smoking was still seen as a major tool to undermine the German body.

Who poisons whom with tobacco? The debate about Jews and the nervous illnesses caused by smoking was found beyond the case study of intermittent claudication. In seeking a root cause for the degeneracy perceived as tied to life in the modern world, tobacco was also designated as one of the origins of hysteria and, by Theodor Billroth, the great Viennese surgeon, of the "nervousness" of modern society.[38] This nervousness was the result of the competition for survival and the result that "tired nerves need the stimulation of tea and alcohol and strong cigars" to function.[39] Jews—and here it must be stressed that these were Jewish men—were seen as the ultimate victims of the modern world since they were congenitally unable to deal with the pressures of modern life. Not only did the non-Jewish scientists of the age believe this, but also Jewish physicians such as the early Zionist and physician Max Nordau accepted this. In the nineteenth century Jewish men are assumed to be a group highly predisposed to specific forms of mental illness such as hysteria. And indeed, there was the view that one of the primary forms of undiagnosed mental illness of the fin de siècle was "Nicotinismus mentalis."[40] Smoking caused hysteria and male Jews from the East were, according to common medical wisdom, the classic hysterics. Yet, if excessive smoking caused nervousness, Leopold Löwenfeld saw moderate smoking, three cigars a day, as a potential therapy to "reduce nervousness."[41] Jews were seen as those who most suffered from all forms of diseases of the modern world and smoking might actually cure them!

The diseases of modern life included the cancers attributed to smoking, especially the smoking of cigars. Certainly the most famous case was that of Sigmund Freud, who was diagnosed with buccal cancer in 1923. For Freud, a cigar was much more than a cigar. He even attributed his ability to work to tobacco.[42] Being without a cigar "was an act of self-mutilation as the fox performs in a snare when it bites off its own leg. I am not very happy, but rather feeling noticeably depersonalized," he writes to Sandor Ferenczi in 1930 after another heart attack.[43] The cigar was a central attribute of his own sense of self; without it he ceased being a complete human being.

For Freud, his father was the model for the productive smoker: "I believe I owe to the cigar a great intensification of my capacity to work and a facilitation of my self control. My model in this was my father, who was a heavy smoker and remained one for his entire life."[44] In Vienna it was the Eastern Jew of Jacob Freud's generation who was understood as an abuser of tobacco.[45] By the close of the nineteenth century, traditional Hasidic views dismissed the smoking of cigars as mere vanity.[46] By Freud's own generation of westernized Jews, cancers of the hard palate had come to be called "rich man's cancer" because of the cost of purchasing the 15 to 20 cigars a day deemed necessary to cause the cancer.[47] In the popular mind, cancer of the buccal cavity became a sign of success, much as did cardiac infarctions during the 1980s in the United States. It was no longer understood as a sign of inferiority but of acculturation. What had been qualities (both smoking and illness caused by smoking) ascribed to foreign Jews became qualities associated with a specific economic class, as Jews became more and more integrated into the economic life of Vienna. Freud, himself a displaced Eastern Jew, saw the smoking of cigars as marking a specific place for himself in Western society. Indeed, from 1900 to 1930, about the time that Freud's cancer was discovered, Jewish scientists, such as Maurice Sorsby, recorded that the incidence of cancer among Jews, except for genital cancer, seemed to be approaching the level of the non-Jewish population.[48] By becoming ill, they were becoming like everyone else.

A predisposition to specific diseases among the Jews, including a predisposition to irrationalism, are seen to be triggered by smoking. These illnesses are an intrinsic aspect of the image of the

Jewish body from the eighteenth century through the twentieth
century. It is also internalized into the Jewish self-image at that
time. As science began to define the Jew as a race, problems associated with smoking that were present in the religious and cultural
models of Jewish identity were transformed into medical categories. This world of mythmaking is far from any real association
of individual Jews with the actual world of tobacco farming, curing, sale, and manufacture.

The fascination with the "special" relationship between Jews
and tobacco has not vanished. Recent medical studies that focus
on illnesses attributed to tobacco use, such as lung cancer, have
also seen tobacco addiction as a cause of death among Jews at a
greater rate than the general population.[49] The contemporary argument focuses on the urban concentration of Jews more than on
any sense of predisposition to tobacco addiction. In contemporary
Israel, the role of tobacco as a source of disease went virtually un-
heeded until the founding in 1999 of Ma'avak Be'tabak (Struggle
Against Tobacco) by Dov Rabinowitz, an immigrant from
Boston.[50] Tobacco-related illnesses are a public health problem in
Israel as 28 percent of the adult population of Israel smoke and
10,000 Israelis die each year from smoking-related causes, making
it the leading single cause of death in the country. The focus is, as
in the Enlightenment, to reach the most religious members of the
Israeli community. Rabinowitz, who is modern Orthodox, believes
that "there is incredible dissonance between being an Orthodox
Jew and smoking. Jews are not allowed to damage their own or
others' health. But you can't get the message across to them in the
general media." Religious authorities agree with him. The Ashkenazi chief rabbi, Yisrael Meir Lau (a former smoker), has condemned smoking and pleaded for legal intervention: "There is no
doubt that smoking is a dangerous addiction that can be and
should be prevented. One should not set down laws that the public
cannot observe, but it would be good and right if international or-

ganizations take action to reduce the cultivation of tobacco and to-bacco advertising and to minimize—if not to halt—the production and marketing of cigarettes."[51] Sephardi spiritual leader Rabbi Ovadia Yosef was even more outspoken: "If the rabbinical courts ruled, every person who smokes would get 40 lashes. To make a living, you're living at the expense of people who die. Managers of tobacco factories are sinners and will receive divine retribution. They will suffer on their day of judgment."[52] Importing the American antitobacco model of hygiene marks a tendency toward modernization even among the religious authorities in the Jewish state. The image of the Jew as associated with growing, manufacture, and consumption of tobacco that was part of an exoticism of Jewish identity as long as tobacco was seen positively vanishes once smoking is seen only as a source of illness.

CHAPTER FOUR

A FRENCH FRONTIER

Proust's Nose

IN 1889 THE AUTHOR OF AN ARTICLE IN THE *ARCHIVES IS-raèlites* chastised those Jews who try too hard to fit into mainstream French society by Frenchifying their names and downplaying their ethnic background. While such gestures were well known in other Diaspora societies that demanded Jewish acculturation, there is one rather surprising claim: that the practice of wearing fake noses (*faux nez*) would bring no good to those who indulge in such activities. With the rise of modern political anti-Semitism, Paris again became a frontier for Jews before and after the Dreyfus affair, with the authenticity of their very bodies drawn into question.

Almost a hundred years later, on January 30, 1983, in a lecture remembering the famous Chicago Reform Rabbi Emil G. Hirsch, Rabbi Howard Berman of Chicago's Sinai Congregation retold the following anecdote. In the 1940s Hirsch used to tell his debutantes who wanted nose jobs that "you can change your noses, but you can't change your Moses."[1] In remembering Hirsch, Berman stressed the significance of the Jewish nose as a hallmark of his opposition to simple-minded acculturation. Hirsch was one of the first generation of Reform rabbis who were also Zionists. He saw Jewishness as unalterable: Jewish authenticity was tied to the unalterability of a Jewish identity, represented by the Jewish body.

How can one bridge these two moments: the desire to alter the Jewish face before the beginnings of modern aesthetic surgery of the nose and its seemingly widespread practice among Jews following the Shoah? How can one recognize the desire to mask and the simultaneous desire to reveal? As a cultural historian, I mentally raced through my readings of Marcel Proust.[2] In his *Remembrance of Things Past*, a series of novels written to recapture the world of the 1880s and 1890s, there is a self-reflexive passage in the novel entitled *Swann's Way*. Here the narrator is talking about the arrival of the immediately identifiable crypto-Jewish character Charles Swann at the dinner hour, disrupting his schedule:

> After two shy peals had sounded from the gate, she would inject and vitalize with everything she knew about the Swann family the obscure and shadowy figure who emerged, with my grandmother in his wake, from the dark background and who was identified by his voice. But then, even in the most insignificant details of our daily life, none of us can be said to constitute a material whole, which is identical for everyone, and need only be turned up like a page in an account book or the record of a will; our social personality is a creation of the thoughts of other people. Even the simple act which we describe as "seeing someone we know" is to some extent an intellectual process. We pack the physical outline of the person we see with all the notions we have already formed about him and in the total picture of him which we compose in our minds those notions have certainly the principal place. In the end they come to fill out so completely the curve of his cheeks, to follow so exactly the line of his nose, they blend so harmoniously in the sound of his voice as if it were no more than a transparent envelope, that each time we see the face or hear the voice it is these notions which we recognize and

to which we listen. And so, no doubt, from the Swann they had constructed for themselves my family had left out, in their ignorance, a whole host of details of his life in the world of fashion, details which caused other people, when they met him, to see all the graces enthroned in his face and stopping at the line of his aquiline nose as at a natural frontier . . . [3]

The point of Swann's nose is clear: for Proust it is a map of the world in which the Jew is the boundary marker that defines the limits of what is French. This boundary is risky to traverse and more over, in spite all other protestations of equality, still visible. The nature of this self-consciously constructed and internalized identity of the Jew as diseased, as polluting, is reflected in his physiognomy.[4] The new nose (*faux nez*) is a mask identical to the new persona adopted by the Jew. Proust recognized that such a view possessed such power that even Jewish writers like himself (i.e., writers who felt themselves stigmatized by the label of being "Jewish") needed the mask to disguise the nose. (Proust's uncomfortable relationship to his mother's Jewish identity haunted his life almost as much as did his gay identity.)

Swann is more than a visible Jew who desires some form of invisibility. He is also a member of the elite who marries a courtesan. This link between Jew and prostitute is mirrored in Proust's manner of representing the sexuality of the Jew. For Proust, being Jewish is analogous to being gay—it is "an incurable disease."[5] But what marks this disease for all to see? For to the turn-of-the-century mind, syphilis in the male must be written on the skin, just as it is hidden within the sexuality of the female. Proust, who discusses the signs and symptoms of syphilis with a detailed clinical knowledge in *Cities of the Plain*, knows precisely what marks the sexuality of the Jew upon his physiognomy. It is marked upon his face as "ethnic eczema."[6] It is the infectious nature of that "incurable disease," the sexuality of the Jew, that Proust's Jew fixated upon his courtesan. (This is an interesting reversal of one of the subthemes of Zola's *Nana*. There Nana, like Moll Hackebout, is first the mistress of a Jew, whom she bankrupts and drives to suicide.) The Jew's sexuality, the sexuality of the polluter, is written on his face in the skin disease that announces the difference of the Jew. For Proust, all of his Jewish figures (including Swann and Bloch) are in some way diseased, and in every case, this image of disease links the racial with the sexual, much as Proust's image of the homosexual links class (or at least, the nobility) with homosexuality. ("Homosexuality" is a "scientific" label for a new "disease" coined by Karoly Benkert in 1869 at the very same moment in history that the new "scientific" term for Jew-hating, "anti-Semitism," was created by Wilhelm Marr.)

The image of the infected and infecting Jew also had a strong political and personal dimension for Proust. And yet, how can one reconcile the notion that the internalization of the image of the Jew is a reflex of a false set of values generated by society and internalized by the powerless (even though they are wealthy and well-placed)? For the ability to "see" the Jew who was trying to pass as a non-Jew within French society is one of the themes of the novels, a theme which, after the Dreyfus affair in the late 1890s, had overt political implications. Seeing the Jew was seeing the enemy within the body politic, the force for destruction. And Proust's "racial" as well as sexual identity was tied to his sense of the importance of class and society for the definition of the individual. Thus, Proust's arch Jew, Swann, was visibly marked by him as the heterosexual syphilitic, as that which he was not (at least in his fantasy about his own sexual identity). But was syphilis a disease of the body or of the soul?

One clear problem is the notion, which develops at midcentury, that the reconstruction of the face is the reconstruction of the face not of the Jew, but of the syphilitic. In 1834 the Berlin surgeon Johann Friedrich Dieffenbach, the central figure in nineteenth-century facial surgery, wrote that " . . . a man without a nose [arouses] horror and loathing and people are apt to regard the deformity as a just punishment for his sins. This division of diseases, or even more their consequences, into blameworthy and blameless is strange. . . . As if all people with noses were always guiltless! No one ever asks whether the nose was lost because a beam fell on it, or whether it was destroyed by scrofula or syphilis."[7] The surgeon's moral imperative was evident: correct and hide the fault, no matter what its cause, so as to allow the individual to pass as whole and healthy.

Theodor Billroth, the famed nineteenth-century Viennese surgeon, often carried out "plastic operations with artistic ability to correct defects of beauty (*Schönheitsgebrechen*) . . . one could see his joy when he was able to successfully improve the appearance (*verschönern*) of a damaged person, so that that person was no longer the object of pity or horror."[8] Whatever the cause of their disfigurement, Billroth's Viennese patients struck their observers with the same pity and horror, the classical hallmarks of ancient tragedy, as did the victims of syphilis. One of his most distinguished students, Vincenz Czerny, pioneered the modern reconstruction of the saddle nose, a nose without a bridge. Recounting a case in 1895, Czerny stressed that the patient came from "a healthy family (without a history of rickets or lues) and had suffered a depression of the osseous nasal skeleton through a fall on his nose, when he was 3 years old."[9] It was a childhood fall (as in Sterne's *Tristram Shandy*) and not inherited syphilis that was the cause of the child's deformity. But all deformed noses (and souls) in this world were assumed to be syphilitic in nature! Even Socrates's proverbially ugly nose is read in the nineteenth century as a clinical sign of syphilis.[10] (It seems odd since Socrates had his nose long before the illness was introduced into Europe in the fifteenth century—but this argument was made by a scholar arguing against Columbus having "discovered" syphilis in the Americas and having carried it back to Europe!) The unclean nose embodies all of the horrors associated with the illness and the bad character of those who have it.

According to nineteenth-century medical science, the Jew had a special relationship to syphilis (through the agency of the prostitute). But this special relationship could literally be seen on the Jew. The British pamphleteer Joseph Banister saw the Jews as bearing the stigmata of skin disease (as a model for discussing sexually transmitted disease): "If the gentle reader desires to know what kind of blood it is that flows in the Chosen People's veins, he cannot do better than take a gentle stroll through Hatton Garden, Maida Vale, Petticoat Lane, or any other London 'nosery.' I do not hesitate to say that in the course of an hour's peregrinations he will see more cases of lupus, trachoma, favus, eczema, and scurvy than he would come across in a week's wanderings in any quarter of the Metropolis."[11] The image of the Jew's nose is a delicate anti-Semitic reference to the phallus. For the nose is the iconic representation of the Jew's phallus throughout the nineteenth century. Indeed, Jewish social scientists, such as the British savant Joseph Jacobs, spend a good deal of their time denying the meaning of "nostrility" as a sign of the racial cohesion of the Jews. It is clear that for Jacobs (as for Wilhelm Fliess in Germany) the nose is the displaced locus of anxiety associated with the marking of the male Jew's body through circumcision, given the debate about the primitive nature of circumcision, and its reflection on the acculturation of the Western Jew during the late nineteenth century. Indeed, even the putative blackness of the Jew's skin reflected the infection of the Jew with syphilis! Jews bear their diseased sexuality marked on their skin like the leper.

This view is to be found in Adolf Hitler's discussion of syphilis in fin-de-siècle Vienna in *Mein Kampf* (1925). Hitler links the Jew, the prostitute, and the power of money:

> Particularly with regard to syphilis, the attitude of the nation and the state can only be designated as total capitulation. . . . The invention of a remedy of questionable character and its commercial exploitation can no longer help much against this plague. . . . The cause lies, primarily, in our prostitution of love. . . . This Jewification of our spiritual life and mammonization of our mating instinct will sooner or later destroy our entire offspring.[12]

Hitler's views also linked Jews with prostitutes and the spread of infection. Jews were the arch pimps; Jews ran the brothels; but Jews also infected their prostitutes and caused the weakening of the German national fiber. Jews are also associated with the false promise of a "medical cure" separate from the "social cures" that Hitler wishes to see imposed: isolation and separation of the syphilitic and his/her Jewish source from the body politic. (Hitler's reference here draws upon the popular belief that particularly the specialties of dermatology and syphilology were dominated by Jews, who used their medical status to sell quack cures.)

Between the eras of Proust and Hitler began the aesthetic medical alteration of the Jewish nose. The means to change the nose, and perhaps the character, was supplied by Jacques Joseph, a highly acculturated young German Jewish surgeon practicing in fin-de-siècle Berlin. Born Jakob Joseph, he had altered his too-Jewish name when he studied medicine in Berlin and Leipzig. Joseph was a typical acculturated Jew of the period. At the university he had joined, like many Jewish students, a conservative dueling fraternity and bore the scars of his saber-dueling with pride. (Jews were at that time admitted to the general fraternity systems in Germany.) Indeed, he must have appeared much like Kunz, the oldest Jewish sibling in Thomas Mann's vaguely anti-Semitic novella *The Blood of the Walsungs* (1905), "a stunning tanned creature with curling lips and a killing scar,"[13] who remains, as Mann describes him, essentially Jewish in spite of his scar.

Like many acculturated Jews, such as Theodor Herzl, the founder of Zionism, Joseph "relished the test and adventure of the duel, the so-called *Mensur*, which was considered manly and edifying."[14] The scars (*Schmisse*) from the *Mensur* were intentionally created. Students challenged each other to duels as a matter of course, without any real need for insults to be exchanged; being challenged was a process of social selection. "Without exclusivity—no corporation," was the code of the fraternities as late as 1912.[15] The duelists had their eyes and throats protected, but their faces were purposely exposed to the blade of the saber. When a cut was made, it was treated so as to maximize the resulting scar. The scar that Joseph bore his entire life marked him as someone who was *satisfaktionsfähig* (worthy of satisfaction), someone who had been seen as an honorable equal and thus had been challenged to a duel. Marked on the duelist's face was his integration into German culture.

The more marginal you were the more you wanted to be scarred. In 1874 William Osler, then a young Canadian medical student visiting Berlin, described "one hopeful young Spanish American of my acquaintance [who] has one half of his face—they are usually on the left half—laid out in the most irregular manner, the cicatrices running in all directions, enclosing areas of all shapes,—the relics of fourteen duels!"[16] Such scarring was not extreme among the medical students of the day. The scar marked the individual, even within the medical faculty, who was seen as a hardy member of the body politic. This was the context in which the Jewish fraternities (most of which did not duel) sought to reconfigure the sickly Jewish body into what the early Zionist Max Nordau called the "new muscle Jew." The Jewish fraternity organization stated in 1902, that "it desires the physical education of its members in order to collaborate in the physical regeneration of the Jewish people."[17] For some Jews, a dueling scar marked the socially healthy individual.

At the very close of the nineteenth century, after Joseph and
Herzl left the university, Jewish men were strenuously excluded
from Christian dueling fraternities. Being a member of a fraternity, like being an officer in the army, was a badge of truly belonging to the in-group in the society. It was a sign of being a German.
With the expulsion of the Jews from the dueling fraternities, this
sign of belonging was denied Jewish men. In 1896 the Christian
dueling fraternities had accepted the following proposal:

> In full appreciation of the fact that there exists between Aryans
> and Jews such a deep moral and psychic difference, and that our
> qualities have suffered so much through Jewish mischief, in full
> consideration of the many proofs which the Jewish student has
> also given of his lack of honor and character and since he is
> completely void of honor according to our German concepts,
> today's conference . . . resolves: "No satisfaction is to be given to
> a Jew with any weapon, as he is unworthy of it."[18]

Jews are different and thus dishonorable; they are unworthy of satisfaction, even if those with facial scars, look just like "real Germans." The visible scar advertises and guarantees the purity of the
group. Because Jews cannot be pure, they must be denied the right
to scar and to be scarred in duels. For a Jew to bear a facial scar is
to hide his sickly essence from the mainstream. This duplicity is
what is meant by "Jewish mischief."

By the 1920s such seemingly false scarring comes to be part
of the German discourse on aesthetic surgery. The aesthetic surgeon Ludwig Lévy-Lenz tells the tale of a young man who, having won money in the lottery, came to him and wanted him to
create artificial dueling scars through a cosmetic procedure.[19] In
this way, he could pass as someone who was worthy of being challenged to a duel. Lévy-Lenz refused to do the surgery and the
young man went to a barber who scarred him with a straight
razor and in doing so severely damaged his salivary glands. The

visible scar enabled the young man to pass as a man of honor. But was it an authentic mark of honor or merely cosmetic?

The scarred Jacques Joseph was trained as an orthopedic surgeon under Julius Wolff, one of the leaders in that field. In 1893 Wolff had developed a surgical procedure to correct the saddle nose, which followed up James Israel's earlier work repairing the syphilitic nose in the mid-1880s. Wolff's major surgical innovation was not cutting the graft from the forehead, thus avoiding a telltale scar.[20] More important, he established the "law of the transformation of the skeleton." This argued that every function of the skeleton could be described through the laws of mechanics and that any change in the relationship between single components of the skeleton would lead to a functional and physiological change of the external form of the entire skeleton.[21] Wolff's wide-ranging contributions to the practices of his day included developing a therapeutic procedure for correcting a club foot with the use of a specialized dressing that altered the very shape of the foot.[22] Orthopedics, more than any other medical specialty of the period, presented the challenge of altering the visible errors of development so as to restore a normal function.

Joseph's interests did not lie with the foot, even though the feet were often considered another sign of Jewish inferiority, but elsewhere in the anatomy. In 1896 he undertook a corrective procedure on a young child with protruding ears, that, while successful, caused him to be dismissed as Wolff's assistant. Joseph's procedure was his own, but it paralleled the work of the American otorhinolaryngologist Edward Talbot Ely who had corrected a "bat ear deformity" on a twelve-year-old boy in 1881. Ely undertook the procedure because the child had been "ridiculed by his companions."[23] In Berlin in the 1890s, this sort of operation was seen as "beauty" rather than "real" surgery. When Joseph was dismissed, he was told by his Jewish supervisor Wolff that one simply did not undertake surgical procedures for vanity's sake. A child's protruding ears were not in the same class as a functional disability, such as a club foot or the reconstruction of the external ear, which had been a major problem for surgeons from the earliest written accounts.[24] (The congenital absence of the external ear [microtia] was often attributed to hereditary syphilis. This would have been grounds to operate!)

Yet, according to the child's mother, the boy had suffered from humiliation in school because of his protruding ears. It was the child's unhappiness with being different that Joseph was correcting. Abnormally big and protruding ears alone might account for the child's unhappiness. But it was the specific cultural meaning of protruding ears at the close of the nineteenth century that really added insult to injury. They were understood in Central Europe to be a sign of Jewish identity.

An old European trope about the shape of the Jew's ears can be found throughout the anti-Semitic literature of the fin de siècle. The racial anthropologist Hans Günther summarizes the turn-of-the-century view that Jews, especially the males, have "fleshy ear lobes" and "large, red ears" more frequently than other peoples do. They have "prominent ears that stick out." According to Günther, prominent ears are especially prevalent among "Jewish children; one refers to them in Austria as 'Moritz ears.'"[25] Moritz (Morris) was a typical Jewish name of the day. They are the "elongated ears" that appear as the "ill-shapen ears of great size like those of a bat," according to an English-language anti-Semitic text of 1888.[26]

In his major paper of 1910 on the correction of "prominent ears," William H. Luckett of New York comments obliquely about the "odium attached to these ears."[27] In the American cultural context, these may have been the jug ears that dominated the caricatures of the Irish (and which contemporary Irish aesthetic surgeons continue to treat aggressively in modern Eire). They may also have been the ears of the Jewish immigrants on the lower East

Side. The stigma they evoke is repugnance at a visible sign of difference, a difference ascribed to the character as well as to the body. Luckett reports that one of his patients suffered "the constant harassing by classmates [which] frequently is the cause of so much distress as to produce a very bad mental condition in the child as well as in the parents, and to warrant our surgical interference." The strife that a big-eared child sows among his classmates spreads so much unhappiness in the world that the surgeon's larger duty, as well as the needs of his patient, demands that he operate.

The "scientific" belief in the visibility of the ear as a racial marker is also a major subtheme of one of the major works satirizing the world of turn-of-the-century Prussia, Heinrich Mann's *Man of Straw* (1918).[28] In that novel, Mann's self-serving convert, Jadassohn (Judas's son?) "looks so Jewish" (85) because of his "huge, red, prominent ears" (86) which he eventually has cosmetically reduced. He goes to Paris to have this procedure done. Mann clearly intends the ugly ears to be read as a sign of the Jew's lack of good character. They give the lie to any claim of conversion away from Jewishness. They mirror the shallow characterlessness of the Jewish parvenu. Jadassohn is put down as merely "witty," (87) as other Jews in the novel are "too clever" (57). The ears of the Jew are a sign of his superficiality, a sign recognized by the other characters in the novel as a reason to mock and taunt him.

Heinrich Mann sends his character to France for surgery rather than to Berlin. He saw the difference represented by Jadassohn as physical and identified it with the "foreign," which during World War I meant "France." "Like cures like," to follow the homeopathic model evoked in the novel. Mann also uses the name of one of the most prominent German Jewish dermatologists-syphilologists, Josef Jadassohn, for the name of his character. The association of Jews with syphilis is not merely a fantasy of anti-Semitic rhetoric, which classified them either as carriers of the illness or as being immune to it. This also reflects disapproval of notable Jewish scientists such as Adolf von Wassermann and Jadassohn for choosing to study and treat such a disreputable disease.

This image of the "Jewish ear" flourished into the twentieth century. Adolf Hitler was convinced that Joseph Stalin was Jewish (as he claimed all Bolsheviks were) and arranged to have photographs analyzed to see whether his ear lobes were "ingrown and Jewish, or separate and Aryan."[29] Race is written clearly on the body—especially on the ear. As late as in the 1970s in Central Europe "men request plastic operations of the ears more frequently than do women."[30] No wonder. A standard textbook on physical anthropology published in 1974 still listed the ear as a sign of Jewish racial identity: "The ear is large, wide in its upper part, and provided with a large lob."[31] From its inception the operation on the ear is a deracializing operation that is gendered in complex ways. It comes to have the same significance for Jewish males as the Jewish nose and the circumcised penis. It is a sign of the male child's humiliation. The desire to pass as normal, which is the result of the felt need to be completely "male," created the need for a new specialty that would dispel psychic pain by intervening in the body of the male child. For Jewish women and girls with big ears, long hair obviated surgery and allowed them to pass.

After being dismissed from Wolff's clinic, Jacques Joseph had opened a private surgical practice in Berlin. In January 1898, a twenty-eight-year-old man came to him, having heard of the successful operation on the child's ears. He complained that "his nose was the source of considerable annoyance. Wherever he went, everybody stared at him; often, he was the target of remarks or ridiculing gestures. On account of this he became melancholic, withdrew almost completely from social life, and had the earnest desire to be relieved of this deformity."[32] The symptoms were analogous to those of the young boy whose ears Joseph had repaired.

Joseph took the young man's case and proceeded to perform his first reduction rhinoplasty, cutting through the skin of the nose to reduce its size and alter its shape by chipping away the bone and removing the cartilage. On May 11, 1898, he reported on this operation before the Berlin Medical Society. In that report Joseph provided a detailed scientific rationale for performing a medical procedure on an otherwise completely healthy individual: "The psychological effect of the operation is of utmost importance. The depressed attitude of the patient subsided completely. He is happy to move around unnoticed. His happiness in life has increased, his wife was glad to report; the patient who formerly avoided social contact now wishes to attend and give parties. In other words, he is happy over the results."[33] The patient no longer felt himself marked by the form of his nose. He was cured of the "disease of nostrility." In his own eyes, he looked less different from the group he desired to join, the non-Jews. Joseph had undertaken a surgical procedure that had cured his patient's psychological disorder! Yet, he had left scars that pointed to the procedure itself, and this became a major concern of Joseph. He warned his colleagues that "disclosure to the patient on the problem of scarring is very important. Many patients, however, will consider even simple scars too conspicuous."[34] He raised the specter of a court case in which the "unsightly scar might represent a greater degree of disfigurement than the enlarged cartilage [of the nose] presented previously" (35). More centrally though, surgical scars, unlike dueling scars, reveal the inauthencity of the body and the effort to pass by means of medical intervention.

On April 19, 1904, Joseph undertook his removal of a hump from within the nose using cartilaginous incisions. He retrospectively commented that in 1898 he had used the extranasal procedure which "caused a scar, but this scar will be hardly visible after a short time, assuming that the incision is sutured exactly."[35] But "hardly visible" was not sufficient. Even the slightest scar was enough to evoke a visual memory of the too-big nose. The invisibility of the patient hinged on the elimination of the scar. Both patients needed to become (in)visible to pass, and Joseph had learned that only invisibility left his patients happy.

Joseph's claim to fame was his solution to the problem of the visible scar. His procedure to remove the excess bone and cartilage intranasally (from within the patient's nose) is still used today, as are the surgical tools he used to carry out the procedure. But others also claimed to have recognized this problem earlier and to have corrected it. His priority as the first surgeon to use the intranasal procedure was challenged in 1923 by the Berlin surgeon Friedrich Trendelenburg, who described undertaking (and documenting) such a procedure in 1889.[36] Joseph's procedure also paralleled one developed by John Orlando Roe in upstate New York. In 1891, his patient, a Miss C——, came to him for a "winter cough" but used this apparent excuse to complain to him about the "angular, bony projection of the top" of the nose. Roe developed a procedure to shorten the nose intranasally and corrected the source of her perceived ill health and present unhappiness.[37] Roe's procedure, like that of Trendelenburg, did not leave scars and this was a major difference from Joseph's initial attempts at reduction rhinoplasty. In his 1892 paper on "sunken noses," Robert F. Weir presented a case of "monomania" focusing on the too-large nose and his detailed attempts to cure it by the reduction of the size of the nose.[38] But it was Joseph's procedure that dominated the field because his patient population among the Jews in Central Europe was extensive, exposed, and anxious about their nostrility.

Large numbers of Joseph's patients needed to become invisible to become happy, but the men and women had different visions of happiness. In his summary paper on the reduction of the size of the nose published in 1904, Joseph commented on the psychology of his male patients: "The patients were embarrassed and self-conscious in their dealings with their fellow men, often shy and unsociable, and had the urgent desire to become free and unconstrained. Several complained of sensitive drawbacks in the exercise of their profession. As executives they could hardly enforce their authority; in their business connections (as salesmen, for example), they often suffered material losses. . . . The operative nasal reduction—this is my firm conviction—will also in the future restore the joy of living to many a wretched creature and, if his deformity has been hindering him in his career, it will allow him the full exercise of his aptitudes."[39] According to Joseph, the patient "is happy to move around unnoticed." The visibility of the Jew (often defined in the nineteenth century in terms of his mercantile ability) made it impossible for him to compete equally with the non-Jew in the economic world at the turn of the century. Only vanishing into the visual norm and passing as non-Jewish in terms of his appearance enabled the young Jewish male to become part of the general society. Passing thus meant functioning more fully as a male, because masculinity was defined in economic terms.

Such a transition became possible in late nineteenth-century Germany when the legal restrictions, which limited the Jew (and especially the Jewish male), were lifted. Jewish women were still bound by the limitations applied to women in late nineteenth-century Europe, but Jewish males generally could enter into the world of masculine endeavors as long as they were not too evidently Jewish. No law bound them (unlike African American males in the United States at the same moment) from becoming officers, doctors, lawyers, or businessmen in the general society, but the powerful social stigma associated with the Jews continued in spite of civil emancipation. Thus one did not want to appear Jewish—one needed to be able to pass as German or French. A twentieth-century commentator notes about Joseph's procedures that: "Even today, 70 years later, one often hears the erroneous remark that rhinoplasty is an operation for vanity's sake. That is not true. Vanity is the desire to excel. The average rhinoplasty patient wishes to be relieved of a real or imagined conspicuousness of his nose."[40] The route to happiness lay not in standing out but in blending into the dominant group whose silently taking no notice of one was the key sign of one's acceptance. Being (in)visible is being intensely visible, but as a member of a group which defines itself as the norm, as beautiful and healthy. Friedrich Nietzsche quite insightfully noted that we are only aware of our bodies when we become ill. This was the boundary Joseph's patients desired to cross. They wished to forget their bodies, to become one with those they imagined had no worries about the acceptability of their bodies. This is the essence of passing and it set the model for all aesthetic surgery for the future. In order for such a model even to appear effective, all awareness must be on the level of consciousness; no unconscious desire or hidden goals can influence the individual. Physical change must alter consciousness. But the male Jew's hope of passing, of vanishing into the world of the German or the French, depended not just on the alteration of all-too-visible ears and noses, but on the surgeon's ability to alter the most hidden and secret aspect of the male body.

Proust's fascination with the Jewish body was a reflection of this European, scientific discourse about the fixed nature of the body and the desire of Jews to alter their own visibility. His ambivalent sense of belonging to high culture in France was heightened by the split in his cultural world by the Dreyfus affair. As much as Franz Kafka on the eastern frontier of the Austro-Hungarian empire, Marcel Proust, hidden away in his cork-lined room in Paris, saw his own body (Jewish, gay, French, Catholic) as the object of contestation.[41] For Proust, syphilis marked the Jewish body. As we shall see, the other side of the argument was where Kafka imagined his own Jewish body situated. As Kafka did, Proust wrote this into his literary creations, a permanent cultural monument to debates about Jewish physical difference that so dominated his own times.

CHAPTER FIVE

A DREAM OF JEWISHNESS
ON THE FRONTIER

Kafka's Tumor and "A Country Doctor"

FRANZ KAFKA KNEW HIS FREUD. FRANZ KAFKA GREW UP and into the age of Freud on the frontier that was Prague in imperial Austro-Hungary. Freud had been moved as a small child from the provinces to Vienna. He had crossed the frontier for those acculturated Jews in the provinces who oriented themselves toward Vienna (or even Berlin). Kafka was as much at home in Prague as he was anywhere. As with Freud in Vienna, Kafka's sense of being on the frontier had much more to do with an awareness of his own body that was shaped by what it meant to be Jewish (read: ill) in a world of health (read: non-Jewish bodies). This was Kafka's sense of the frontier, as it was of many Jewish thinkers in his time.

Much as the surrealists such as Max Ernst and André Breton "invented" Freud, finding in Freud "scientific" proof of their own manner of seeing the world, Kafka too created his own Freud. And in his deepest fantasies about the psyche, Freud invented the world in which Ernst and Breton and Kafka could be imagined. Like Freud's own "dream book," which Kafka read and annotated,

Kafka's diaries are full of real, invented, or desired dreams.[1] Indeed, in complex ways and in spite of his struggle with psychoanalysis and his avoidance of psychotherapy, Kafka's fascination with the dream as a key to his own internal life remained consistent over his adult life. But as often as not, Kafka's dreams (like that of his creation Gregor Samsa) are waking dreams: "I can't sleep. Only dreams, no sleep," he writes in July 21, 1913.[2] These waking dreams are constructed from what Freud calls "day residue," the images left over from daily experience. Kafka knows this category and writes on February 11, 1914, to Grete Bloch: "This type of sleep I have is superficial, truly not fantastic, rather constructed from the thoughts of day; they are exciting, repetitious dreams that are more lively and exhausting than being awake" (18). On March 22, 1922, Franz Kafka enters in his diary the following dream: "In the afternoon a dream of a tumor on the cheek. The continually trembling border between the normal life and the seemingly more real horror" (62). Let us imagine with Kafka where such a dream can be located in the world of K.K. (imperial Austrian) culture and dreaming. As Karl Grözinger has shown, such dreams can have Jewish as well as psychoanalytic roots, a mixture that is not atypical after the turn of the century.[3]

On March 7, 1913, Julius Tandler, a Jewish professor of anatomy and a Viennese city councilor, addressed the German Society for Racial Hygiene (that is, eugenics).[4] (It is Tandler who in 1924 interceded for the terminally ill Franz Kafka at the behest of Kafka's friend Franz Werfel and enabled Kafka to get a bed at the Kierling Sanatorium, where he ultimately died.[5]) In this basic address, he attempted to align a series of concepts that were loosely used at the turn of the century—among them constitution, predisposition, and race. Tandler assumed that these aspects define the human being and that they are present simultaneously. For him, all of these categories are "predetermined at the moment of conception" (13). Anything that can be altered by environment is not constitutional. Constitution is the variation that is present in an individual once the qualities of type and race are subtracted. This would have included any "inherent relative abilities" such as the specific "disposition" for an illness. Thus, there are "tumor races" (20). (There is a slippage from constitution to race in Tandler's argument). According to Tandler, there are races that develop specific forms of tumors.

Who are the tumor races and why are tumors the sign of their racial difference? What is a tumor on the cheek for Kafka in 1922? In 1838 Johannes Müller had discovered that the cell structure of a tumor is inherently different from normal cell structure. In Berlin Hermann Lebert then was able to describe in detail the morphology of the cancerous cell. By the 1860s Rudolf Virchow's view that only cells could give rise to other cells, and, therefore, that cancer was not a foreign intrusion into the body was accepted. Cancer was an inherent, degenerative cellular disease which, by 1886, was believed to be limited by the specific origin of the cell from which the tumor sprang.

But what caused cancer? The views were as diverse as the theories themselves. With the acceptance of Louis Pasteur's view on the bacteriological origin of certain diseases such as rabies, one focus was on bacteria. The fascination with local inflammation and the realization that it seemed to produce tumors gave rise to the alternative view that cancer was a disease resulting from scarring. Given the central importance of the science of race in medicine, it is little wonder that at the beginning of the twentieth century the focus turned to the question of race and its role in the origin of cancer.

In 1914 Theodor Boveri, professor of zoology at the University of Würzburg, published his study of the origin of malignant tumors which argued that carcinomas had their ultimate origin in an error of the chromosomes that could be caused through either mechanical or chemical means.[6] This view augmented earlier

work by David von Hansemann, who saw in the growth of malignant tumors a parallel to that of normal cells. He understood cancer as a type of developmental response to external stimuli.[7]
Cancer was to be understood as a somatic mutation that could,
therefore, be inherited, rather than as the result of some unknown
infectious disease.[8] This view had been widely discussed in the
course of the late nineteenth century. Greater knowledge about
the mode and means of inheritance, following the rediscovery of
Mendelian genetics at the beginning of the twentieth century, led
to the reestablishment of this view as one of the central theories
for the origin of cancer. By the 1930s this view of cancer as a disease of the chromosomes had become part of eugenics' cadre of
inherited diseases that could be eliminated by careful breeding.[9]

During the course of the nineteenth century the question of
race becomes one of the means of distinguishing those at risk from
those who were seen to be immune from the disease. From the
very beginning, the Jews were labeled as a tumor race. In the
1860s the Italian Jewish scientist Cesare Lombroso had begun to
study the question of the comparative mortality of the Jews of
Verona in the context of the death rate of the non-Jewish population. He observed that Veronese Jews suffered from double the
number of cases of cancer than did Veronese Christians.[10] Lombroso's statistics supported the contention that Jews were a separate and unique race, whose medical anomalies rested in this
separateness. They were, to quote one early twentieth-century
study, " . . . a race of considerable purity of stock, [which] . . . by
their ubiquitous presence . . . supply the interesting phenomenon
of a racial unit subjected to widely-differing geographical influ-
ences."[11] In Berlin during 1905, 8.6 percent of all deaths among
Jews was attributed to cancer, while the rest of the population evi-
denced a 6 percent death rate from cancer.[12]

At the close of the nineteenth century the predominant view
came to be quite the opposite. British physicians such as James

Braithwaite at the fin de siècle made the simple reversal of Lombroso's claim about a Jewish predisposition to cancer.[13] Their view, that "cancer occurs rarely among Jews," was quickly refuted by further statistical evidence to the contrary.[14] But if Jews were neither immune nor predisposed to cancer, they certainly were seen as a group that presented very particular manifestations of the disease.[15]

By the beginning of the twentieth century the question was no longer whether or not Jews suffered from cancer but whether Jews were predisposed to or immune from certain types of tumors. There was a growing statistical literature that discussed the Jewish predisposition and immunity to specific forms of cancer. In 1890 W. S. Bainbridge could cite the case of a sarcoma in a Jewish woman as a pathological curiosity.[16] But in 1909 in Munich, Adolf Theilhaber saw the social rather than the racial role of his patients as a major factor in the frequency that any group develops specific carcinomas, such as uterine tumors.[17] Religious practices of the Jews, such as circumcision, were felt to play a role in the lower incidence of uterine cancer.[18] The Jewish neurologist Leopold Löwenfeld reinterpreted Theilhaber's findings very differently. He saw the lower incidence of uterine cancer among Jewesses as a reflection of types, rather than of race. The earlier menarche of Jewish women reflected the predominance of a specific type (the plethoric) among the Jew: the increased amount of blood in the organ resulted in lower incidences of uterine cancer.[19] As we have seen, the replacement of racial arguments with typological arguments was a common one in the fin de siècle.

The work of Felix Theilhaber, Adolf Theilhaber's son, on the decline of the Jewish birthrate had begun with his interest in cancer while he was at his father's proprietary hospital for female diseases in Munich. He documented the complex literature on the relationship of cancer to race, stressing the much lower rate of cancer of the uterus and cervix for Jewish women and, as his father had also stressed, and the much higher rate of cancer of the stomach for Jewish men.[20] He clearly saw that this was in no way tied to the question of class, as the Jews he examined came from many social classes. He also discounted the prevailing views about the lower rate of uterine and cervical cancer. For him, because Jewish women tended to have more children (his figures were from Budapest), a lower birthrate could not account for the lower cancer rate. They were admitted to hospitals more frequently (which would tend to provide a higher rather than a lower reporting of incidence), and they were exposed to the same surgical procedures as non-Jewish women. He noted that the "Jews are a purer race than those people among whom they live," and they suffer from many fewer cases of cervical cancer.[21] Theilhaber assumed the lower cancer rate was related to the etiology of the tumors.

The Theilhabers make little distinction between "racial," i.e., endogenous, and "social," i.e., exogenous, causes for cancer and its localization, but certain overall views can be extrapolated from their findings. For the Theilhabers, the localization of specific cancers makes it possible to speak of a gender-based difference in the types of cancer among Jews. The stated rationale for the lower incidence of uterine and cervical cancer among Jewish women is sexual practices of the Jews, specifically the "strict observance of the Mosaic Law regarding marital relations."[22] The laws that govern abstinence among Jewish women during and following their menstrual cycle decrease the amount of "continued irritation" which is seen as "a potent causative factor" in the etiology of cancer. Hidden within this argument is the assumption that one further cause is the ritual circumcision of male Jews as well as their lower incidence of sexually transmitted disease.[23] For there is a strong assumption in the course of the late nineteenth and early twentieth centuries that cervical or uterine cancer had a parasitical origin that could be sexually transmitted.[24] The etiology for the higher incidence of stomach cancer among Jewish men is the pace of life; the lower rate of cervical cancer among women is due to the sexual practices of the Jews. Contemporaries would have had access to a summary of this debate in Felix Theilhaber's essay on cancer and the Jews in the *Jewish Lexicon*.[25] It is fascinating to measure this discussion and its literary reception against the counter argument that not only Jews were the primary carriers of syphilis, infecting Western Europe, but they had a heightened proclivity for the disease themselves. The skin diseases attributed to the Jews, as reflected in Marcel Proust's representation discussed in the prior chapter, illustrate how anti-Semitic stereotypes cover all cases. But these skin diseases also show that the response by Jewish physicians about Jewish immunity comes to be seen as an answer to the charges of their great risk for sexually transmitted diseases. Kafka and Proust share a complex legacy of claims of physical difference of the Jews.

Certainly the debate about the localization of cancer in both male and female Jews focused on the central biological marker of the Jew, the circumcised penis, and its implications.[26] There is a detailed literature on the relationship between penile cancer and circumcision. Penile cancer accounted for between two and three percent of all cancerous tumors in the male during the nineteenth century and was one of the most physically and psychologically devastating diseases. As early as 1882, the British surgeon Jonathan Hutchinson related the occurrence of cancer of the penis to the appearance of phimosis, the constriction of the prepuce, in infants. He also encouraged the practice of circumcision as it "must necessarily tend to cleanliness."[27] This relatively rare anomaly became one of the standard rationales for the advocacy of universal male circumcision by the end of the century and its introduction in the United States.[28]

In 1907 J. Dellinger Barney, of the Harvard Medical School, published a study of one hundred cases of cancer of the penis in which he noted "that not a single circumcised Jew was found in the hundred cases. This seems to my mind a most convincing argument in favor of circumcision."[29] Benjamin S. Barringer and Archie Dean added 36 cases to the literature on cancer of the penis in 1923 and noted early in their paper that "no Jews appear in this series."[30] Abraham Wolbarst of New York asked the most evident question: "Is circumcision a prophylactic against penis cancer?" His study which considered 675 males, who with few exceptions were Jews, found "not a single case of cancer of the penis."[31] The reason Wolbarst gives is the "cleanliness" that circumcision affords.[32] In Austria, the work of V. Föderl at von Hochenegg's surgical clinic in the University of Vienna in the 1920s argued precisely the same point: he reported on 40 cases from his clinic over a period of 24 years, none of which were in Jewish males. In addition he related 276 cases of cancer over 11 years among men from the Viennese Jewish Hospital in which not a single case of penile cancer was recorded.[33] Further studies in Vienna done over the years 1921–1927 record 2,252 cases of cancer in Jewish males, but of these, not a single case of cancer of the penis was found.[34] These statistics implied not only that there was an immunity to penile cancer afforded by circumcision but, that taken together with Theilhaber's work on cervical cancer, cancer of the genitalia was substantially less frequent among Jews than among the general population. Circumcision was a prophylaxis against cancer and was a sign of sexual hygiene. Here, the implications of the debate about Jews and the transmission of syphilis lurked in the background.

There is a complex interrelationship among many of these views concerning Jewish immunity or propensity for specific forms of disease. Given the debate about the lower (or higher) incidence of syphilis among Jews, it is little wonder that this view is linked to statistics concerning specific forms of cancer. Thus, cancer of the mouth was assumed to be the result of scarring left by syphilis. In the standard nineteenth-century handbook on syphilis, there is an extensive discussion that "in the case of the tongue, the association of the two [cancer and syphilis] is so common, that it is difficult to avoid an impression, that syphilis must exercise some degree of predisposing influence. . . . In attempting to lay down rules for the differential diagnosis between cancer and syphilis, I am most anxious to insist, as already done, on its extreme difficulty. . . . Cancerous processes may be simulated by syphilis in the closest possible manner."[35] In one study, 30 percent of all of the cases of cancer of the mouth were claimed to have a syphilitic origin.[36] Maurice Sorsby used this as an illustration to rebut the assumption that the Jewish immunity to certain forms of cancer was hereditary: "A low incidence of [cancer of the tongue] among Jews would lend no support to the suggestion of racial immunity to it among Jews, for it its well known that cancer of the tongue is frequently excited by syphilis, and syphilis is by no means so common among Jews as it is among non-Jews; indeed, in the past it was almost completely absent."[37] Indeed, there was the assumption that there was a low incidence of cancer of the buccal cavity (the soft tissues of the mouth and tongue) among Jews.[38]

For the period from 1924 to 1929 Sigismund Peller documented a greater incidence of death from buccal cancer among Jewish men than among Jewish women. (In Peller's sample, 28 Jewish men died as against 9 Jewish women. For every 100 cases of cancer reported, 2.5 Jewish men suffered from buccal cancer and .7 Jewish women as opposed to 3.5 non-Jewish men and .4 non-Jewish women. In the overall statistics 37 Jews and 319 non-Jews died of buccal cancer, a ratio of 1 to 8.5.) Peller notes that Jewish men are much less likely to have cancer of the oral cavity and Jewish women much less likely to have cancer of the genitalia than their non-Jewish counterparts.[39] Later work contrasted cancer of the mouth and cancer of the breast in men and women: cancer of the mouth was five times more frequent among men and cancer of the breast was seventeen times more frequent among women.[40]

What the breast represented for the female, the mouth represented in the male. Reproduction defines the "woman" within nineteenth-century medicine. The image of the Jewish male as possessing and using language as a weapon defines him in anti-Semitic thought as far back as (at least) Immanuel Kant. Jewish males had a substantially lower rate of buccal tumors than the general population, but higher than Jewish women. Disease was gendered as much as it was categorized by race.[41]

Are tumors of the cheek racial signs or are they signs of syphilitic infection—or both? Are they male or female illnesses? Following these chains of associations may lead to an understanding of the day residue in Kafka's dream. Kafka had been diagnosed with tuberculosis in 1917. Tuberculosis was, like syphilis, a "social disease" according to the French physician Jules Héricourt.[42] However, it was not considered to be a Jewish disease. Indeed, Jews were seen in Central Europe as relatively immune to the disease (at least until the horrible winter of 1916–1917).[43] But tuberculosis was associated with the stigma of a disease written on the body. The *habitus physicus*, the tubercular body with its sunken chest and lanky, bony frame was Kafka's body. These stigmata only revealed the innate nature of the body. Tuberculosis is the result of "the privations and the fatigue undergone by men of weakly constitution [that] end by reawakening attenuated or torpid cases of tuberculosis" (viii). (Read: Jews.) Héricourt's British translator, Bernard Miall, provides the ultimate rationale for a eugenics that would separate the healthy from these sick but hidden bodies, the beautiful from the potentially ugly:

> We need a religion of beauty, of perfection. It would be a simple
> matter to teach children to worship perfection rather than hate
> it because it reveals their own imperfection. For we cannot teach
> what beauty is without making plain the hideousness of egoism.
> Beauty is the outward and visible sign of health—perfection—

virtue. Pleasure is the perception of beauty, or some of its elements. What makes for the fullness and perfection of life, for
beauty and happiness, is good; what makes for death, disease,
imperfection, suffering, is bad. These things are capable of
proof, and a child may understand them. Sin is ugly and painful.
Perfection is beautiful and gives us joy. We have appealed to the
Hebraic conscience for two thousand years in vain. Let us ap-
peal to the love of life and beauty which is innate in all of us. A
beauty-loving people could not desire to multiply a diseased or
degenerate strain, or hate men and women because they were
strong and comely and able.... The balance of the races is
overset, and only the abandonment of voluntary sterility by the
fit, and its adoption by the unfit—which is eugenics—can save
us. (244–5)

In this view, it is the Hebrews (not the Hellenes) whose fantasy of
the body has condemned modern man to the world of self-
loathing and disease.

And yet it is not evident when one looks at the Jew that he is
diseased. The reason for this is that Jews have over the years undertaken certain ritual practices that have left them unmarked by
certain ailments such as tuberculosis:

All these peculiarities in the comparative pathology of the Jews
are not due to any ethnic, "biostatic," or racial characteristics of a
purely anatomical or physiological nature in relation to non-Jews.
They have their origin in the past history of the Jews, in their
habits of life, and in the fact that syphilis and alcoholism have but
rarely been seen among them. When the Jew is commingling
with his Christian neighbors and adopts their customs and habits
of life, he sooner or later loses his "racial characteristics," and his
comparative pathology presents no special peculiarities.[44]

Only in the acculturated Western Jew (such as Franz Kafka) do the
signs of disease (tumors, cancer, tuberculosis, and syphilis) become

immediately evident, for these Jews have shed their supposed immunity as they left ritual behind them. It is the hidden Jew within the Western Jew that appears, revealing the inherently diseased nature of the male. It is the reconciliation of the seemingly contradictory association (or nonassociation) of Jews and syphilis that marks the self-representation of the modern, acculturated Jew as "diseased." Here Kafka, in his obsessive concern with his own body, is little different than Proust. The fear that the body must betray to the world the Jew hidden within is translated into concern about disease and hygiene.

Even before his diagnosis with tuberculosis in 1917, Kafka begins to understand this notion of a diseased Jewish body that fails when it is acculturated. Kafka's feet increasingly prevent him from undertaking the strenuous physical activity that he needs to reform and transform his body, a hopeless task given the body's persistence. In early October 1910, he dislocates his big toe. He writes that "the foot in particular is enormously swollen—but it is not very painful. It is well bandaged and will improve."[45] The physical foot may improve, but Kafka's symbolic foot never will: it will inexorably become the lame foot of the Jew. It represents an inability to be a real man; it is a sign of the Jew, the devil, and the cripple: "I frightened Gerti [Kafka's young niece] by limping; the horror of the club foot."[46] The limping Jew is the evil Jew.

The limp foot is conspicuous in anti-Semitic discourse of the time. In Oskar Panizza's fin de siècle drama, *The Council of Love*, the Devil appears as a Jewish male, his corruption written on every aspect of his body including his foot: "The Devil stands before them, leaning on one foot and supporting the other with his hands. He wears a black, close-fitting costume, is very slender, close-shaven with a fine-cut face, but his features wear an expression that is decadent, worn, embittered. He has a yellowish complexion. His manners recall those of a Jew of high breeding. He leans on one foot, the other is drawn up."[47] The "yellowish" skin color, the limping leg, the degeneracy of the Jew form Panizza's image of the seducer of humankind. His limp signifies his Jewish illness and effeminacy.

At the fin de siècle, it is the syphilitic who limps, as the Parisian neurologist Joseph Babinski showed in 1896 when he proved that a diminished plantar reflex was a sign of neurosyphilis. The limp of Panizza's Devil's reveals him to be a syphilitic Jew. He thus prefigures the central theme of the play—the introduction of syphilis into Renaissance Europe. He is already infected with his disease, his Jewishness, and he will presumably spread it by using the Jews as intermediaries. Syphilis was actually considered a Jewish disease as early as its first modern outbreak in the fifteenth century, and Panizza as well presents it as such, personified in a Jewish, male Devil.[48]

The symbolic association of Jewish or Satanic limping with syphilitic limping was already well established in the culture of the late nineteenth century, by means of the intermediate image of the "yellow" skin of the Jew. His yellow, Oriental skin is also part of the standard image of the diseased Jew. Otto Weininger, the quintessential Jewish self-hater of the turn of the century, had stressed that Jews "possess a certain anthropological relationship with both Negroes and Mongolians."[49] From the former, they get their "readily curling hair," from the latter, their "yellowish complexion." This is an unchanging racial sign. For Kafka this yellow color later marks a disease process in the bearded "friend in Russia," in his tale "The Judgment" (1913), whose "skin was growing so yellow as to indicate some latent disease."[50] He bears the symptoms associated with the diseased Jew, including his skin color: "Even three years ago he was yellow enough to be thrown away" (87). This yellowness suggests the jaundice that signals a number of Oriental illnesses such as malaria and thalassemia but is also associated with the skin color of the syphilitic in European popular belief.

Kafka's world is a world of bodies and of images of bodies. Having seen the complexity of that tumor about which Kafka dreamed (and wrote), let us turn to a literary tale that employs fragmented aspects of this chain of images, and use the model that Freud proposed, a model that both revealed underlying fantasies through images and disguised the meaning of the images. Kafka knows this model. Whether he accepts it in its totality is doubtful, but the devices he uses (and that Freud presents) belong to the shared turn-of-the-century notions of hidden meanings in dreams and texts. These are, however, meanings exposed through the verbal account of visual images.

Kafka's "A Country Doctor" appeared in 1919 but was most probably written during the war winter of 1916–1917 that preceded Kafka's diagnosis of tuberculosis (and that saw a spectacular increase of the disease in Prague).[51] It is an account of a failed cure and the meaninglessness of modern, Western medicine. One evening a country doctor, actually the regional health officer, is called out on an emergency. At a loss as to how he is to get to his patient, a groom suddenly appears. Magic horses also appear out of his abandoned pigsty to pull his carriage. As he is about to depart, the groom suddenly turns on the doctor's maid, Rosa: "Yet hardly was she [Rosa] beside him when the groom clipped hold of her and pushed his face against hers. She screamed and fled back to me; on her cheek stood out in red the marks of two rows of teeth" (221). The mark on the cheek is the first sign of something wrong with the representations of the characters' bodies in the story, a sign of something being out of joint. It is a visible sign of the destruction presented by the introduction of illness into the tale, for without the call to the ailing patient, none of the magic would have been needed. We, through the eyes of the country doctor, see the marks on Rosa's cheek and we know their causation—the bite of the groom. But this is, of course, only the proximate cause, the sign now written on the body. The ultimate cause seems to be the illness of the patient. It is the doctor's diagnosis, the identification of the cause of illness, that fails at this point.

While the doctor threatens the groom with a beating, he is also made internally aware that the groom has appeared to *help* him to reach the patient and therefore cannot be punished as the patient must (according to the Hippocratic oath) take precedence. We read this in his thoughts as revealed by the narrator. So he is forced to abandon Rosa to the further attacks of the groom as the horses carry him to his patient. The "tumor on the cheek" enters the tale in the form of the groom's bite; sexuality, destruction, and illness are all suggested by the wound. This image is also indicative of the problem of Western medicine in trying to understand its multiple roles in a complex society.

When the doctor magically reaches his patient, he provides us with an account of the patient's appearance: "Gaunt, without any fever, not cold, not warm, with vacant eyes, without a shirt, the youngster heaved himself up from under the feather bedding" (221). Having made this physical examination, the doctor dismisses the patient as a malingerer until he is forced by his family to examine him further. At that point he discovers the tumor: "In his right side, near the hip, was an open wound as big as the palm of my hand. Rose-red, in many variations of shade, dark in the hallows, lighter at the edges, softly granulated, with irregular clots of blood, open as a surface mine to the daylight" (223). This is the description of a cancerous lesion as well as a syphilitic one, at least in its literary provenance. It is the grail king's wound to be healed by Parzifal (with Richard Wagner's music being quietly hummed in the background). The wound in the groin marks the appearance of illness, sexuality, and destruction. Its *rose*-color links it to the maid's cheek visually and literally, a link echoed in the visualization of the word as well as the color. And the doctor now feels that he cannot act at all; the case is hopeless. When the patient asks to be left alone to die, the doctor suddenly thinks about that other hopeless case, Rosa, whom he had abandoned some ten miles away.

Instead of going to Rosa's aid, the doctor continues to examine the lesion. In it he finds a further proof of the impossibility of cure. The wound is full of "worms, as thick and as long as my little finger" (223). The maggots in the wound are read by the doctor as a sign of putrefaction, of the inevitability of his patient's death from the now open tumor. He, of course, was wrong in this reading. He was brought to the bedside by the magic horses and through the actions of the magic groom not to evoke the powers of Western medicine but to bring his shamanic authority as a healer. The medical world that he has entered is the world of folk medicine. His modern, Western, enlightened skills may well be useless, he thinks, more because of his own ambivalence about them than because of any innate problem with the medicine itself. It is the doctor not the medicine that is at fault. The model of modern medicine that he brings into the country house forces him to misconstrue the meaning of the larva he sees in the wound. The maggots are not a sign of decay but of cure.

Maggot therapy is an old folk (and, in special cases, present-day clinical) remedy for cleaning precisely such ulcerations as those found in his patient. It had been recognized as a successful means for the debridement of wounds in folk medicine for at least four hundred years before Kafka wrote his tale.[52] By the 1920s the use of maggot therapy had even become part of Western clinical practice.[53] The line between folk medicine and clinical practice is always slippery but, from the perspective of the clinician, must always be distinguished from "quackery." The doctor's misdiagnosis of this folk remedy shows him that his only role is to become part of the magical treatment of the child. He is lifted up by the family and laid in the patient's bed magically to warm and cure the child's lesion. When he is laid on the bed, the boy says to him: "'I have little confidence in you. Why, you were only blown in here, you didn't come on your own feet'" (224). The image of the foot suddenly reappears in the text as the definition of a "real" doctor.

In this magical world of dreams structured according to Kafka's reading of Freud, dreams reveal as they dissemble. The images are condensed accounts of complex narrative that reach beyond themselves into the past. Kafka knows this. All of the images that Kafka uses deal with a complex of cultural fantasies about Jews. The wounded body of the woman and the diseased body of the child both represent classic turn-of-the-century anti-Semitic views embedded in the popular (and clinical) medical discourse of the day. Is the wound cancer or is it syphilis or is it a cancer caused by syphilis? The doctor too takes on the coloration ascribed to the Jew during the late nineteenth century. His feet reveal him. Standing on one's own feet is impossible for the acculturated Jew suspended between the belief systems of religion and the fantasies about the diseased Jewish body inherent in the rational world of medical science.

It is clear that Kafka is not writing "A Country Doctor" as a tale about Jews, even though his uncle Siegfried Löwy may have served as a model for the protagonist.[54] His vocabulary of images that deal with illness and bodily decay is taken from the vocabulary of his own world. How could it be otherwise? What is removed is the Jewish aspect in Kafka's bodies. All else is left. Kafka's dream of the tumor is the dream in which all of the qualities of race, so central to the world in which Kafka lived, vanish. I have argued elsewhere in my study of Kafka that one of the resulting moves of universalizing the literary discourse of Kafka's texts was to deracinate it.[55] While some of his contemporaries, such as Richard Beer-Hoffmann and Arnold Zweig, were moving in precisely the opposite direction by thematicizing Jewishness, Kafka was removing the overt references to the Jewish body from his work.[56] What is left, of course, are the images without their racial references, and yet they would have been present in any contemporary reading of the text. The association between sexuality and disease, the association of specific predisposition to specific forms of tumors were part of the legend of the Jewish body at the turn of the century. One further association that is quite powerful is the image of the Jew as physician that haunts the anti-Semitic literature of the time as well as the work of Jewish physicians such as Arthur Schnitzler.

In Kafka's tale of the country doctor, the Jewish references are totally missing, yet their traces, following Kafka's reading of Freud's theory of the dream, are still present. Let us imagine that Kafka *consciously* adapts a Freudian model rather than thinking that this is all a process of unconscious forces. Kafka knows clearly that his texts are avant-garde, that the model he strives for is a reading of his texts not as a Jewish writer with all the anti-Semitic taints ascribed to that category, but rather as a modern writer. The imagery he draws on are the images from which he wishes to distance himself. They are present in a gestural language: the tumor of the cheek and the lesion in the groin mark the presence of disease. The unsure-footedness ascribed to the physician and his inability to read the folk medicine he sees (and becomes part of) mirror the sense of being caught between rival claims. On the one hand (foot?) was the Enlightenment claim of the Jew as rational being, espousing a scientific religion that prefigured much of modern medicine. On the other hand (foot?) was the desire of Central European Jews at the turn of the century to be different, to express their Jewishness in their own manner, even to revel in the irrational and the magical. Leopold Sacher-Masoch had presented this dichotomy in 1892 in his key text on the nature of Austrian Jews, called "Two Doctors," contrasting and reconciling the two types.[57] For him, a late Enlightenment (and non-Jewish) writer, modern medicine is recognized by the practitioner of folk medicine as preferable and wins the competition. Jews of Kafka's generation are no longer so secure in this assumption. Perhaps the lost truths of ancient belief and practice were in their particularism more valuable for the modern Jew than acculturation. In "A Country Doctor," Kafka too uses the physician as the model for the conflict between rationality and irrationality but is quite clear as to which force will win. The forces of the irrational triumph because the doctor cannot understand what he sees through the lens of his rationality. This too was the dilemma seen by Jews of Kafka's generation from Martin Buber to Walter Benjamin, from Georg Lukacs to Gershom Scholem. It echoes in their writing and their desire for a place for the irrational, for the messianic, for the transcendental in the world. Kafka's engagement with this model of Jewish identity is written into the bodies of his characters as the irrational nature of the meanings attached to their (and our) bodies.

CHAPTER SIX

PRIVATE KNOWLEDGE

Jewish Illnesses and the
Process of Identity Formation

BODIES ON EVERY FRONTIER ARE CONTESTED. THEY ARE drawn into question as ill or are seen as healthy. The new frontier in biology and medicine is that of genetic knowledge. How do we, as human beings in specific cultural settings, imagine being ill on this frontier? And how does this new moment echo many of the concerns that we have seen raised about the differences of bodies in the nineteenth and early twentieth centuries?

Recently scholars and the press have given much attention to the expanding implications of genetic knowledge in the public sphere.[1] What happens when your employer or the state has information about real or imagined anomalies in your genetic makeup—especially when those anomalies can be defined as diseases, whether current or future, whether yours or your off-springs'? It is clear that the negative impact of such public knowledge, at least in the light of our present inability to effect "cures" for genetically transmitted illnesses, seems to outweigh the public good. Employers in the United States now screen over a quarter of potential employees for genetically transmitted ill-nesses of all types in order to eliminate individuals at risk from their insurance pool. While seemingly in violation of existing laws, such sharing of information, as Dorothy Nelkin shows in two coauthored works, creates a new category of the "potentially ill" who are stigmatized and have virtually no ability to alter their now cryptopublic status. This is equally true of individuals with geneti-cally transmitted illnesses who are assumed to pass these illnesses on to their children. In a society that defines health as the norm, the moral implications of such an identity as someone at risk are clear. If being healthy is the norm, then being sick is abnormal. Being abnormal is a value-ridden concept that denies people con-trol and power over their own lives.

The very concept of "at risk" is complicated with interlocking aspects of definition. There are those who are at risk for a disease themselves. This may be because the category of illness present in their families has been redefined as "genetically" predisposed, as certain forms of breast cancer have recently been, whether or not a specific genetic test is now or ever will be available. There are those at risk because they have been tested for a conventionally defined, genetically determined disease, such as Huntington's chorea. This may also mean that these individuals are simultane-ously seen and see themselves as at risk for transmitting such dis-ease to their offspring, whether or not they have the potential of acquiring the disease themselves. And finally, there are those who have children with a disease defined as genetically determined, who suddenly recognize that they were at risk for having transmit-ted the illness. All these individuals are at risk but often times in different or overlapping ways. A parent who suddenly discovers that he or she is free from a disease that appears in their offspring has a different relationship to the idea of being at risk than does someone suffering from the disease itself. Yet these are clearly linked categories that compose the identity of those at risk.

Suddenly we are confronted with new communities of the potentially ill. Those labeled as bearing the seeds of illness are now seen in the public sphere as at risk. This label is also internalized by those individuals who are so defined in public. They become the potentially ill or the parents of potentially ill children. What has often happened with the public knowledge of their state is that the potentially ill have created an "imagined community" (to use Benedict Anderson's term in a very different context[2]) through which to control and comprehend their anxiety about their or their children's existing or potential illness. Those who see themselves as healthy (that is, not at risk) define this community as ill. They attempt to exclude or marginalize those now labeled as having the *potential* for disease. Those labeled as ill in complex ways accept this label and turn it into a mark of identity. For is there anything more redolent of identity in the age of the human genome than our biological code? In an age of biologization, have not our genes become the ultimate definition of who we believe we are? Indeed, the recent discovery at the beginning of 2001 that human beings have about half the number of genes as was predicted seems to strengthen the argument for adaptation of the genome through life experiences. It is interesting that the popular response to this discovery was a strengthened sense that the mapping of the genome will lead to cures for a wide range of diseases now understood primarily as genetic.

Such an imagined community of the ill is intergenerational. It connects the past with the present and the future. It becomes greater than the nuclear family through which it has been diagnosed. It is always present even when the focus of the community is horizontal, i.e., of the same generation. The ghost of the past is always present in the way that the present-day community is imagined. It is constructed by those family members who create a clearly defined social subset with whom they identify and onto which they are thus able to displace the stigma of responsibility for the disease. Not we alone are at risk, but all of our new extended family—the family unit now defined by a shared disease. All sufferers come to be members of this constructed family. "We are not alone" is their answer to the charge that they are at risk; "here is the community of the ill into which we fit." Such a bridging of the private sphere (nuclear family) and the public sphere (imagined community of the ill) is one of the most fascinating results of the new discussion of genetically transmitted disease.

What happens to the construction of such categories of potential or imagined genetically transmitted illness when we turn from the public sphere to the private sphere? What happens in the (self-constructed) private sphere of the nuclear family to the private knowledge of such risk? How is such knowledge understood within the family, i.e., what meaning is given to it? Does knowing about the potential for genetically transmitted illness alter the nature of intrafamilial relationships? What function does such constructed knowledge have on how families explain the potential of genetically inherited illness? Is ignorance better than knowing in such contexts? Are these problems analogous or different from the problems confronted in the public sphere, in, for example, the adoption process?

Recent work on the question of genetic knowledge in the case of adoption presents the middle ground between the purely public sphere questions and those intrafamilial questions raised by the claimed ability to use genetic information as predictors of pathology. (No one in the scholarly community seems to be interested at this point in positive predictors such as high intelligence or large stature. This, however, will surely play a role in future discussions as there is more and more desire to identify the genetic components of such qualities, even if they do not exist.) The present debate seems to focus on the impact of genetic information on the nuclear family as now constituted through adoption. For the psychologists Susan Michie and Theresa Marteau, any genetic information on potential

adoptees should be withheld, even from the adoptive parents, because of fear of impacting the private sphere. Such knowledge "may
distort the child's upbringing; expectations . . . may be affected."[3]
Also, there is the implied public sphere problem that adoptive parents may have greater knowledge of the genetics of the biological
parents than they have of themselves. Michie and Marteau come
down on the side of supplying virtually little or no information to
potential adoptive parents as this information may well skew the
adoption process at its very inception. Parents may be unwilling to
adopt a child who may develop a disease in the future.

The British physician J. A. Raeburn, on the other hand, advo-
cates the sharing of genetic information about the child with the
potential adoptive parents, but he places a major and ambiguous
caveat on that claim. He grounds his belief in the view that "adoptive parents should not expect to receive more information about
the adopted child than birth parents would have about their own
child."[4] What exactly does this mean? For Raeburn, the idea of a
community governed by knowledge means that the history of each
member defines the family.

Raeburn distinguishes between "secretive" and "open" families and argues that "candor and openness is usually in the best interests of any child whether adopted or not" (190). Thus if you
have information (or can get information) about the imagined
community of the ill it should be shared with the child (and by extension with the child's adoptive parents). Open is good; secretive
is bad. This, of course, presupposes that Michie and Marteau's
anxiety is baseless. Their belief is that such shared information
might skew the adoptive process in favor of those children with
clean genetic records or no genetic information whatsoever.

We seem to be caught between a rock and a hard place. In the
public sphere the decision to share information or disclose it is seen
as a consequence of a newly evolving public policy concerning
adopted children's right to know. This right to know is postulated

on the existence of an imagined community into which the child fits "naturally" because of the child's biological inheritance. Raeburn's evocation of the "best interest of the child" is a claim based on the discourse of rights, not of community. Within the potential adoptive family, the advocacy of intrafamilial privacy issues is stressed when the development and socialization of the child is at stake. The sharing of genetic information often comes down on the side of the child's rights to an unstigmatized life within another imagined community, now the healthy community of the adoptive family. (It is unimportant if the family is itself truly healthy; the assumption is that only healthy families adopt children. "Healthy" is another term for "acceptable.") For the nuclear family, newly constituted by adoption, needs to understand the child as integral to it rather than part of the public sphere beyond itself. The new child has to be healthy as the family is defined as healthy. What are the problems that arise within a nuclear family when genetic information concerning future pathologies is made available to the family?

There are two recent studies that attempt to answer questions about intrafamilial response to genetic information. T. M. Marteau and T. J. Peters at King's College (London) interviewed the parents of 24 children with familial hypercholesterolaemia, an inherited predisposition to heart disease.[5] Here the perception tests determined the parents' attitude toward the nature of the disease. When the parents saw the test as measuring heightened cholesterol levels, it was understood as measuring diet, and therefore under the control of the parents and less threatening. Diet can be changed within the family. When the test was seen as part of genetic screening, it was seen as uncontrollable and more threatening. Genetic predisposition was seen as inalterable and beyond the control of the family. The sense of parental guilt was thus ameliorated if the disease was understood as situational rather than as inherited, as part of the imagined community of the diseased. This seems also to be the case in an older study concerning colorectal cancer in which "the gene test is imbued with meaning beyond determination of gene status in families who choose gene testing."[6] The guilt of being the source of the illness was greater if the source was perceived as inherited rather than from the life style of the individual. Thus, in a sense, the community of the ill was perceived as more dangerous than the actions of the individuals, perhaps because it was seen as beyond the control of those defined as ill. Change your life style and end your risk, seems to be the mantra of modern medicine. But even life style changes can often not alter the course of illness.

T. J. Wilcke and his colleagues inquired about the impact of sharing such information about genetically transmitted illness among families with a member with alpha 1-antitrypsin deficiency (A1AD) as well as a control group.[7] Like familial hypercholesterolaemia, A1AD is an illness in which disability can be prevented by a change of life style or by careful management. Individuals with A1Ad lack a protective protein called alpha–1 antitrypsin that protects the lungs from a natural enzyme (called neutrophil elastase) that helps fight bacteria and clean up dead lung tissue. If allowed to progress, the lungs are damaged and a form of emphysema becomes chronic and may lead to death. It thus offers a multiple reading quite different than that offered by illnesses such as Huntington's chorea, which have at present a specific fatal course and little possibility of intervention (and therefore reinterpretation).

When individuals with severe A1AD were asked whether their sisters should be screened and told of the results, 66.8 percent said that they should be told of the results; 58 percent saw this as a means of preventing illness; 41 percent saw this as a means of "maintaining openness in the family and to avoid uncertainty." Given the question of the transmission to the next generation, such sharing with sisters marked a clear desire for information prior to planning a family of their own. "Openness" is itself a coded term and is a given a positive value in this society. Here, it refers to the revelation of the real or potential sharing of an illness. This sharing would take place within the extended family structure in the light of transmission to future generations. It presents the image of an imagined community of sufferers extended into the past as well as into the future.

The findings of these two recent studies are not particularly startling. It is clear that all stigmatizing illnesses are read to ameliorate the sense of guilt attached to them. When illnesses are understood as stigmatizing, they create inner conflicts among those who are labeled (correctly or incorrectly) as the cause of the illness. The construction of a greater community into which such illness can be read moderates the immediate effect of the role that the nuclear family has in being the cause of the illness. This is analogous to the anxiety felt in the adoption of children with potential genetically transmitted illnesses. There the fantasy of adoptive parents is to construct an imagined community of the potentially ill into which the child can be placed that is different from the biological inheritance of the adoptive family. In the nuclear family the desire is to construct a world beyond the nuclear family into which the illness can be projected and given meaning. The genetic identity of the adopted child is by definition different than that of the adoptive parents. However, it should not be seen as worse than the adoptive parents biological self-definition.

If we look at the discussion within nuclear families with ill children today, something similar occurs. The illness comes to define the family from within, in ways that limit the meaning of the illness through the construction of an imagined community. Public discussions of genetically transmitted illness are now haunted by images of the family, the traditional definition of the private sphere. I have drawn on a series of family websites that deal with the occurrence of a genetically transmitted illness. I understand that these websites are in the public sphere and are indeed intended to provide information to a broad public about genetically transmitted diseases using first-person accounts. Yet they also represent an odd opening on intrafamilial self-representations. For this purpose, let me take two self-representations of families with genetically transmitted diseases: one that has had two children who have died of the complications from Fanconi anemia; the other with a child afflicted with Tay-Sachs disease.

The first family, the Frohnmeyers, has a third child with the initial symptoms of Fanconi anemia. Named for Swiss pediatrician Guido Fanconi, Fanconi anemia is a recessive disorder, one of the inherited anemias that leads to bone marrow failure (aplastic anemia). Often marked by specific symptoms at birth (such as mental retardation or anomalies of the extremities), it is usually fatal before the child reaches adulthood. After their first child's death in 1983, they "struggled for two years with grief, anger, loss, isolation, and depression" since they "knew of no other similarly affected family."[8] They organized a support group in 1985 that now has 460 affected families. The need to see one's family as not unique is part of the discourse in this family, a way of affirming that the parents do not bear the responsibility for their children's disease. The child suffers from an aliment that, while rare, is not limited to one family and is therefore not "their fault." The number of such support groups for genetically transmitted illness has increased with the proliferation of information about the nature of the diseases themselves. Support groups may have many functions in the public sphere, but they also answer the Frohnmeyer's cry that they cannot be alone, they cannot be the only cause of their children's illness.

The creation of a cohort (like the equation of Jews and diabetes in the nineteenth century) in which genetically transmitted illness can be located and thus given meaning may have inherent ramifications not first grasped. The Tay-Sachs case has equally interesting dimensions in this regard. The Cassadys had a child in 1997 who showed the initial symptoms of Tay-Sachs shortly before his first birthday. Diagnosis was delayed because the Cassadys were both of Irish descent and Tay-Sachs is seen as a Jewish disease (although it is also found among Francophone populations in Quebec and Louisiana). Here finding a "community" to define the illness was difficult for the Cassadys: "The disease was predominately in the Jewish community for years. They do testing in most families where they feel the general public needs to be made aware of this disease." Specifically "a simple blood test can tell if you are a carrier to inform you before you have children."[9] Here the problem of "not belonging" meant that the illness could not easily be diagnosed because the family was not associated with the cohort. Ashkenazi Jews know they are at risk; they test to prevent the conception of children with Tay-Sachs but, goes the argument, we Irish did not have that luxury.

In the United States the National Foundation for Jewish Genetic Diseases has identified nine genetic diseases as "being the most common among Jews of Eastern European or Ashkenazi descent."[10] The diseases include Tay-Sachs; Bloom's syndrome, in which about 10 percent of those affected also have diabetes; Canavan disease, a progressive neurological disorder; dystonia, which affects movement control; Fanconi anemia and familial dysautonomia, both of which will be discussed below; Gaucher's disease, a metabolic disorder; Niemann-Pick disease, a neurodegenerative disorder; mucolipidosis, a neurological disorder and the most recently discovered Jewish genetic disease, first identified in 1974. Labeling these diseases "Jewish" especially in the public press, has created the impression that only Jews (defined as an ethnic, religious, or racial group) carry and manifest these diseases. The reality of patterns of reproduction and the dissemination of illness, as in the case of the Cassadys, belies this totalizing claim. Orthodox Jews have created a Committee for the Prevention of Jewish Genetic Diseases (Dor Yershorim) that provides anonymous genetic

testing (Tay-Sachs, cystic fibrosis, and Fanconi anemia) for potential brides and bridegrooms prior to any arranged marriage. This
would technically alert both parties and cause the marriage not to
take place, therefore slowly eliminating these diseases from the
genetic pool of Orthodox Jews. Thus it would come to be a Jewish
but not an Orthodox Jewish problem. Howard Markel observed
the problems of this Jewish bias in his op-ed piece in the *New York
Times* about the testing for Tay-Sachs.[11] After his wife, Kate, was
pregnant with their first child, she was tested for Tay-Sachs, "a
rare genetic disease that clusters among Askenazi Jews, of Central
and Eastern European descent." She tested positive and the question was whether he too carried the gene which would pass the illness on to their unborn child. Markel noted that before genetic
screening was available, about 1 in 3,500 children of eastern European Jews were born with this fatal disease; today about 95 percent
of the pregnancies are terminated once the disease is identified in
prenatal screening. The good news was that he was not a carrier;
the pregnancy was carried to term. Here, too, the promise of the
reduction of this illness now through termination reflects on the
identification of the illness as being limited to a specific cohort, for
only those perceived at risk will be tested for the disease. The Jews
as a social construct represent the extended family suffering from
the illness. This category excludes all others from this newly constructed family.

The notion of the family of children with inherited diseases as
part of a cohort, a new imagined community, is central to this self-
representation.[12] The case of familial dysautonomia can be taken
almost as paradigmatic. This genetically transmitted disease seems
to be limited to Eastern European Jews. The internet image of the
disease is made to reflect this quite literally: "Our logo shows a
small case 'fd' to reflect the medical expression of the autosomal
recessive nature of FD genetics. The letters are in an upswept Star
of David to symbolize our optimism for the future; the Star of

David in recognition of the predominantly Jewish inheritance of this disorder (our 'founder' who had the first mutation several hundred years ago undoubtedly lived in a Polish *shtetl.*)"[13] This becomes a Jewish disease and all of its sufferers become part of an extended family, an imagined community linked solely by their experience of having children with familial dysautonomia. Thus, all of the sufferers whether they have the disease or whether their children have the disease are cousins in illness:

> Since 99% of the kids who have FD have the exact same gene sequence at 9q31–33, it means that someone years ago had a spontaneous mutation (perhaps his mother ate too much borsht!). That mutation was inherited by his/her children and passed down through the years to us. Our FD children in turn inherited the affected gene from both parents. In other words, we are all truly related. Not just theoretically, but in reality. Distant cousins. Don't know if that makes things easier or not, but unlike Gaucher's Disease Type I, where there are at least 4 mutations, we are all from the same family. As such, I hope we can all work together to benefit our children! Signed: Your cousin, . . . [14]

The construction of an extended family of sufferers changes the very meaning of the private sphere and private knowledge. Inheritance means, in common usage, relationship; here, the relationship is via shared suffering. There is no question that the establishment of such cousinship is a means of sharing the burden of knowledge in all of its complexity.

One mother with an FD child wrote that she saw a particularly Jewish difficulty in constructing such an extended, public family: "My armchair theory is that Jewish families have some difficulty accepting children who do not have a bright future (as opposed to, in general, Catholic families). In the Hasidic community, kids with FD are often 'hidden' (according to the main doctor who treats the disorder)." This strikes me as perhaps a misreading of the construction of the extended FD family as a Jewish family. Here too, Jewishness is the collective quality given to the group of sufferers. Whether the social structure of Jewish communities is less flexible in this regard is doubtful. Jewish social organizations have traditionally dealt with the disabled, beginning with the Home for the Orthodox Feeble Minded in the late nineteenth century to contemporary organizations such as Keshet: Jewish Parents of Children with Special Needs. The sense that the Jewish community can serve as a public referent for the collective into which these families can now fit themselves seems important, no matter how Jewishness is interpreted in such contexts.

The need to construct a cohort through which the family and its expectations of genetically transmitted illness can be understood is evident. The power of this construction of the cohort is indicated in the two recent studies discussed above. But there are also interesting historical cases about the reading of genetically transmitted illness and their implications for individual identity within familial structures. What happens when one is defined within the family or, indeed, when the family is defined as diseased? There is an historical model in the view of diabetes, which was understood as transmitted within specific racial groups (in the scientific language of the nineteenth century: races) such as Blacks and Jews. Diabetes is a good case study for such questions because it is a disease that has two forms, one of which is clearly transmitted genetically; the other which may be present as a genetic predisposition (with a strong environmental factor) or as the sequelae of pregnancy or obesity.

In the nineteenth century, in the public sphere, labeling Blacks or Jews as a "diabetic race" was a means of labeling these groups as inferior. Thus, the Parisian neurologist Jean Martin Charcot explained to Sigmund Freud in the fall of 1888 about the predisposition of Jews for specific forms of illness, such as diabetes, where "the exploration is easy" because of the intramarriage of the Jews.[15] Jewish "incest" left its mark on the Jewish body in the form of diabetes as well as on the Jewish soul. (In his letter to Freud, Charcot used the vulgar "juif" rather than the more polite "Israélite" or more scientific "sémite."[16])

But how does the nineteenth-century Jew respond? Certainly there is the old Jewish joke about the Russian, the Frenchman, and the Jew stranded in the desert, slowly dying of thirst. They find a town and a bar. Stumbling in the Russian gasps that he is so parched that he must have vodka; the Frenchman that he must have wine; and the Jew, that he must have diabetes. Jewish scientists of the turn of the century, such as Felix Theilhaber in 1909, accepted the racial stigmatization of diabetes.[17] Other Jewish scientists, such as Joseph Jacobs, had seen diabetes as the result of the inferior social and economic position of the Jews: "So far as these [hemorrhoids and diabetes] are due to sedentary habits."[18] The American physician Maurice Fishberg saw (like Charcot) intramarriage as the cause. He writes that "the Jews have not had the advantage of draining the pure fresh country blood for the rejuvenation of their own . . . as a final result we find that most of the diseases that increase with the advance of civilization, particularly the neuroses and psychoses and also diabetes, are relatively more frequent among the Jews than the non-Jews."[19] Some physicians, such as Arnold Pollatschek in 1902 (working in the spa town of Carlsbad), saw this predisposition to diabetes merely as an artifact of the Jews' hypochondriacal mind-set and their financial ability to pay for diagnosis and treatment of the disease.[20] In other words, the attempt is always to understand the group predisposition to illness from within the group in the terms of a model that provides the individual researcher the most control of the present and/or future while taking into consideration the prevailing stereotypes of racial difference.

The cohort—here, the family—is defined either socially or biologically. The imagined community of the Jews with diabetes, like the notion of the family of sufferers today, moves the responsibility to a level beyond that of the individual. We know today that diabetes can be both a result of inheritance (type I) as well as life style (type II). Recent work shows that the cultural component may be telling. In work compiled over a decade, one researcher found an increase in cases of diabetes among Yemenite Jews who had migrated from a region where no sugar was eaten to one where their diet included sugar.[21] The researcher arrived at the conclusion that diabetes appeared in this group because of its entry into the "modern" world of sugar-rich diets and abundant food, not the fact that the group was Jewish or had a genetic predisposition. Today, the general consensus is that diabetes is not particularly a Jewish illness. Research being done now follows the so-called "thrifty genotype" hypothesis suggested in 1964: when mice are transferred from a harsh to a benign environment, they gain weight and are hyperglycemic. First generation groups of immigrants to either the United States in the late nineteenth century or to Israel today exhibit a substantially higher rate of diabetes. The initial groups, such as the Yemenites, showed an extremely low index of diabetes prior to their arrival in Israel. Thus, diabetes and obesity seem to be an index of a failure to adapt rapidly to the new environment.[22] It is in no way a Jewish genetic disease.

In the nineteenth century the image is of the "sick Jew" as part of a community of the ill. The result of this within Jewish communities in the West (from the mid-nineteenth century on, beginning in Hamburg) was the founding of Jewish hospitals, where Jewish patients had equal access, where Jewish physicians could research and practice. They were also, however, places that treated the illness perceived to be the illnesses of the community, not merely the illness of the individual. Jews in the twenty-first century, in an age where it seems that genetic markers label them as at risk, react no differently than other groups so marked. They create Jewish families of the ill. However, the historical context of this makes it a dangerous practice, for it sets off Jews as a collective at risk, thereby retaining the older relationship of race with that of disease. The new genetic frontier is one in which identity too is formed and the odd echoes of the past shape the response to the new categories. "Race" has reappeared as a category of analysis, as if the pseudo-anthropological definitions of race of the nineteenth and twentieth centuries are completely coterminous with the idea of genetic alleles in contemporary science. Indeed, the very notion of race now having a primary place in the categorization of scientific research (as well as in the development of a literature and centers for the study of Jewish genetic diseases) flies in the face of the misuse that this category has had over the past two hundred years. While any individual Jew may show the impact of any number of genetically transmitted diseases, by binding this evident fact in a homogenous category of the "Jew" leads to misrepresentations and bad science.

Today, the model of the support group, the therapeutic community, or the family of sufferers provides an analogous outlet for the desire of the individual to place him- or herself or their offspring into a context greater than that of an individual with an illness. The unspoken anxiety about having had a child with a genetically transmitted illness and the potential of bearing children who themselves will carry this "stain" on to future generations creates a phantom that haunts these families. It is the phantom of the cohort experience.[23] Not I, says the individual, but my family (however defined or constructed) is the cause of this illness and bears a covert responsibility with me to help me deal with it. Thus, anxiety is controlled by its displacement onto other levels of the community. The families with the private knowledge of inherited illness exorcise the ghost hidden within the gene by trying to create and thus understand the cohort into which the illness places them. And, as in the case of the Jews in the nineteenth century, the manner of doing this is to use the cohort to provide some type of meaning for the origin and form of the illness.

The construction of the cohort is also inherent in the self-understanding of the individual and the family with a genetically transmitted disease. By creating a cohort into which the family experience must be fitted, the onus of responsibility is lifted from the nuclear family unit and placed on the genetic allele. Such narratives of a constructed group identity come then to form and to haunt the narratives of those families that understand themselves retrospectively or prospectively at risk for genetically transmitted illness. The phantom in the machine here is the story of the cohort into which the family must insert itself. That story means that there is rarely private knowledge that is not immediately transmuted into public knowledge. For all such explanations move the image of the disease beyond the family into the greater world. Thus, it is not only possible but also necessary to create a science of such diseases, as in the nineteenth century, or websites advocating for the families with such disease in the twenty-first century. All of these are the public manifestations of private knowledge.

PART III

JEWISH BODIES ON THE
MULTICULTURAL FRONTIER

CHAPTER SEVEN

"WE'RE NOT JEWS"

*Imagining Jewish History and Jewish Bodies
in Contemporary Multicultural Literature*

MULTICULTURALISM AND THE JEWS

BY THE END OF THE TWENTIETH CENTURY A NEW FRON-
tier had come into being on which Jews were imagined to have a
special function. That new frontier was called multiculturalism
and it defined itself quite literally in terms of real or perceived
boundaries. It was, according to contemporary self-defined multicultural thinkers such as Gloria Anzaldúa, the space where "this
mixture of races, rather than resulting in an inferior being, provides hybrid progeny, a mutable, more malleable species with a
rich gene pool."[1] Contemporary multicultural theory provides a
further rehabilitation of notions of continually crossing ideas of
race at the frontier. The Canadian filmmaker Christine Welsh effects a similar, necessary rehabilitation of the anxiety about being
Métis, of mixed race: the *Métis* becomes one type on the Canadian
frontier.[2] By positing the "cosmic race" as "healing the split at the
foundation of our lives," she removes the stigmata of illness from
those at the borderlands.

And yet the multicultural is also the antithesis of hybridity. It can just as frequently be the reification and commodification of ethnic identity. It may stress the boundaries and borders between ethnic, cultural, religious, or class groups. If the *Métis* is hybrid, then hip-hop is multicultural. (And "world music" can be both!) While multiculturalism can allow for and indeed celebrate the merging of cultures so as to eliminate boundaries, one of its strongest claims (in the new global culture that is both hybrid and multicultural) is its insistence that each of us has a "culture" in a concrete ethnic or class sense, and that the products of these cultures can be displayed, sold, consumed, and exchanged across borders. More importantly, central to both models of multiculturalism is that culture is the basis for our identities. Biological difference, the difference of the older and some of the present views of race is displaced onto a symbolic cultural level. But at the same moment, this cultural heritage is commodified and thus made available for all consumers.

In such a world, how do writers who self-consciously see themselves as multicultural members of a clearly delineated group (ethnic, social, religious), or see themselves as inherently hybrid of such groups, imagine minorities such as Jews? Recently there has been an explosion of studies on this topic, contrasting African American images of Jews and Jewish American images of Blacks.[3] And yet this multicultural theme seems to have its limits in emphasizing the boundaries between the groups rather than the possibility of hybridity (to be found, for example, in the intertwined history of jazz and klezmer in the United States). But is multiculturalism an American problem? What groups count as multicultural? What happens when this project is extended beyond the Blacks-Jews paradigm and beyond the borders of the United States? What happens when other groups are brought into the discussion of multiculturalism? And what happens when it crosses national, even linguistic, boundaries? What happens when a writer

self-consciously representing her or his work as the voice of a multicultural writer needs to define difference? The reception of these
works is often very much in line with the self-definition of the author. The specific subject position of the text is seen as part of the
fiction itself. Each multicultural text takes as one of its themes the
creation of a multicultural voice in the novels, whether it is that of
the narrator or of the protagonist. It labels itself as functioning on
the imagined frontier of the multicultural.

In many of these multicultural texts, the figure of the Jew, defined within the world of the fiction, is a key to understanding the
very nature of the multicultural society represented. This figure
takes on different contours based on the existing stereotypes
within each culture and each ethnic cohort. The core concepts
that shape the image of the Jew are the age-old ones: the Jew as
foreign and victim; the Jew as cosmopolitan and successful. How
these concepts function in a multicultural context as expressed in
the ancient fantasy about Jewish physical difference is the subject
of the present question.[4] Are Jews inherently different? That is,
can there be a difference beyond history and culture that is inscribed on the body? The error embedded in this question is that
it elides the fact that bodies themselves both in fantasy and in reality are historically constructed objects. Suffering and success shape
the body as do hunger and affluence. The fantasy about the
uniqueness of the Jew's body, however, postulates that the difference of the body reflects an essential difference in the mind or
soul. What happens when such tropes are used, if only ironically,
in contemporary multicultural literature? One can ask with Audre
Lorde, can such texts dismantle the master's house, anti-Semitism,
with the master's tools, irony?

Each of the texts examined below uses the Jew as a litmus
test to define a particular multicultural world in terms of the
physicality of the Jew. They have a specific Western origin, having been first published in England, South Africa, the United

States, Germany, and Belgium. They also appeared at approximately the same time, at the end of the second millennium. It was (and is) a moment in Western literary culture where the issues of multiculturalism have become a central concern (pro or contra) to the writer as well as to the literary world. It is as much a question of what is written as what is published now for a wider, even global audience.

All of these texts provide a sense of how the Jews figure in the collective fantasies of other actually or potentially successful minorities. (This in marked contrast to the case of the African American writers' image of the Jews from the fiction of Richard Wright to Spike Lee's 1990 *Mo' Better Blues.* Such images assume a world in which African Americans remain marginalized and subjected to discrimination.) Multiculturalism is also a space where the contrast been the haves and the have-nots is played out. The more you can claim the status of victim, the stronger your case for primacy in this world in which "all animals are equal, but some are more equal than others." In the past decade, the Jews have been imagined as a successful minority. This perceived success came at exactly the time, as Peter Novick has noted, that the Shoah became the touchstone for all histories of persecution and genocide.[5] Jewish American writing has focused on the Shoah for the past forty years, ever since Bernard Malamud, Philip Roth, and Saul Bellow inscribed it on the American literary consciousness. The centrality of this topic in defining the Jew in literature has a literary dimension beyond Jewish American writing. More than Anglo Jewish or German Jewish writing, Jewish American culture is an example of how a successful multicultural presence in a national literature can be established. From Saul Bellow to Steven Spielberg, the introduction of Jewish subject matter by self-consciously Jewish cultural figures has made the representation of the Jew part of the American mainstream of both high and mass culture. These multicultural texts of the late 1990s and early 2000s represent how the image of the Jew functions in contemporary fantasies of a multicultural society partially in light of the success and power of Jewish American writing, which by then had become mainstream American writing.

READING JEWISH DIFFERENCE

In the Anglo Pakistani novelist and screenwriter Hanef Kureishi's short story "We're Not Jews" (1997), the representation of the Jew within a multicultural context is given an exemplary formulation.[6] Kureishi, born in Kent, was raised in London and made his first mark as the author of the multicultural film *My Beautiful Launderette* in 1984. His story "We're Not Jews," retrospectively set in the 1960s, centers on a mixed marriage between an English woman and a Pakistani man, a laborer with pretensions of becoming a writer. Their son is torn between the two worlds of England and Pakistan. At the beginning of the story the woman has gone to school to complain about her son Azhar having been bullied by her neighbor's son. Confronted by her ex-Teddy boy neighbor and his bully son on the bus, Azhar's mother tries to ignore their taunts. Each character has constructed the other. England in the Teddy boy's fantasy is the land of the white and the English; there is truly no Black in their Union Jack.[7] Pakistan in the tale is defined by a new nationalism and its Muslim roots. Yvonne, Azhar's mother, may be English but her class identity as marginal even to the working class puts her at the lowest common denominator of what is English. Azhar's father had lived in China and India but had never actually been to Pakistan. He is Pakistani only in the sense of belonging to an Urdu-speaking, Muslim cultural diaspora.

The child's confusion becomes manifest when his mother teaches him to answer "Little Billy's" bullying by denouncing him as "common." Class is defined by etiquette. The Teddy boy's response is "But we ain't as common as a slut who marries a darkie"

(43). The extended family that she has married into is different but is still a full step above the most liminal figures in English society. " . . . Mother always denied that they were 'like that.' She refused to allow the word 'immigrant' to be used about Father, since in her eyes it applied only to illiterate tiny men with downcast eyes and mismatched clothes" (45). Her choked response to being taunted: "Mother's lips were moving but her throat must have been dry; no words came, until she managed to say, 'We're not Jews'" (45). Big Billy, the bully's father answered: "You no Yid, Yvonne. You us. But worse. Goin' with the Paki'" (45). Who is the "Yid" in Kureishi's vocabulary of constructs? The "Yid" is even more pathetic than the victims of apartheid, as the father notes, "where people with white skins were cruel to the black and brown people who were considered inferior" (49). The Jews are the ultimate victims because they appear to be white but are really not. The Jew is the foreigner everywhere. Azhar had heard his father say "that there had been 'gassing' not long ago. Neighbour had slaughtered neighbour, and such evil hadn't died. Father would poke his finger at his wife, son and baby daughter, and state, 'We're in the front line'" (45). For his parents, the memory of the Shoah is written onto their own experience and they thus understand how easily they too could become the victims of racial persecutions. They have the potential of becoming "Yids." The Shoah defines a difference that is not merely victimhood, but an odd sort of Orientalism, that casting of the exotic East as the place from which those who are inherently unassimilable come. What liminal characters share in the diaspora is their Oriental fate, that of victims.

The marker for the difference is not only skin color but also language. Just as Big Billy mangles spoken English, so too does Azhar's father, whose desire to become a writer is limited by his lack of a "sure grasp of the English language which was his, but not entirely, being 'Bombay variety, mish and mash.' Their neighbour, a retired schoolteacher, was kind enough to correct Father's spelling and grammar, suggesting that he sometimes used 'the right words in the wrong place, and vice versa'" (47). The story ends with the child listening to his father and his father's family shouting in Urdu during a cricket match on the radio. "He endeavoured to decipher the gist of it, laughing, as he always did, when the men laughed, and silently moving his lips without knowing what the words meant, whirling, all the while, in incomprehension" (50–1). Language confusion, exile, cosmopolitanism are all qualities of the image of the Jew in the world of Kureishi's characters. To identify with them, however, means accepting the potential of a cosmopolitanism that is tainted by the failure of language as a marker of belonging.

Yet Kureishi's image of the Jew's language is tied closely to physicality. The Jews are "illiterate tiny men with downcast eyes and mismatched clothes" (45). This is a very English manner of seeing the Jews and therefore is ascribed to Azhar's mother, whose prejudices are English even though (or because) she is married to a South Asian. The image she uses is analogous to one ironically employed by author Julian Barnes in a description of one of his protagonist's Jewish friends:

> Toni far outclassed me in rootlessness. His parents were Polish Jews and, though we didn't actually know it for certain, we were practically sure that they had escaped from the Warsaw ghetto at the very last minute. This gave Toni the flash foreign name of Barbarowski, two languages, three cultures, and a sense (he assured me) of atavistic wrench: in short, real class. He looked an exile, too: swarthy, bulbous-nosed, thick-lipped, disarmingly short, energetic and hairy; he even had to shave every day.[8]

After the Shoah, the Jew's physical state is a result, in the eyes of the character, of their history, but it is also written on their bodies. Kureishi's operative concept of the immigrant is close to that of the stranger, who is, to paraphrase the Berlin sociologist Georg Simmel, one who comes and then stays and stays and stays.[9] The Jewish immigrants to Great Britain who haunted the East End of London had set the pattern in the 1960s. But even more so, those immigrants who had escaped or survived the Holocaust marked for the British sensibility the outcast invited for a short time who becomes a permanent part of the society. Azhar, Kureishi's narrator, needs to feel that he is English in spite of (or because of) the class system. While his parents are stuck in their world of difference, he is not. He can become a real writer (like Kureishi himself) and move into an intellectual world of the 1990s in which the multicultural is prized. He is not merely a "Yid" whose difference transcends all class difference. How true this remains can be seen in 2001. After race riots in the north of England during the spring of 2001, when South Asians and members of the white-only British National Party clashed, reporters were driven from a South Asian housing estate with shouts of "Jews," followed by a "barrage of unprintable remarks about Jews." In the end, all non-South Asians are Jews.[10]

The complexity of such a multicultural discourse about the Jews can be seen in another work published at more or less the same time as Kureishi's short story. Achmat Dangor's novella *Kafka's Curse* is set in South Africa before the election of 1994.[11] The theme, like that of Philip Roth's *The Human Stain* (2000), is passing, specifically a "colored" man passing as "white" by becoming a "Jew." It is a text rooted in the ideology of a specific multicultural diaspora, that of South Africa under apartheid where Dangor was born in 1948. He was a member of the Black cultural group Black Thoughts and banned for six years in the 1970s. He notes: "In addition to those inexplicable inner urges to tell stories, I was influenced by my upbringing in a staunch, if not dogmatically 'fundamental' Muslim environment. In addition to the conventional Western school, I attended 'madressa' (Islamic school) each day."[12] One might add that the school was most probably full of the most intense anti-Jewish rhetoric given the fact that he attended it during the height of the Arab campaign against Israel, a campaign in which the full armament of anti-Jewish images were used. Dangor uses and undermines these images in his representation of the Jew.

Dangor's novella is his literary fantasy of the meaning of multiculturalism projected back into the world of apartheid. The protagonist of the tale, Omar Khan, changes his name to Oscar Kahn because he was able to pass as white: "I was fair, and why not, my grandmother was Dutch. This oppressive country had next-to-Nazis in government, yet had a place, a begrudged place but a place nevertheless, for Jews. Can you believe it? For that eternally persecuted race? Because they were white." (23) In Kureishi's world, Azhar's mother does not regard the "Yid" as truly white. The Jews of South Africa however, became white only after the beginning of the twentieth century; before that they were labeled as "colored," as they seem to be in Kureishi's world. They became white because they became a successful minority and had the economic clout to demand being labeled "white."[13]

In South Africa, as in Great Britain, there is a set of images of the Jew that shape Dangor's representation. Kureishi represents the "Yid" only from the perspective of the outsider, as the projection of all that is said about the South Asian. In Dangor's world, the Jew is a trickster always cheating the non-Jew. He may, as quoted by Milton Shain writing about anti-Semitism in South Africa, "always be known to a farmer by the shape of his nose, the many rings on his fingers, and by the tongue being too large for his mouth."[14] This comment was made in an early twentieth-century article in the English Language *Cape Punch*, about the "Boereverneuker," the Jew who cheats the Boer, himself a stereotyped figure. The physiognomy reflects his character. Here Jew and Boer, cheat and victim, are seen as separate from the Anglophone writers and readers who are, from their perspective, clearly superior to both in terms of their command of the language of power. The image of the Jew's "tongue being too large for his mouth" is a trope found in European science of the day. Its reflection on the inability of the Jew to command the language of the culture—and still be able to cheat the Boer—takes on a specific local coloration as seen from the perspective of English speakers' hegemonic claims on real culture.

Jews are a race apart, like the Boers and, by extension, the Blacks. Even Jews who do not look Jewish, who look white, will eventually reveal their inner nature in their appearance. They look white for "as yet the stress of trade had not awakened the ancestral greed, which would one day dominate his blood and modify his physiognomy" (Shain 25). At that point the Jew becomes a "Peruvian," an odd, turn-of-the-twentieth-century term for a Jewish trader in South Africa. "Peruvian" perhaps because of his non-Western, nonwhite exoticism that puts the Jew on the very margins of the known world. And the Peruvian, the Jew who "looked worth no more than the clothes in which he stood," was "still muttering in Yiddish" (Shain 51). Language marks the difference of the Jew from the Boer and the Anglo. Here is the reflection of Kureishi's image, now placed in a society in which multiculturalism ignores the colored inhabitants and focuses only on the nuances of what can be defined as white.

And yet, there is the constant anxiety about Jewish superiority in South Africa, given the history of the country's gold fields and diamond mining. Here, the myth of Jewish hyperintelligence that haunts the medical and psychological literature of the nineteenth century takes on its South African specificity. The Jew wins over the non-Jew "due to his shrewdness and wit" (Shain 73); this is playwright Stephen Black's phrase in the context of a fin-de-siècle representation of the Jew as a successful entrepreneur. Given the central role of the mercantile system in defining success among the British in South Africa, the questionable position of the merchant is projected onto the Jews, who are shown to have no class but to be shrewd and therefore successful. True success, it is implied, comes with having both culture (language) and money—and Jewish characters can never have this.

The Jews may appear to acculturate themselves but the acculturation is only superficial. They are malleable when conditions permit them to be. They then appear to "merge into the political life of the country, without abandoning their own racial loyalty" (Shain 70). Even when they put on the mask of culture, they remain racially Jews and are therefore different under the clothes they wear or the language they seem to acquire. Put them to the test—such as the litmus test of war—and they will reveal themselves as merely Jews in all of their racial identity.

The very term "Jews" has a South African dimension evoked only in passing by Dangor. For while there are some Sephardic Jews and some Central European Jews in this story, South Africa evinces a uniformity of the term "Jew" in its social history that parallels the cohesive representation of the Jew in Afrikaans and Anglophone non-Jewish culture of South Africa. For the greatest majority of Jews who came to South Africa were Lithuanian Jews (*Litvaks*) whose language was Yiddish. The language politics of South Africa during the early twentieth century presented the two dominant languages of power—Afrikaans and English. No other language would be acceptable, and what these two languages had in common was their alphabet.

In the Cape Colony in 1902 an Immigration Restriction Act was passed in order to limit the settlement of people from the Indian subcontinent. Only Europeans, defined by the alphabet of the language they spoke, were to be given the privilege of immigration to South Africa. Yiddish, needless to say, was not accepted as a European language. Since only languages written in the same alphabet as Afrikaans and English were "white," Hebrew became "colored."

The "Hebrews" entered into the world of Southern Africa with its overwhelming Black population not as members of the privileged, hegemonic white race, but as a marginal colored race. This view was of course very much in line with late nineteenth-century racial theory in Europe. Houston Stewart Chamberlain, Wagner's son-in-law and the most widely read popular racial theorist of the day in all of Europe, argued that the Jews were a mongrel race for having mixed with Blacks in their Alexandrian exile, and this fact could be read in their physiognomy.

The urban environment gave the Jews both visibility and protection. Falling on the wrong side of the color bar during the colonial period (which eventually led to the institution of apartheid) could have been fatal for Jewish cultural and political aspirations. There would have been no hiding in the protective environs of the city. Thus, Jews lobbied against the categorization of the Cape immigration bill and had Yiddish reclassified as a European language. Yet, Cape censuses continued to differentiate between "Europeans" and "Hebrews."

In Dangor's, *Kafka's Curse*, his protagonist, Oscar Kahn, defines his whiteness by moving into a white neighborhood. He had left the Indian township of Lenasia and moved to a Johannesburg suburb, passed as a Jew, and married Anna Wallace, who was of impeccable British ancestry. He suffers from their anti-Semitism. "Anna's mother hated me. I think she suspected even my Jewishness. Prejudice has unerring instincts" (32). For Anna's friends, he is a sexual object but not a potential husband because of his visible difference: Oscar is "all brown bread and honey! Good enough for bed . . . but to marry?" (11). Marriage and reproduction and the difficulty of passing are at the heart of this tale. Her friends know that he is different: "Are you Indian?" . . ."No, the Kahn here is a good old Jewish name" (31). *Nomen est omen*, but how does one become Jewish?

Oscar is eventually employed by a Jewish architect, Meyer Lewis, who trains him and slowly makes him over into a image of himself: "In my dreams I often slit Meyer's bulbous throat and danced with naked feet in the pools of his hot blood. . . . I began to hate his hybrid South African Yiddisher tongue, his sharp contemptuous eyes. . . . Meyer was short and stocky" (24–25). Language and physicality define the real Jew in the tale. Meyer, like Oscar, is a successful Jew, yet he is still marked by his linguistic and physical difference. He is a successful version of Kureishi's "illiterate tiny men with downcast eyes and mismatched clothes."

When Oscar buys a house in a white-only suburb, it is a house marked in an odd way by his Jewishness. When he courted Anna, she would watch him masturbate: "[Anna] was not surprised that I was circumcised; a Jewish custom after all" (31). Muslim men, like Jewish men, are physically different. This difference becomes the stain that mars the image of Oscar's house in the white suburb. It is a 90-year-old house. Oscar insists that it cannot be altered in any way. It has an odd configuration. When you approach it, you are faced with: "a strange fountain that stood in the centre of the path leading to the front door, forcing people to confront the sorrowful sight of a castrated David, his drooping stone penis broken at the tip like a child's pee-pee. *It was an integral part of the house's nature*, Oscar said" (11). The fountain of the "young boyish David had water piped up through his foot and out his penis. The piping was made of metal and it rusted. Over time the rust coloured the water until he appeared to be peeing blood" (37). The ancient fantasy of male Jews bleeding regularly had been the origin of the idea of Jewish ritual murder from early modern times to the present. Jewish men were believed to need Christian blood to heal their bloody discharge. This view persisted into the late nineteenth century.[15] It was raised again at the turn of the century in a powerfully written pamphlet by a professor of Hebrew at the University in St. Petersburg, D. Chwolson, as one of the rationales used to justify the blood libel. Chwolson notes that it was used to "cure the diseases believed to be specifically those of the Jews," such as male menstruation.[16] The house that Oscar occupies is a Jewish house with its bleeding David. While Oscar is circumcised, as a Muslim he is not condemned to bleed.

The earlier inhabitant of the house, a little boy called Simon, was embarrassed by the blood-peeing David; he took a garden spade and "lopped David's penis off" (38). Again, in the Western image of the Jewish body, circumcision is a form of real or attenuated castration.[17] The power of the image of Jewish circumcision in the West is such that it actually elides any reference to the practice by other peoples, such as the Muslims. When Oscar buys the house, one of his first tasks is to repair the statue and have it working again. It begins to pee blood again. Oscar believes that he probably tore the new plastic tube when he inserted it. His daughters read it differently: "The girls blushed. The elder one said that David was peeing monthlies" (38). Dangor makes an association between the Jewish body, here clearly not a white body but a successful body nevertheless, and the mythmaking inherent in Western society about Jewish physical difference. It was just as present in the legends of Jewish difference in South Africa a hundred years before as it was in the Muslim propaganda concerning the Jews in the 1970s and 1980s.

After Oscar dies, his children discover that his mistress, Elizabeth Marsden, is a sculptress "with a gift for pissing Davids. Young erotic Davids. Fashioned in our father's image" (115). Oscar has become Jewish even though it is this mistress who knows Oscar's secret. His mistress "was the only one who really saw that Oscar was not Oscar, smelled his bastard genes, the oily stench of his 'coolie' ancestry" (112). In becoming a Jew, he also becomes one whose success marks him as only superficially white. Oscar's therapist, Amina Mandelstam, notes that "the name he took—Oscar—defined his personality" (47). It made him into a Jew and defined his body. Amina's husband is also physically marked by his Jewishness: "The cripple Jew was being questioned [about Oscar's death]. But there was no photo of him. I wonder what a cripple Jew looks like?" asks one of Oscar's relatives (103). The Jew is defined by his crippled (circumcised) body, but it is also simultaneously the body of the Muslim man.

Hybridity is the centerpiece of this magic realist tale in which the protagonist eventually develops symptoms of an unknown disease, Kafka's curse, that transforms him virtually into a tree, breathing carbon dioxide and expelling oxygen. As with Kafka, as I have argued elsewhere, it is the fantasy of Jewish physical difference that defines the Jew, no matter whether he is Jewish or not.[18] Like Coleman Silk, the protagonist of Roth's *The Human Stain*, Oscar becomes a Jew and therefore adopts all of the perceived physical differences of the Jew, giving proof to Jean-Paul Sartre's claim that societies makes their own Jews through the discourse of anti-Semitism. The society here, that of apartheid South Africa, roots its image of the Jew in the discourse of a false cosmopolitanism that is merely the world of the Oriental, here again defined as the Eastern Jew, the *Litvak*, in a Western society. Dangor's image of apartheid South Africa evokes the world of Nazi Germany with all the anxiety about passing. Writing from a postapartheid perspective, Dangor can present the image of the Jew into which his protagonist has transformed himself in the most ironic manner. It is also clear that this transformation, like that of Gregor Samsa, is a failure because of its very necessity.

The multicultural view labels the Jews as the ultimate victims because of their experience in the Shoah. And this is tied to their difference. Jewish difference is the inability to integrate into a society, to be able to claim true command over language, culture, and physical difference. Sadly, whether through ironic recapitulation or simple repetition, these images are the images that existed prior to the Shoah in Western culture. In Kureishi's world, the Jewish experience is the litmus test for essential difference. In Dangor's world, it is the key to a form of belonging. For Zadie

Smith, it becomes something quite different and still much the same. Her brilliant first novel, *White Teeth* (2000), is perhaps the most complicated comic novel yet written on the multicultural frontier.[19] Born in northwest London in 1975, she is herself a product of multicultural London. She was born into a mixed-race family—her mother is from Jamaica and her father is English—and is a graduate of Cambridge University in English. Her first novel has been spectacularly successful, winning such awards as Best Book and Best Female Newcomer at the BT Emma Awards (Ethnic and Multicultural Media Awards), the Guardian First Book Award, the Whitbread Prize for a first novel in 2000, the James Tait Black Memorial Prize for Fiction 2000, the W. H. Smith Book Award for New Talent, the Frankfurt eBook Award for Best Fiction Work Originally Published in 2000, and both the Commonwealth Writers First Book Award and Overall Commonwealth Writers Prize. The operative question that Smith asks in her satire of late twentieth-century England is how can one define "Englishness," and this is much the same theme as that of Kureishi. How can one be different without being a victim? And can that difference be a positive rather than a negative quality?

Smith's novel presents a multigenerational account of the development of Englishness. It begins with the older generation, Archie Jones, who is a working-class Englishman married to a Black immigrant from Jamaica, and his friend Samad Iqbal, a Muslim from Bangladesh. They had been friends since they both served in the same tank with the British army in Romania in World War II. The twin sons of Samad (Magid and Millat) and Archie's daughter (Irie), who were all born in England, represent the second generation. All are foreigners there because of their visibility and in spite of their seeming hybridity:

> This has been the century of strangers, brown, yellow, and white. This has been the century of the great immigrant exper-

iment. It is only this late in the day that you can walk into a playground and find Isaac Leung by the fish pond, Danny Rahman in the football cage, Quang O'Rourke bouncing a basketball, and Irie Jones humming a tune. Children with first and last names on a direct collision course. Names that secrete within them mass exodus, cramped boats and planes, cold arrivals, medical checkups. It is only this late in the day, and possibly only in Willesden, that you can find best friends Sita and Sharon, constantly mistaken for each other because Sita is white (her mother liked the name) and Sharon is Pakistani (her mother thought it best—less trouble). Yet, despite all the mixing up, despite the fact that we have finally slipped into each other's lives with reasonable comfort (like a man returning to his lover's bed after a midnight walk), despite all this, it is still hard to admit that there is no one more English than the Indian, no one more Indian than the English. There are still young white men who are angry about that; who will roll out at closing time into the poorly lit streets with a kitchen knife wrapped in a tight fist.[20]

The new world of England is a world of hybrids, reflected in their very names, but it is also a world still dominated by class. For, as we shall see, even those labeled as middle class, the Jews, do not really belong to the true corridors of power in this world.

The economically successful hybrids are not Archie Jones and Samad Iqbal but the Chalfens, upper middle class, liberal, and the very definition of English. "Marcus and Joyce, [are] an aging hippie couple both dressed in pseudo-Indian garb" who are very outspoken at the meeting of parents in the school attended by all of the children (110). They are successful: "the father is something of an eminent scientist and his mother is a horticulturist" (252). They are the most English people we meet to this point in the novel. Their Englishness is defined by their class status as well as by their hippie clothing.

We are very slowly introduced to their son Joshua Chalfen. At first sight he is "pasty, practically anemic, curly-haired, and chubby" (226). He is very white. But he is also revealed to be "Josh-with-the-Jewfro" (247). He is a Jew if only by the very definition of his body. He too is a hybrid: "a cross pollination between a lapsed-Catholic horticulturist and an intellectual Jew" (258). Being Jewish is being a misfit. Joshua is a "smart Jew," an outsider, who immediately identifies Irie as "one of his own" (247). His "own" is a collection of physical misfits with whom the very bright but very tall Irie seems to belong. She is more or less adopted into the Chalfen clan as a sign of their social commitment to racial equality. Liberal, English, and yet visibly different, Joshua and his parents are the cosmopolitan insider as outsider.

Ironically, the Chalfens interact only with those who have "good genes." And that is, by definition, the Chalfen family, "two scientists, one mathematician, three psychiatrists, and a young man working for the Labour Party." Success becomes the measure by which intelligence is judged. They rarely visit Joshua's maternal grandparents, the Connor clan, "who even now could not disguise their distaste for Joyce's Israelite love-match." Other than Irie, they have no friends (261). The Chalfens are not only hybrids, they are also strangers and sojourners, no matter how they deny it: "the Chalfens were, after a fashion, immigrants too (third generation, by way of Germany and Poland, né Chalfenovsky). . . . To Irie, the Chalfens were more English than the English" (273). They are, of course, merely disguised Orientals, Eastern Jews who appear to fit into this new English world better than most of the other hybrids. From the very moment of civil emancipation in the eighteenth century, Jews are seen as having a natural mimicry as part of their difference. They can transform themselves into any nation or people. By doing this, they prove that they remain Jews.

Jewish difference is understood as a physical difference. As Joyce notes about her husband's appearance: "that's Dr. Solomon

Chalfen, Marcus's grandfather. He was one of the few men who would listen to Freud. . . . The first time Marcus showed me that picture, I knew I wanted to marry him. I thought: if my Marcus looks like that at eighty I'll be a very lucky girl" (293). Physical difference trumps everything else. It is seen as palpable, even if it is defined as beautiful. Joshua is the product of the assimilation of his father into the England represented by the Irish clan of the Connors. Once you become English, you forfeit any right to be anything else but different:

> These days it feels to me like you make a devil's pact when you walk into this country. You hand over your passport at the check-in, you get stamped, you want to make a little money, get yourself started . . . but you mean to go back! Who would want to stay? Cold, wet, miserable; terrible food, dreadful newspapers—who would want to stay? In a place where you are never welcomed, only tolerated. Just tolerated. Like you are an animal finally housebroken. Who would want to stay? But you have made a devil's pact . . . it drags you in and suddenly you are unsuitable to return, your children are unrecognizable, you belong nowhere. (336)

They have become what Georg Simmel called sojourners, who cannot belong and who cannot return. Joshua is one of these sojourner children who remain different as his origin is in history, not in geography. His father has no nostalgia for Poland or Germany. He is English, but only from his own perspective and that of the other multicultural figures.

It is twentieth-century Jewish history, specifically the Shoah, that dominates the novel, not the history of Jamaica, nor the history of South Asia: "Because this is the other thing about immigrants (fugees, emigres, travelers): they cannot escape their history any more than you yourself can lose your shadow" (385). The plot, much too convoluted and funny to recapitulate, reveals that the

mad Nazi doctor that Archie Jones and Samad Iqbal were to have
captured in Romania, but whom Archie lets escape, is the master-
mind behind Marcus Chalfen's plan to manufacture "Future-
Mouse," a genetically engineered mouse that will live forever.
Joshua is seduced into sabotaging the experiment and releasing
the mouse by the Keepers of the Eternal and Victorious Islamic
Nation, an organization plagued by its "acronym problem"—
KEVIN is hardly an alternative to British blandness. The line between the medical experiments at Auschwitz and the attempt to
create a perfect human being today is shown to be clear. Marcus
turns out to be the natural ally of the Nazi because of his emphasis
on genetic inheritance and rationality. His actions can only be redeemed by his son, who is misled by sexual desire into opposing
his father. At the conclusion of the novel, almost as an after-
thought, Zadie Smith has Irie and Joshua marry, for "you can only
avoid your fate for so long" (448). Yet Irie's daughter is the offspring of one of Samad's twins. In this play of multiculturalism, it
seems that the family that most relied on genetics for its identity,
the Chalfens, will remain without offspring. It is the old model
that the hybrid is sterile. The utopian end to the novel sees the
FutureMouse scampering away, proving that random hybridity is
better than scientific planning—but also showing that visibility is
the key to defining difference.

The history of the Jews and the medical and eugenic experiments of the Third Reich frame the very definition of difference
in Smith's novel. The common history of Archie and Samad is
their experience fighting fascism. The history of the struggle
against the Nazis becomes background for the contemporary
struggle against homogeneity. The Jews, the victims of the Nazis,
become their (unwitting) accomplices at the end of the millennium. Joshua's rebellion against the scientific ideals that his father
represented is his means of putting himself, no matter how misunderstood, on the right side of the issue. Yet he remains suspended

between all of the groups, not smarter, not more cosmopolitan, not different from them. The transparency of his character shows that he exists more than most other characters in the light of a history, merely an Eastern European Jew not quite aware of his own limitation even though it is literally inscribed on his body.

Astoundingly, Zadie Smith returns to the question of a Jewish hybridity in her most recent novel, *The Autograph Man* (2002).[21] Its protagonist is Alex-Li Tandem, half-Chinese, half-Jewish. His father's name was Tan but "someone thought 'Tandem' sounded better. . . . Mother, Sarah . . ." (65). The protagonist is literally in tandem, being both Chinese and Jewish, and yet more than either of these. His body is that of the Jew who "has grown and filled; he's now soft-bellied, woman-hipped, and sallow. His new glasses magnify the crescents of his eyes—does he look more Chinese?" (4). The protagonist is introduced as part of a triplet of Jews, which also includes his friend Mark Rubinfine, whose accountant father wants him to become a rabbi (and he does), and Adam Jacobs, of a family of "black Harlem Jews, claiming the tribe of Judah. Dressed like Ethiopian kings!" (11). Here the book of these multicultural Jews is interchangeable with the Jewish mystical text, the Kabbalah, and seems to structure the novel; being Jewish frames and shapes this story of multiculturalism.

Also giving context, the story contrasts the introduction of the main characters with a page of extracts from the Jewish-American comedian Lenny Bruce listing what is Jewish and what is not: "Dig: I'm Jewish. Count Basie's Jewish. Ray Charles is Jewish. Eddie Cantor's goyish. B'nai B'rith is goyish; Hadassah, Jewish. . . ." What is cool and what is in, is Jewish, such as the Kabbalah that reappears through the novel, framing each subsection and each change in plot. Smith uses Jewish mysticism to structure the world of her novel, but it is the pop Jewish mysticism of the 1990s, watered down to become a universal experience separate from its Jewish religious context. It is the Kabbalah of

Madonna and of Hollywood. Being Jewish itself is being hybrid—
being "in." Thus, it is Esther, Adam's "Ethiopian" sister, who becomes Alex-Li Tandem's lover. As in her earlier novel, the Jewish
experience—here made ironic and universal—is the human experience. Here, too, one of the oldest canards appears as part of the
plot line consistent with the Jewish nature of the novel in that
Alex-Ti's profession is an autograph collector and seller. His pas-
sion has been for the mysterious, Garbo-esque Kitty Alexander, a
"Russian-Italian-American" (180). Alex-Ti discovers her in New
York and spirits her away to London, where he reads her obituary
in the American media. (It has been planted by her jilted man-
ager.) Based on the announcement of her death and the rarity of
her signature, Alex-Ti, is able to sell a number of her autographs
at auction, knowing full well that his actions are criminal. But
white-collar crime, too, is part of the image of the Jew in this
world. It is, to paraphrase Lenny Bruce, "Jewish." Likewise, Zadie
Smith's world of Kabbalah and the Jews is central to the formulation of the story, as are her representation of the Jews that echo
many of the Jewish stereotypes acceptable in the world of multicultural fiction.

The Shoah forms the background of Zafer Senocak's novel
Dangerous Relations (*Gefährliche Verwandtschaft;* 1998).[22] For Senocak, the theme of the Jew as the Oriental or Eastern Jew and as the
hybrid, which is evoked in Zadie Smith's novel, is part of a theme
of Turkish acculturation into contemporary German culture. (It
has an analogy in *The Story of the Last Thought* [*Das Märchen von
letzten Gedanken;* 1991] by the Jewish survivor-author Edgar
Hilsenrath. This account of the Armenian massacres ends in
Auschwitz because the Armenian protagonist, a survivor of the
massacres as an infant, looks too Jewish as an adult.) Senocak provides the reader with a novel about Germany after the Shoah that
is also an account of the tribulations of modern Turks in that Germany. Senocak, born in Ankara in 1961, has lived in Germany

since he was nine years old. He writes in German from a self-consciously and ironically multicultural perspective.

Senocak's novel recounts the adventures of Sascha Muchteschem, the son of a German Jewish mother and a Turkish middle-class father. After the death of his parents, he inherits a box with the notebooks of his Turkish grandfather, which he cannot read as they are written in Arabic and Cyrillic script. These unreadable texts start him on the search for his roots just as he begins to write his first novel. Central to this novel are both of his grandfathers, the German Jewish Orientalist and the Turkish adventurer.

Senocak represents a hybrid author in his own novel who is in his own estimation therefore the exemplary cosmopolitan German: "I don't have an identity. People in my world have more and more problems with this. It is as if the fall of The Wall, the collapse of the old order, did not only have a liberating function. Without The Wall one no longer feels oneself protected. Identity is a substitute concept for being protected" (47). He is, however, seen in the Berlin Republic as a Turkish writer. "Are you a foreigner? I am asked when I spell my name. Earlier I spelled it without being asked. Indeed, according to the passport I am German" (128). He is seen as Turkish, nevertheless: "Do you write in Turkish? I offer many contradictory answers to this question if only to confuse those who are already confused. Who could know that I hardly speak a word of Turkish . . . ? Colleagues of mine, who are more evidently foreigners than I, who are dark skinned or speak German with an accent, seem to have little problem with their reception as Foreign Writers" (130). Thus, it is visibility (skin color) and language that define difference. He is seen as different and the assumption is that his language must also be different. He, however, does not see himself as appearing different because of his Jewish background. For him, but not for the Germans, this appears white.[23]

Sascha Muchteschem is very dismissive of Germanness. "Am I a German? This question never interested me. It seems to interest no one. The question about a German identity was an old-fashioned question, a theme heavy with clichés and stereotypes, a type of heretical question, that any intelligent person would dismiss with a gesture that indicated that it was unimportant" (127). Yet, of course, the history of the German Jews who saw themselves as Germans haunts his own family: "In the family of my mother there were no survivors. One didn't speak about this. My mother crossly answered the questions that I asked about the photos I found in the drawers in the library. She took the photos away and, as I later learned, called aunts and cousins merely strangers or friends of grandfather" (59). This vanished family wanted to be German, which did not mean that they wanted to become Christian. "My grandfather was one of those German Jews for whom Judaism was nothing more than the belief of their fathers. My maternal family felt itself for generations indebted to the Enlightenment. . . . It would have never occurred to him to convert to Christianity, because this religion was just as passé as Judaism" (57). Could one be a German who just happened to be a Jew, just as the narrator desires to be a German with Turkish and Jewish ancestry? The historical answer is clearly "no."

Certainly, the narrator sees his Jewish grandfather as a German. He reads his way through the library that his grandfather had built up in the 1920s and that survived the Nazis. It is filled with authors such as Thomas Mann (59). He shares the cultural prejudices of the Germans toward other peoples, especially the Turks. His mother accepted his father, who was upper middle class and well educated, only after a five-year courtship: "The arrogance and disdain for the poor and primitive Turks that the German Jews expressed was a sign of their assimilation. . . . Many Orientalists were German Jews. They attributed to the Orient eternal tyranny, fatalism, immutability, and difference. Who would have thought that their grandchildren would become Orientals like their ancestors" (92). The irony is double-edged. For the Orientals (i.e., the Turks) are simultaneously becoming Germans as the Jews are becoming Israelis—and they are becoming Israelis because the project of their becoming Germans failed horribly.

Belonging to the German cultural sphere is not sufficient to define Germanness. There is the double problem, as Gershom Scholem noted: the Jews never really belonged in the eyes of the Germans but the Jews fantasized that they were included. Will the Turks simply replicate this error? "One day a woman said to me, who lived in a very elegant and very well kept house in Dahlem, that today's Turks are much worse than the Jews of the past. The Jews would have masked themselves in Germanness. They acted as if they were Germans. One didn't believe them. But that was their problem" (66). The mask is central to the German Jews in Senocak's image of history. It is a mask as seen by the Germans, but it was the only face that the German Jews, such as the narrator's grandfather, actually had.

To understand the distinction between appearance and reality of Jew and Turk is the key to the novel. The narrator enters into an exchange with his friend Heinrich, who is an expert on nineteenth-century German Jewish history, as to what defines a human being:

> "The body is the only home that a human being has," Heinrich claimed categorically.
> I contradicted him. "Language is essentially more important. Only in language can you be at home."
> "Language alienates man from himself." He argued, "Man is a being without name." (82)

For Senocak, it is in the body that the essence of Jewishness lies for the Germans; language, the utopian space of the writer, is secondary. (Remember author Stefan Zweig's claim, shortly before his suicide in Brazilian exile, that language is the only home of the writer.) The body betrays even as it changes:

> Many generations of German Jews have concerned themselves with the question, when and how a Jew can overcome his Jewishness in order to become a total German. Lightening the skin and the hair, Germanizing language and belief did not free the Jews from the Jewish illness that they brought from Germany. The Jews took over these tortuous questions from the German society in order to belong to that society. They made them more sophisticated and asked them again. And they became the same questions in return. And so on. This reciprocal process continued until the question was reformulated in: "When will Germany be free of its Jews." (89)

Historically this is quite accurate, if teleological, in that nineteenth-century anti-Semitism led directly to the Shoah. By the latter half of the nineteenth century, Western European Jews had become indistinguishable from other Western Europeans in matters of language, dress, occupation, location of their dwellings, and the cut of their hair. Indeed, if Rudolf Virchow's extensive study of over 10,000 German schoolchildren published in 1886 was accurate, they were also indistinguishable in terms of skin, hair, and eye color from the greater masses of those who lived in Germany. Virchow's statistics sought to show that wherever a greater percentage of the overall population had lighter skin or bluer eyes or blonder hair, a greater percentage of Jews also had lighter skin or bluer eyes or blonder hair.[24] Although Virchow attempted to provide a rationale for the sense of Jewish acculturation, he still assumed that Jews were a separate and distinct racial category. George Mosse has commented that "the separateness of Jewish schoolchildren, approved by Virchow, says something about the course of Jewish emancipation in Germany. However rationalized, the survey must have made Jewish schoolchildren conscious of their minority status and their supposedly different origins."[25] Nonetheless, even though they were labeled as different, Jews came to parallel the scale of types found elsewhere in European society. They became German in their very bodies, but these bodies were distrusted by the culture in which they found themselves.

At the close of the twentieth century, it is the turn of the Turks. Can Turks, even hybrids like the narrator, really become Germans? According to Senocak's Heinrich, "The Germans have learned nothing from history . . . now they have brought the Turks here. And they never came to terms even with the Jews" (82). Physical assimilation through surgery or intermarriage seems to be no prophylaxis in Senocak's world. Hybridity, such as that of the protagonist, means only that one is exposed to a double risk. One is in the end an Oriental, no matter what one's identity or language. Being hybrid only reinforces this. The protagonist desires not to be cosmopolitan, just simply German. This is denied to him by his Turkish identity; and, in his own estimation, his Jewish ancestry reinforces this.

Of all the self-consciously multicultural writers in Germany, Thomas Meinecke is perhaps the most explicit in terms of the function that he sees the figure of the Jew playing in the modern, multicultural world. For Meinecke, the Jew must be part of the multicultural mix. Born in 1955 in Hamburg and now living in a small town in Bavaria, Meinecke is the author of a series of novels that employ the notion of the hybrid as the ideal for the contemporary world. His first novel, the winner of the Heimito-von-Doderer prize for young novelists in 1997, was *The Church of John F. Kennedy* (1996), which chronicles a young German's car trip from New Orleans to Amish country. What is striking about this first novel, a novel of travel and education in the older model of Laurence Sterne and Jean-Paul Sartre, is its extraordinary humor in dealing with the complex hybridity of American society. Meinecke places his protagonist into this mix by stressing the often forgotten role of the Germans in the American mix. He highlights this suppressed role by quoting throughout the novel passages from letters and diaries of nineteenth- and twentieth-century German emigrants to America. These authentic texts comment, like snapshots, on the world that the protagonist (and the author) visits at the end of the twentieth century. Jews figure throughout this novel as part of the mix that defines America.

In his novel *Tomboy* (1998), Meinecke addresses the question of the slipperiness of gender designations. (He had begun this already in his long novella *Wood* [*Holz*] of 1988 in which a Jewish bisexual figure is introduced as one of the central characters.) The question of what makes a man a man centers on the definition of the Jew provided by American professor of Talmud Daniel Boyarin, whose work concerns masculinity and Jewish identity. In addition, Meinecke uses Judith Butler, Boyarin's colleague at the University of California at Berkeley, as one of his pivotal figures. Lesbian, Jewish, and a strong advocate of the notion that all gender is performative, Butler serves as the key to the novel's concern with the construction of gender identity.[26] Rarely has multicultural theory been appropriated in such a direct way in modern fiction. Again it is the Jew that serves as the fulcrum for Meinecke's observations about the flexibility of gender.

Meinecke's most recent novel, *Bright Blue* (*Hellblau*) (2001) does much the same thing with ideas of ethnicity and multiculturalism as *Tomboy* undertook with gender. Also set in America, the novel deals with the question of how ethnicity and race is defined. His initial question relates to Mariah Carey, the pop singer: Is she white or Black? She has a Black father and a white mother but what is she actually? Society sees her as Black and yet she is a hybrid. In Meinecke's fiction, the question of race eventually focuses on the Jews; Boyarin and the protagonist in this novel serve as touchstones for this question. The Jewish body appears to define difference as much as does the Black body of Mariah Carey.

What happens in a world defined by hybridity, in which all groups intermix with each other and yet maintain some sense of difference, to those groups that hold themselves apart? Meinecke picks up on the debate, outlined in an earlier chapter of this book, about the genetic illnesses of the Jews. His protagonist and friends ruminate about the idiosyncrasies of the Orthodox Jews of Borough Park, in Brooklyn. One relates that researchers at Johns Hopkins University had discovered the breast cancer gene, the result of "century old religious rules." What happens to such self-isolating groups, the character notes, is that their very isolation increases their risk of disease and eventual extinction. Jews, or even those bearing a Jewish name, come to bear the stigma of these illnesses. Indeed, in 1998, the Satmar Rabbi Joseph Eckstein ordered the dissolution of more than 200 marriages because both partners carried the gene for the same genetically transmitted disease. "The majority of these," the character says, "would not have originally voluntarily married one another."[27] Arranged marriages within the group "cause" genetic illness and thus those who most want to avoid the "healthy" mixing of a hybrid culture are condemned to eventually vanish.

Certainly the most striking recent literary representation of the anxiety about identification with the Jews in an American context (beyond African American literature) is to be found in Gish Jen's novel *Mona in the Promised Land* (1996).[28] Jen ironically comments on the Chinese American construction of the acculturation of Jews and Asians. Set in suburban Scarsdale in 1968, the novel chronicles the adolescence of a Chinese American woman whose family moves into a Jewish neighborhood in its quest for upward social mobility. Their neighbors are "rich and Jewish": "they're the New Jews, after all, a model minority and Great American Success. They know they belong in the promised land" (3). The protagonist identifies strongly with the Jews in her peer group and sees her body in terms of their own anxiety about their physical visibility. The Chinese desire in this novel to become a "model minority" like the Jews, and this is measured by their economic and cultural success.

One day Mona and her friends sit around and discuss aesthetic surgery. "'Do Chinese have operations to make their noses bigger?' someone asks." Yes, Mona replies: "She too envies the aquiline line . . . in fact she envies even their preoperative noses. . . . 'You can't mean like this schnozz here?' somebody says, exhibiting his profile. . . . She nods politely. 'And your eyes too.'" She continues to explain that Chinese Americans often have "operations to make single-fold eyelids into double-folds" (92). In the course of this discussion, Gish Jen supplies an ironic environmental explanation of how and why Oriental eyes have their specific form but concludes with a comment by one of the Jewish boys about Mona's eyes: "You look like straight out of Twilight Zone" (93). The exoticism of the "too small" nose and the "too Oriental" eyes is a clear marker for the Jews of their sense of their own difference.

It is no surprise in this world seen from Gish Jen's perspective that it is not Mona who gets the new nose or Western eyes: "Barbara Gugelstein is sporting a fine new nose. Straight, this is, and most diminutive, not to say painstakingly fashioned as a baby-grand tchotchke" (124). While Mona "admires her friend's nostrils, which are a triumph of judiciousness and taste," she herself is not moved to have aesthetic surgery. What Mona does is to convert to Judaism! But, as one of the African American characters disparagingly comments, becoming a Jew in religion but not physically is difficult in her world. For in order to be a real Jew "that nose of yours has got to grow out so big you've got to sneeze in a dish towel" (137). Jewishness means belonging to a visible outsider group. For Mona, this has become an insider group, which defines her sense of her own body. The role of aesthetic surgery is to reshape the external visibility of that group. Yet, as the novel shows, it is a sign of false acculturation. Barbara's nose job is faulty; it "runs extraordinarily when she cries" (237). Jews with short noses remain marked as Jews in this seemingly hostile world, and the Chinese, such as Mona's physician-sister, acculturate with the rise of multiculturalism by becoming Asian American, a form of alteration of identity without the alteration of the body. Happiness is becoming something else, something identifiable as Asian that is not too Chinese.

Still, Jewish visibility does not simply remain as the sign of success: it is haunted by history. Early in the novel Mona's mother tries to explain to her about the Japanese invasion of China when she announces that she has a Japanese boyfriend: "Are you sure? In school, they said the War was about putting the Jews in ovens" (15). For Mona, it is the Shoah that defines the past. Later in the novel the success of both the Chinese and the Jews is measured against those, such as the African Americans, shown to be in a permanently liminal position in American society. History fixes the positions of the Jews and those "wanna-be" Jews, such as Mona (just as in Senocak's novel, Sascha Muchteschem is condemned on a talk show as a "Wannabe-German" [130]). The more one wants to belong, the more the dominant society in these stories feels a greater sense of importance and the fact of the protagonist's true difference. In complex ways that is the moral of Gish Jen's account of the Asians as a model minority in the United States. Hybridity leads to assimilation and a loss of individual identity, even when a character such as Sascha Muchteschem actually has a dual cultural inheritance.

Fitting into American society means having the right kind of nose. In the fictional world representing the imaginary body of the American Jew, the retroussé Oriental nose comes to be an ideal. But for the Chinese American, according to Gish Jen's portrait, it is a sign of the new Asian identity: one nose *does* fit all. In this world, aesthetic surgery is a sign of middle-class rather than American identity, though one could argue that there is a fatal parallelism between these two ideas of imagining oneself as different. Thus, among Asian Americans in California, double-fold eyelid surgery has become "the gift that parents offer their daughters when they graduate from high school or college."[29] This parallels the experience of Jewish Americans in the 1960s. For the Vietnamese and Koreans in America, aesthetic surgery becomes a means of defining identity as flexible rather than permanent. Hybridity now means reshaping the body to make it more American. Yet the end result is not an American body but an Asian American body. The diasporic body remains marked as different and, just as Black became beautiful in the 1960s, so too is Asian beautiful today.

If Gish Jen's Westchester posits the Jews as an ironic norm of beauty, ("Jewish is beautiful"), Oscar Hijuelos's novel *A Simple Havana Melody (from when the world was good)* presents a Cuban American fantasy of the Jewish body.[30] It echoes the physical difference of the Jews and the impact of the Holocaust in a way more than slightly reminiscent of Achmat Dangor's *Kafka's Curse*. Hijuelos was born in 1951 of Cuban parentage in New York City, and has received the Pulitzer Prize and numerous other awards for earlier fiction that stressed the theme of Cuban culture seen through American eyes. The protagonist of this novel, Israel Levis, is a pious Catholic ("an individual, blessed by a Catholic God"), who composed the hit song "Rosas Puras" in the 1930s. At the opening of the novel, we see him having returned to Havana, old and very ill, after the war: "On his arm seven numbers in green ink" (23). He has been in Buchenwald. How he got there is at the heart of this fiction.

In the isolated country of Cuba, Levis had assumed that he, "a Cuban Catholic with a name like Israel Levis, was immune to the terrors descending upon the Jews of Europe" (37). Hijuelos stresses in the novel (following Jean-Paul Sartre's fantasy in the late 1940s) that any one could be made into a Jew, and yet Levis is in complex ways already "Jewish," even before he confronts Nazi racism in the 1940s. His name is redolent of his hidden nature. For although his family "had been for generations, quite irretriev-ably Catholic," he may well have had a "distant Catalan ancestor, who may or may not have had some Jewish blood" (49). He is Catholic in all senses, but in Spanish or Cuban terms, it can also mean that he is multicultural: his "Jewish" ancestor (real or not) marks him as different. Yet the Jew in his lineage is much closer. After his father (and siblings) die, his mother in a moment of mad-ness announces to him, "'My son, the idea has come to me that perhaps your father was a Jew. And that is why God has been act-ing so cruelly to us.' Then: 'We must make up for this with our prayers'" (81). The Jew is the victim; the one who is punished for having crucified Jesus and who will be punished for all eternity.

It is not just Israel Levis's lineage that marks him as the hid-den Jew—his body is even more of an identifier. Thin and emaci-ated when he returns to Cuba after the war, he was equally as huge before the war. Indeed, his nickname then was "El Gordo," the fat one, but most extraordinary about his body was the exaggerated size of his penis. Even as a small child "the manifestation of his fu-ture virility [was such] that their house maid, Florencia, when bathing him, often remarked, 'What a wonder!'" (53). And as he matures, his sexuality is extraordinarily compromised, even though his body is highly sexualized. Attracted to men but ob-sessed with the singer Rita Valladrares, he can only perform with paid prostitutes. His ambiguous sexuality points to a reading of his physical size as an indicator of his difference. Only much later, when he moves to Paris in 1932 to escape Havana and his mother, does the huge Israel Levis find love and sexual satisfaction with a Jewish woman named Sarah Rubenstein. With her, he is for the first time fully sexual as a male.

Israel's stay in Paris brings him in direct conflict with the Nazis. While his music is "degenerate," it is also very popular (254). With the fall of France in the spring of 1940, suddenly

Israel Levis, whose ancestry and body imply something Jewish in the Cuban context as depicted by Oscar Hijuelos, is transformed into a Jew by the Nazis. He aids Sarah and her daughter in escaping from Paris, but he remains there, ensconced at the Grand Hotel, which has become a German headquarters. He goes to mass each day at Notre Dame as a good Catholic should. He remains popular. He performs at parties, at one of which he meets the head of the Paris Gestapo who speaks to him in Spanish, noting that he had heard him many years ago in Vienna (273). With the beginning of the terror against foreign Jews, his Cuban passport is seized. He is ordered to go to the Gestapo office because of his obvious "Jewish" name, which labels him as a Jew. But we the readers know he is not one, whatever the multicultural references to his Jewishness have been in the novel to that point. The questioning quickly turns to the heart of the matter, to Levis's physical difference, to his penis. At this point in the novel, only its size has been revealed to the reader. At the Gestapo's inquisition he is asked if he is circumcised: "It happened that with his birth his father, Doctor Leocadio Levis, had thought of the minor operation as a preventative against the possibility of cradle-borne infections" (275). His claim that he is not a Jew is dismissed: "The police were amused—how could any man with a name like Israel Levis be anything but a Jew, no matter what his protests?" (275). Even more so, his Jewish body reveals his true nature to them. He is to be placed on a train to the death camps, but is rescued by the Gestapo general who sends him to Buchenwald, instead. Here, he is granted a special status, as he often plays for the camp officers on a "grand Bosendorfer piano under an enormous chandelier and gilded ceiling" (37). Still, the horrors of the camp turn his huge body into a shell, a survivor.

The novel, a Cuban American novel of Havana, becomes a novel of the Cuban as a Holocaust survivor. The multicultural image of the Jew remains that of the ultimate victim. The Cuban history that marks him, such as the political despotism of the Cuban dictatorship of Machado, is paralleled with the rise of the Nazis. The random murders in Havana that drive Levis to Paris, foreshadow the street brawls and beatings of the Jews that he sees on a trip to Munich. The fusion between the Cuban, seen through the eyes of the Cuban American writer, and the Jew in the Shoah is complete. For the American reader and writer, the Jew is a sign of the Holocaust. The Holocaust also defines the victim status of the protagonist. All of Levis's difference is that of the Jew. The imaginary Jew is again a disguise for the multicultural experience of the victim. The Jew does not truly exist except in the fantasy of the persecutors. Israel Levis takes on the mantle of the Jew in this multicultural novel. His actual difference as a fat man, as a bisexual man, as a creative genius is in the end is still defined by his difference as a Jew.

We began with Kureishi's identification of the Jew as marked to be permanently different. In the United Kingdom Kureishi saw, at least in his fantasy of the 1960s, a particularly good example of a culture in which the transition to a multicultural, perhaps even hybrid, society had begun from what had been perceived as a purely class-based society. The Jew at this point was the litmus test for immutability and difference. By the mid-twentieth century, British Jews, as opposed to immigrant Jews, had made it into the highest reaches of the British class structure. Assimilation, even conversion, marked their path from Benjamin Disraeli to the Rothschilds. And yet they remained "foreign" even in their movement up the class ladder.

Another answer to the identity dilemma is suggested by the Francophone novelist and scriptwriter Philippe Blasband's short story "A True Exile" ("Une exil véritable").[31] Born in 1964 in Teheran to a Jewish family, he was educated in Brussels. His first, autobiographical novel won the Rossel prize in 1990. In this monologue, we seem to have a similar set of expectations to those

of Hijuelos's Levis. The narrator, speaking to his friend who seems
to be mired in a false nostalgia for a lost Iran, describes himself as
having a Belgian father, a Belgian passport, and French is his
mother tongue; he professes ignorance of most things Iranian. Yet
he is, in his account, the perfect hybrid, the man between two
worlds who has begun to integrate his Iranian ethnicity into his
sense of Belgian identity. This Belgian identity is clearly Walloon;
it is French in all its aspects, and thus masks the split that still
haunts Belgian culture today, a split that equates ethnicity and language. For the choice of becoming truly Belgian means for him
becoming French-speaking rather than Flemish-speaking. At the
close of this monologue, he defines himself yet again as "not a bad
Iranian, not much of an Iranian at all, neither truly Belgian, nor
truly a Jew" (109). This is the fantasy of the Jew as merely part of
the multicultural mix, a mix defined as Francophone and therefore
beyond the struggle for linguistic hegemony that is still modern
Belgium. This simplification seems to be possible only when an
author such as Blasband has also written a novel on the fate of a
Jewish family that moves from Teheran to Brussels.[32] It reflects
the old joke about a pitched battle between French and Flemish
speakers in Belgium during the 1960s in which both sides are sep-
arated by the police, who order the Walloons to one side of the
street and the Flemish to the other. A Jew walks up to a policeman
and asks: "And where do we Belgians go?" The answer, in the discourse of contemporary multiculturalism, is: any place you want
but not here.

The privileged position of being a "real Belgian" enables the
multicultural writer to observe the complexity of a world in which
the Jews seem to be omnipresent. Whether examining the problem of diaspora, of acculturation, of hybridity, or of risk, the Jews
become the touchstone for all of the pitfalls that present themselves to other cultural groups. The Jews are either the ultimate
victim, because of the Shoah, or the worst case for assimilation, as

in the images of the German and American Jews that we have seen. Jewish writers themselves, such as Blasband, tend to amalgamate their image into that of the multicultural world in which the Jews are just one more culture in the multicultural salad bowl. Multicultural writers are torn between the image of the Jews as victims and as the most successful minority community. This is especially the case when they themselves are part of a group (such as the East Asians or South Asians) that are becoming successful. Multiculturalism seems to work best if (like naturalism) it focuses on economic liminality. The Jews are also an odd case precisely because of the Shoah. Hegel could not understand why the Jews continued to exist as a people, while their contemporaries from the Babylonians to the Romans had vanished. So too it seems impossible to imagine the Jews as anything but a symbol for death and destruction after the Shoah. This contrasts in an often bizarre manner with the very notion of Jewish success.

Thus in an age of multiculturalism, when American Jewish writing has become American writing, many American Jewish novelists have trouble with multiculturalism. Philip Roth's novel *The Human Stain* takes on political correctness as one of its central themes, and Saul Bellow has had a constant struggle with multiculturalism over the past two decades. Remember the outrage to his comment on "who is the Tolstoy of the Zulus," about whether there is an African culture?[33] Jews on the brave new frontier of multiculturalism seem always to be the subject of comparison. In the fantasy of the new multicultural author, they belong to a world of power but are also that world's most victimized group. This continuation of older images often makes it difficult for Jewish writers, sensing their distance from such representations, to imagine themselves as part of the multicultural universe. What remains of constant fascination is how many of the older motifs of Jewish difference, including images of the body and the language of the Jews, are internalized in this context. Gary Shteyngart, a Russian

Jew whose family immigrated to New York City in 1978 when he was six, turned his American Jewish experience into his first novel, *The Russian Debutante's Handbook* (2002).[34] His account stresses the impossibility of integration. His protagonist, the Russian Jew Vladimir Girshkin, is employed (in a Henry Miller sort of manner) in an office dealing with immigrants, a position that his middle-class professional parents find well below his potential. While they have integrated themselves into suburban America (in their own fantasy), Vladimir never can. He remains too Russian (and therefore too Jewish) for America. His adventures in New York City, as well as those in Russia where he becomes the "American Jew" for the Russian Mafia, illustrates a sense of never really belonging. *The Russian Debutante's Handbook* is in many ways the exemplary antimulticultural novel. His literary antecedents are to be found as much in the Russian tradition of Goncharov's *Oblamov* as in the North American immigrant novel, such as Mordechai Richler's *The Apprenticeship of Duddy Kravitz*. Shteyngart felt isolated in his new multicultural America and captured that sense of failure in what has turned out to be a very successful novel. When Steyngart (like his protagonist Vladimir Girshkin) actually returned to Russia, he seemed pleased that his accent was heard, not as American but as Jewish. "After I'm in Russia for a while, I lose it."[35] The mark of his hybridity, his accent, vanished and he became neither American nor Jew, just another Russian, like Blasband's Belgian. The brave new frontier of multiculturalism uses Jewish difference, but in ways that often contrast with those Jewish writers who feel that their cultural success is as a mainstream author and not as a marginal voice.

Notes

INTRODUCTION

1. Steven Kepnes, ed., *Interpreting Judaism in a Postmodern Age* (New York: New York University, 1996).
2. Arnold M. Eisen, *Galut: Modern Jewish Reflection on Homelessness and Homecoming* (Bloomington: Indiana University Press, 1986), p. 43.
3. Zeev Sternhell, *The Founding Myths of Israel*, trans. David Maisel (Princeton: Princeton University Press, 1997); Yael Zerubavel, *Recovered Roots: Collective Memory and the Making of Israeli National Tradition* (Chicago: University of Chicago Press, 1995).
4. Sandra Braude, *Windswept Plains* (Cape Town: Buschu Books, 1991), p. 79.
5. Jacob Neusner, *Self-Fulfilling Prophecy: Exile and Return in the History of Judaism* (Atlanta, Ga.: Scholars Press, 1990; 1987).
6. W. D. Davies, *The Territorial Dimension in Judaism* (Minneapolis: Fortress Press, 1991; 1982).
7. See specifically Deborah Bernstein, *The Struggle for Equality: Urban Women Workers in Prestate Israeli Society* (New York: Praeger, 1987); Vicki Caron, *Between France and Germany: the Jews of Alsace-Lorraine, 1871–1918* (Stanford: Stanford University Press, 1988). The central text to rethink history in gendered terms remains Joan Wallach Scott, *Gender and the Politics of History* (New York: Columbia University Press, 1988).
8. Daniel Goldhagen, *Hitler's Willing Executioners: Ordinary Germans and the Holocaust* (New York: Knopf, 1996).
9. Jonathan Boyarin, *Storm after Paradise* (Minneapolis: University of Minnesota Press, 1992), p. xvii.
10. Richard Schusterman, "Next Year in Jerusalem?" in David Theo Goldberg and Michael Krausz, eds., *Jewish Identity* (Philadelphia: Temple University Press, 1993), pp. 291–308.

11. On the history and background of Jewish attitudes toward language, the languages of the Jews, and the image of the Jews' language, see my *Jewish Self-Hatred: Anti-Semitism and the Hidden Language of the Jews* (Baltimore: Johns Hopkins University Press, 1986).

12. Gabriel Josipovici, "Going and Resting," in Goldberg and Krausz, pp. 309–21.

13. Arnaldo Momigliano, "What Flavius Did Not See," in his *Essays on Ancient and Modern Judaism*, ed. Silvia Berti, trans. Maura Masella-Gayley (Chicago: University of Chicago Press, 1994), pp. 67–78. References to other material in this volume are in parentheses.

14. Benedict Anderson, "Exodus," *Critical Inquiry* 20 (1994): 314–27. On the context and continuation of this argument about the relationship between the global and the modern, see Reingard Nethersole, "Models of Globaliztion," *PMLA* 116 (2001): 638–49.

15. Michael A. Meyer, "German-Jewish Identity in 19th Century America," in *The American Jewish Experience*, ed. Jonathan D. Sarna (New York: Holmes & Meier, 1986), pp. 45–59.

16. James Clifford, "Traveling Cultures," in *Cultural Studies*, ed. Lawrence Grossberg, Cary Nelson, Paula Treichler (New York: Routledge, 1992), pp. 96–112 (discussion, pp. 112–16).

17. Homi Bhabha, *The Location of Culture* (London: Routledge, 1994), p. 224.

18. In the major postcolonial version of the English Bible, *The Revised Standard Version*, there are a series of evocations of the frontier. The following verses come to reflect the sense of boundaries, borders, and frontiers. Deuteronomy 2:19 states "and when you approach the frontier of the sons of Ammon, do not harass them or contend with them, for I will not give you any of the land of the sons of Ammon as a possession, because I have given it to the sons of Lot for a possession." Joshua 22:11: " And the people of Israel heard say, "Behold, the Reubenites and the Gadites and the half-tribe of Manas'seh have built an altar at the frontier of the land of Canaan, in the region about the Jordan, on the side that belongs to the people of Israel." 2 Kings 3:21: "When all the Moabites heard that the kings had come up to fight against them, all who were able to put on armor, from the youngest to the oldest, were called out, and were drawn up at the frontier." Ezekiel 25:9: "therefore I will lay open the flank of Moab from the cities on its frontier, the glory of the country, Beth-jesh'imoth, Ba'al-me'on, and Kiriatha'im."

19. Daniel and Jonathan Boyarin, "Diaspora: Generation and the Ground of Jewish Identity," *Critical Inquiry* 19 (1993): 693–725.

20. Stephen Aron, "Lessons in Conquest: Towards a Greater Western History," *Pacific Historical Review* 63 (1991): 125–47, here, p. 128.

21. Kerwin Lee Klein, "Reclaiming the 'F' Word, or Being and Becoming Postwestern," *Pacific Historical Review* 65 (1996): 179–215.

22. Charles Taylor, *Multiculturalism and the "Politics of Recognition"* (Princeton: Princeton University Press, 1992).

23. Hilde Domin quoted in Hans Jürgen Schultz, ed., *Mein Judentum* (Stuttgart: Kreuz-Verlag, 1978), p. 98.

24. This is in the German philosopher Walter Benjamin's terms and analogous to Zygmunt Bauman's argument.

25. Gloria Anzaldúa, *Borderlands/La Frontera: The New Mestiza* (San Francisco: Spinsters/Aunt Lute, 1987), 79–81.

26. Richard White, *The Middle Ground: Indians, Empires, and Republics in the Great Lakes Region, 1650–1815* (Cambridge: Cambridge University Press, 1991).

27. Bruno Latour, *We Have Never Been Modern*, trans., Catherine Porter (Cambridge, Mass.: Harvard University Press, 1993).

28. Zygmunt Bauman, *Modernity and Ambivalence* (Cambridge: Polity Press, 1991), p. 5.

29. Angelika Bammer, *Displacements: Cultural Identities in Question* (Bloomington: Indiana University Press, 1994).

30. Gilles Deleuze and Félix Guattari, *A Thousand Plateaus: Capitalism and Schizophrenia*, trans. Brian Massumi (Minneapolis: University of Minnesota Press, 1987), pp. 291–2.

31. Yael Zerubavel, *Recovered Roots: Collective Memory and the Making of Israeli National Tradition* (Chicago: University of Chicago Press, 1995).

32. Felix A. Theilhaber, *Der Untergang der deutschen Juden: eine volkswirtschaftliche Studie* (München: E. Reinhardt, 1911); Bernard Wasserstein, *Vanishing Diaspora: The Jews in Europe Since 1945* (Cambridge, Mass.: Harvard University Press, 1996); Mitchell Bryan Hart, "Social Science And National Identity: A History of Jewish Statistics, 1880–1930" (diss., University of California, Los Angeles, 1994).

33. R. Po-chia Hsia, *The Myth of Ritual Murder: Jews and Magic in Reformation Germany* (New Haven: Yale University Press, 1988); *Trent 1475: Stories of a Ritual Murder Trial* (New Haven: Yale University Press with Yeshiva University Library, 1992); *In and Out of the Ghetto: Jewish-Gentile Relations in late Medieval and early Modern Germany* (Washington, D.C. and Cambridge: German Historical Institute and Cambridge University Press, 1995).

34. This is an extension of the idea of a contact zone developed in Mary Louise Pratt, *Imperial Eyes: Travel Writing and Transculturation* (London: Routledge, 1992).

35. Marc Shell, "Babel in America; or, The Politics of Language Diversity in the US," *Critical Inquiry* 20 (1993): 103–27.

36. Benjamin Harshav, *Language in Time of Revolution* (Berkeley: University of California Press, 1993).

CHAPTER 1

1. Yehuda Bauer, *Out of the Ashes: The Impact of American Jews on Post-Holocaust European Jews* (Oxford: Oxford University Press, 1989), p. 36.

2. Erica Burgauer, *Zwischen Erinnerung und Verdrängung-Juden in Deutschland nach 1945* (Hamburg: Rowohlt, 1993), p. 19.

3. Wolfgang Jacobmeyer, "Jüdische Überlebende als "Displaced Persons," *Geschichte und Gesellschaft* 3 (1983): 421–52.

4. Eberhard Lämmert, "Beherrschte Literatur: Vom Elend des Schriebens unter Diktaturen," in Günther Rühle, ed., *Literature in der Diktatur: Schrieben in Natioanlsozialismus und DDR-Sozialismus* (Paderborn: Schönigh, 1997), pp. 15–37. On the more general case of the cultural politics of the GDR, see Richard A. Zipser, ed., "Literary Censorship in the German Democratic Republic, II: The Authors Speak," *The Germanic Review* 65 (1990): 118–29; David Bathrick, *The Powers of Speech: The Politics of Culture in the GDR* (Lincoln: University of Nebraska Press, 1995); Wolfgang Jäger, *Die Intellektuellen und die deutsche Einheit* (Freiburg im Breisgau: Rombach, 1997).

5. Jurek Becker, *Ende des Grössenwahns* (Frankfurt am Main: Suhrkamp, 1996), pp. 11–12.

6. Becker, *Ende*, p. 17.

7. What "Jewish" meant in the cultural life of the GDR can be gleaned in part from Thomas C. Fox, "A 'Jewish Question' in GDR Literature?" *German Life and Letters* 44 (1990): 58–70; and Paul O'Doherty, "The Reception of Heine's Jewishness in the Soviet Zone/GDR, 1945–1961," *German Life and Letters* 52 (1999): 85–96; as well as Paul O'Doherty's "The Portrayal of Jews in GDR Prose Fiction," (Ph.D. diss., University of Nottingham, 1995).

8. Frank Beyer, *Wenn der Wind sich dreht: Meine Filme, mein Leben* (München: Econ, 2001), pp. 180–98.

9. On Jewish life and the image of the Jews in the GDR, see the recent work by Mario Kessler, *Die SED und die Juden: zwischen Repression und Toleranz: politische Entwicklung bis 1967* (Berlin: Akademie Verlag, 1995); Lothar Mertens, *Davidstern unter Hammer und Zirkel: die jüdischen Gemeinden in der SBZ/DDR und ihre Behandlung durch Partei und Staat 1945–1990* (Hildesheim: Olms, 1997); Ulrike Offenberg, *Seid vorsichtig gegen die Machthaber: die*

jüdischen Gemeinden in der SBZ und der DDR 1945–1990 (Berlin: Aufbau-Verlag, 1998).

10. Hermann Kant, *Abspann: Errinerung an meine Gegenwart* (Berlin: Aufbau, 1991), p. 433.

11. Zipser, 114.

12. Jurek Becker, *Irreführung der Behörden* (Frankfurt am Main: Suhrkamp, 1982; copyright, Rostock: Hinstorff, 1973), pp. 30–5.

13. Lola Ramon, "Groll mit nichts im Magen," *tua res* 3 (1959): 39–41.

14. Karin Graf and Ulrich Konietzny, eds., *Jurek Becker* (München: Iudicium, 1991), p. 59.

15. Carl Paschek, ed., *Jurek Becker* (Frankfurt am Main: Stadt-und Universitätsbibliothek, 1989), p. 49.

16. Bundesarchiv: Files of the Ministry of Culture / DEFA: DR 117 2998: Letter from Maa<001>.

17. Bundesarchiv: Files of the Ministry of Culture / DEFA: DR 1–4266: Report of Jahrow, February 3, 1966.

18. Bundesarchiv: Files of the Ministry of Culture / DEFA: DR 1–4266: Report of Jahrow, February 21, 1966.

19. Bundesarchiv: Files of the Ministry of Culture / DEFA: DR 1–4266: Plot summary dated February 4, 1966, sent to Maa<001>.

20. Bundesarchiv: Files of the Ministry of Culture / DEFA: DR 1–4266: Letter of transmittal by Bruk (DEFA) to Maa<001>: August 2, 1966, with a detailed account of the chronology of discussion with the Polish authorities and film studio.

21. Ralf Schenk, ed., *Regie: Frank Beyer* (Berlin: Hentrich, 1995), p. 62.

22. Janusz Gumkowski, Adam Rutkowski, and Arnfrid Astel, eds., *Briefe aus Litzmannstadt*, trans. Peter Lachmann and Arnfrid Astel (Cologne: Friedrich Middlehauve Verlag, 1967), pp. 30, 58.

23. Günter Kunert, *Erwachsenenspiele: Errinerungen* (Munich: Hanser, 1997), p. 157.

24. Reiner Kunze, *Die wunderbaren Jahre* (Frankfurt am Main: Suhrkamp, 1977), p. 168.

25. Carl Paschek, ed., *Jurek Becker: Begleitheft zur Ausstellung der Stadt-und Universitätsbibliothek Frankfurt am Main (24. Mai bis 30. Juni 1989)* (Frankfurt am Main: Stadt-und Universitätsbibliothek, 1989), p. 50.

26. Heinz Ludwig Arnold, "Gespräche mit Jurek Becker," *Text + Kritik* 116 (1992), 4–15, here, p. 9.

27. Stasi files: XX/R16 dated August 26, 1968.

28. See Klaus Schlegel, "Tewje und seine Schwiegersöhne. Zur Analyse von zwei Szenen des Musicals *Der Fiedler auf dem Dach* in der Inszenierung von Walter Felsenstein," *Jahrbuch der Komischen Oper* 9 (1971): 65–79.

29. Theodor W. Adorno, "Was bedeutet: Aufarbeitung der Vergangenheit," in his *Eingriffe* (Frankfurt: Suhrkamp, 1968), pp. 143–4.

30. A. C. Bradley, *Shakespearean Tragedy* (London: Macmillan, 1905).

CHAPTER 2

1. See the following interviews: "Art Spiegelman: An Exquisite Sense of Balance," *Art Press* 194 (September 1994), 27–32; "A Conversation with Art Spiegelman," *Artweek* 24 (December 16 1993), 15–16; Michael Silverblatt, "The Cultural Relief of Art Spiegelman," *Tampa Review* 5 (1992): 31–36. The following citations on Art Spiegelman give a sense of the importance of *Maus* in the culture of contemporary American art: "Out of History," *Artweek* 24 (December 16 1993), 14; "The Maus that Roared," *Art News* 92 (May 1993), 63–4; "High Art Lowdown," *Artforum* 29 (December 1990), 115; "When It's a Matter of Life and Death: Art Spiegelman's Diagrams," *Arts Magazine* 65 (October 1990), 83–7. The following critical essays provide various readings of *Maus:* Michael Rothberg, "'We Were Talking Jewish': Art Spiegelman's *Maus* as 'Holocaust' Production," *Contemporary Literature* 35 (1994), 661–87; Richard Martin, "Art Spiegelman's *Maus;* Or, the Way It Really Happened," in Bernd Engler and Kurt Muller, eds., *Historiographic Metafiction in Modern American and Canadian Literature* (Paderborn: Ferdinand Schoningh, 1994), pp. 373–82; Rick Iadonisi, "Bleeding History and Owning His (Father's) Story: *Maus* and Collaborative Autobiography," *CEA Critic* 57 (1994), 45–56; Joan Gordon, "Surviving the Survivor: Art Spiegelman's *Maus,*" *Journal of the Fantastic in the Arts* 5 (1993), 81–89; Stephen E. Tabachnick, "Of Maus and Memory: The Structure of Art Spiegelman's Graphic Novel of the Holocaust," *Word & Image* 9 (1993), 154–62; Robert Storr, "Art Spiegelman's Making of *Maus,*" Tampa Review 5 (1992), 27–30; Marianne Hirsch, "Family Pictures: Maus, Mourning, and Post-Memory," *Discourse* 15 (1992–1993), 3–29; Miles Orvell, "Writing Posthistorically' Krazy Kat, Maus and the Contemporary Fiction Cartoon," *American Literary History* 4 (1992), 110–28; Kurt Scheel, "Mauschwitz? Art Spiegelmans 'Geschichte eines Überlebenden'," *Merkur* 43 (1989), 435–38.

2. Sheva Fogel, "Drawing on Politics and Chutzpah: A Look at Israel's Comics and Cartoons," *The Comics Journal* 141 (April, 1991): 31–34.

3. Frederik L. Schodt, *Manga! Manga! The World of Japanese Comics* (Tokyo: Kodansha, 1986). The plot of Tezuka's novel: it begins with the Japanese newspaperman Sohei Toge in Germany to cover

the 1936 Olympics. When his brother is killed in Berlin, Toge's quest to discover why takes him both to the Nazis' Nuremberg rally and into a Gestapo interrogation room, and puts into his hands a secret that could bring down Hitler. In Kobe, Adolf Kaufman, the half-German, half-Japanese son of a German consulate employee befriends Adolf Kamil, the son of a baker living in Kobe's Jewish community. Toge returns to Japan, where he is pursued both by Japan's secret police, suspicious of anyone less than enthusiastic about Japan's growing militarism, and by the Gestapo officer who murdered Toge's brother, still after the secret papers for which he was killed. Meanwhile, Adolf Kaufman, sent to school in Germany, meets Adolf Hitler. Adolf Kamil's father journeys to Lithuania to offer 500 dispossessed yeshiva students refuge in Kobe's Jewish community. Adolf Kaufman, recruited into the SS, falls in love with a Jewish girl whose family is to be deported to a death camp. Sohei Toge finds new allies in Japan. And the secret of the Toge papers finally falls into the hands of Adolf Kamil.

4. See Joseph Patrick Witek, "'Stranger and More Thrilling than Fiction': Comic Books as History" (diss., Vanderbilt University, 1988); and Bernd Dolle-Weinkauff, "Das 'Dritte Reich' im Comic: Geschichtsbilder und darstellungsaesthetische Strategien einer rekonstruierten Gattung," *Jahrbuch für Antisemitismusforschung* 2 (1993): 298–332.

5. "Laughter at Film Brings Spielberg Visit," *New York Times* (April 13, 1994): B11–1.

6. Peter Novick, *The Holocaust in American Life* (New York: Houghton Mifflin, 1999).

7. For the more recent literature on this topic, see Sidra DeKoven Ezrahi, "After Such Knowledge, What Laughter?" *Yale Journal of Criticism* 14 (2001): 287–313; and David Bathrick, "Rescreening 'The Holocaust': The Children's Stories," *New German Critique* 80 (2000): 41–58.

8. Aristotle's too, if the book on Comedy had not been lost. Aristotle notes in the *Poetics* that comic laughter is critical of the ridiculous, but that it is a ridiculous that "is not painful or destructive." Gerald F. Else, *Aristotle's Poetics: The Argument* (Cambridge: Cambridge University Press, 1957), p. 74.

9. We can mention one exception—the German idea of a comedy without laughter, which builds upon Denis Diderot's idea of the *comédie sérieuse*. Diderot's view dominates the history of "high" German comedy (but not the popular comedy) through the twentieth century. It is actually bad form to laugh during a performance of Lessing's *Nathan the Wise*. See Helmut Arntzen, *Die ernste*

Komödie: Das deutsche Lustspiel von Lessing bis Kleist (München: Fink, 1968).

10. Terrence Des Pres, *Writing into the World. Essays: 1973–1987*. New York: Viking, 1991), p. 1.

11. A. C. Bradley, *Shakespearean Tragedy* (London: Macmillan, 1905).

12. Alan Dundes and Thomas Hauschild, "Auschwitz Jokes," *Western Folklore* 42 (1983): 249–60; Alan Dundes and Uli Linke, "More on Auschwitz Jokes," *Folklore* 99 (1988): 3–10; Alan Dundes and Thomas Hauschild, "Kennt der Witz kein Tabu? Zynische Erzählformen als Versuch der Bewältigung nationalsozialistischer Verbrechen," *Zeitschrift für Volkskunde* 83 (1987): 21–31. See also: Paul Lewis, "Joke and Anti-Joke: Three Jews and a Blindfold," *Journal of Popular Culture* 21 (1987): 63–73.

13. See my *Jews in Today's German Culture, The Schwartz Lectures* (Bloomington: Indiana University Press, 1995) as well as Miriam Maltz, "Depicting the Holocaust: Literary Techniques in Leslie Epstein's *King of the Jews*," *Jewish Affairs* 47 (1992): 79–85.

14. In translating the memories and images of the Shoah at the end of the twentieth century, humor is considered a less appropriate vehicle and laughter is not desirable. In an insightful essay, Mark Cory, professor of German at the University of Arkansas, has argued that when humor is used in representing the Shoah, it has a significant psychological function. "Humor is a psychological response to danger, as well as a coping mechanism and a means of resistance." Within the genre of Shoah literature, according to Cory, the uses of comedic distance in the employment of psychological and emotional coping are wide ranging. From the gallows humor of actual Holocaust survivors to the protest humor of the trickster motif and the "spunky good humor" of Anne Frank, humor seems to be a means by which survivors cope with an event that is overwhelming in its nature. (This seems not to be true of George Stevens' film *The Diary of Anne Frank* [1959] in which humor is clearly absent from Millie Perkins's version of the title figure.) Cory correctly indicates the difference in the function of humor and coping between Holocaust survivors (such as Hilsenrath) and their Americanized children (here he takes Spiegelman as an example). Mark Cory, "Comedic Distance in Holocaust Literature," *Journal of American Culture* 18 (1995): 35–40. And yet he misses the point that the expectation is not that the audience laughs. The nature of humor even in Corey's account is highly marginalized and seems to serve only as a minimal function in providing a model of the control of the uncontrollable. It is, by definition, condemned to failure.

15. See Thomas Kraft, ed., *Edgar Hilsenrath: Das Unerzählbare erzählen* (München: Piper, 1995).

16. Hans-Jochen Gamm, *Der Flüsterwitz im Dritten Reich* (München: List Verlag, 1963); Steve Lipman, *Laughter in Hell: The Use of Humor During the Holocaust* (Northfield, N.J.: Jason Aronson, 1991).

17. See the taped records on David W., 1921-. Holocaust testimony (HVT–1687) [videorecording] interviewed by Helen Cohn and Lidya Osadchey, January 31, 1991, Fortunoff Video Archive for Holocaust Testimonies, Yale University Library, Box 208240, MS1322. He states that he was born in Chzarnów, Poland, in 1921. He notes the "importance of being with his brother, humor, and his barber skills to his survival." See also the interview by Sidney M. Bolkosky with Agatha R., who was born in Mukachevo, Czechoslovakia, Fortunoff Video Archive for Holocaust Testimonies HVT–739, MS 1322, in which she states the role of "inmate humor" in survival.

18. The most succinct summary of this view (on which many books have been written) is Irving Saposnik, "The Yiddish are Coming! The Yiddish are Coming! Some Thoughts on Yiddish Comedy," in Reinhold Grimm and Jost Hermand, eds., *Laughter Unlimited: Essays on Humor, Satire, and the Comic* (Madison: University of Wisconsin Press, 1991), pp. 99–105.

19. See especially Tony Barta, "Film Nazis: The Great Escape" in *Screening the Past: Film and the Representation of History* (Westport, Conn.: Praeger, 1998), pp. 127–48; Yosefa Loshitzky, ed., *Spielberg's Holocaust* (Bloomington: Indiana University Press, 1997); Stephen Lewis, *Art out of Agony: The Holocaust Theme in Literature, Sculpture and Film* (Toronto: CBC Enterprises, 1984). See also Dominick LaCapra, *History and Memory after Auschwitz* (Ithaca, N.Y.: Cornell University Press, 1998; Ilan Avisar, "Holocaust Movies and the Politics of Collective Memory," in Alvin H. Rosenfeld, ed., *Thinking about the Holocaust: After Half a Century* (Bloomington: Indiana University Press, 1997), pp. 38–58; Janet Lungstrum, "Foreskin Fetishism: Jewish Male Difference in *Europa, Europa*," *Screen* 39 (1998): 53–66; Morris Zyrl and Saul S. Friedman, "The Holocaust as Seen in the Movies. A Handbook of Criticism, History, and Literary Writings," in Saul S. Friedman and Dennis Klein, eds., *Holocaust Literature* (Westport, Conn.: Greenwood, 1993), pp. 604–22.

20. A. Roy Eckardt, "Comedy versus tragedy: post-Shoah reflections," Maxwell Lecture, April 24, 1990 (Oxford: Oxford Centre for Postgraduate Hebrew Studies); and Carol Faye Stern Edelman, "Attitudes toward Violence: the Subculture of Violence Revisited;

Conflict and Control Functions of Sexual Humor; Resistance to Genocide: Victim Response During the Holocaust" (diss., University of Arizona, 1987).

21. For the general context, see Lester D. Friedman, *Hollywood's Image of the Jew* (New York: Frederick Ungar, 1982); Neal Gabler, *An Empire of their Own: How the Jews Invented Hollywood* (New York: Crown, 1988); and Mark Winocur, *American Laughter: Immigrants, Ethnicity, and the 1930s Hollywood Film Comedy* (New York: St. Martin's Press, 1993).

22. David Robinson, *Chaplin: His Life and Art* (New York: McGraw-Hill, 1985), p. 485.

23. Leland A. Poague, *The Cinema of Ernst Lubitsch* (Cranbury, N.J.: A. S. Barnes, 1978), p. 90.

24. William Paul, *Ernst Lubitsch's American Comedy* (New York: Columbia University Press, 1983), p. 225.

25. Uwe Naumann, *Zwischen Tränen und Gelächter* (Köln: Pahl-Rugenstein, 1983), p. 292.

26. See Mordecai Newman, "Naughty Nazis: A Review of 'To Be or Not to Be,'" *Jewish Frontier* 51 (March 1984): 24–26.

27. bmi.com/musicworld/features/200106/mbrooks.asp.

28. Caroline Alice Wiedmer, "Reconstructing Sites: Representations of the Holocaust in Postwar Literary, Cinematic and Memorial Texts," (diss., Princeton University, 1994).

29. Lawrence Graver, *An Obsession with Anne Frank: Meyer Levin and the Diary* (Los Angeles: University of California Press, 1995).

30. For the context, see Susan Zuccotti, *The Italians and the Holocaust* (New York: Basic Books, 1987).

31. Beth Pinsker, "Did Another Shoah Comedy Inspire Benigni?" *Forward* (February 5, 1999): 1.

32. Roberto Benigni's model was echoed by Fernando Trueba's *Girl of My Dreams* (*la Niña de Tus Ojos*) (1998) starring Penelope Cruz playing Macarena Granada, a Spanish actress making a film about German-Spanish friendship for the official German studio, UFA, in 1938. The evocation of the Shoah in this context comes when the German extras are judged not to look Spanish enough and Eastern European Jews are brought in from a concentration camp. The actress rescues one of the Jews and flees with him to Paris. Alan Riding, "German Films Treat Nazis More Freely," *New York Times* (February 18, 1999): B1–2. The light touch in this film answers the rather more serious version of the making of the most repulsive of the pseudodocumentary anti-Semitic films of the Third Reich, Fritz Hippler's *The Eternal Jew* (1940), in which Jews from the Warsaw ghetto were made to "star." A further theme was the accu-

sation about Hitler's favorite director, Leni Riefenstahl, and her film *Tiefland* (1940–45, released 1954). She was accused of having gotten Gypsy extras from a concentration camp to act in the filmed operetta and that some were later murdered there. This is echoed in director Thomas Brasch's *Der Passagier—Welcome to Germany* (1988), in which Tony Curtis plays the adult director who had been a child actor in the Nazi film. As for a German film about the Shoah, the taboo of the comic is firmly in place—see David Welch, *Propaganda and the German Cinema 1933–45* (Oxford: Clarendon Press, 1983), and Yizhak Ahren, Stig Hornshoj-Moller, Christoph B. Melchers, *"Der ewige Jude"-wie Goebbels hetzte: Untersuchungen zum nationalsozialistischen Propagandafilm* (Aachen: Alano, 1990).

33. "Life Is Beautiful: An Interview with Roberto Benigni by Prairie Miller," www.allmovie.com/cg.

34. Ibid.

35. See, for example, the discussion in Ralph Tutt, "Seven Beauties and the Beast: Bettelheim, Wertmuller, and the Uses of Enchantment," *Literature/ Film Quarterly* 17 (1989): 193–201.

36. Erica Milvy "The Beautiful Life and Art of Roberto: Italy's Primo Clown Takes a Controversial Look at the Holocaust," *INDIE—the Guide to Independent Film* (September/October 1998): 20–21 (www.salonmag.com/ent/movies/int/ 1998/10/30int.html).

37. Abini Zöllner, "Die Ehe ist ein Fiasko," *Berliner Zeitung* (March 3–4, 2001): 6–7.

38. Pinsker, 1, 14.

39. Bruce Weber, "What's So Funny?: Decoding that Enigma Called Humor and Failing Gleefully," *New York Times* (March 9, 1999): B1, B9.

40. Compare Frank Beyer's recent account that creates a scenario in which Becker comments on the Kassovitz remake of the film that appeared after his death. See Frank Beyer, *Wenn der Wind sich dreht: Meine Filme, mein Leben* (München: Econ, 2001), pp. 180–98 and 368.

41. http://www.spe.sony.com/movies/Jacobtheliar/cast.html.

CHAPTER 3

1. There are many accounts of this. I am quoting from Jerome E. Brooks, *The Mighty Leaf: Tobacco through the Centuries* (London: Alvin Redman, 1953), pp. 12–15. The account is also part of a Jewish history of tobacco in the article "Tobacco," *The Jewish Encyclopedia*, 12 vols. (New York: Funk & Wagnalls, 1905–1926), XII: 164–6.

2. Guillermo Cabrera Infante, *Holy Smoke* (Woodstock, N. Y.: Overlook Press, 1998), pp. 6, 13.

3. The best scholarly article on the early history of smoking stresses this association: Charles Singer, "The Early History of Tobacco," *Quarterly Review* 436 (July 1913): 125–42.

4. Wolfgang Schivelbusch, *Tastes of Paradise: A Social History of Spices, Stimulants, and Intoxicants*, trans. (New York: Vintage, 1993); Jerome E. Brooks, ed., *Tobacco: Its History Illustrated by Books, Manuscripts and Engravings in the Library of George Arents Jr.*, 5 vols. (New York: Rosenback, 1937–1943); Count [Egon Caesar] Corti, *A History of Smoking* (London: George G. Harrap, 1931).

5. Frank Swiaczny, *Die Juden in der Pfalz und in Nordbaden im 19. Jahrhundert und ihre wirtschaftliche Akitivtäten in der Tabakbranche: Zur historischen Sozialgeographie einer Minderheit* (Mannheim: Institut für Landeskunde und Regionalforschung der Universität Mannheim, 1996).

6. Svend Larsen, *Kortfattet beretning om tobakkens historie: fortegnelse over Tobakkens museumsgenstande* (Odense, Danmark: Tobaksmuseet, Hagen & Sørensen, 1948).

7. Joseph von Retzer, *Tabakpachtung in den österreichischen Ländern von 1670–1783* (Vienna: Sonnleither, 1784); Sabine Fellner, Wolfgang Bauer, Herbert Rupp, *Die lasterhafte Panazee: 500 Jahre Tabakkultur in Europa : Ausstellung im Österreichischen Tabakmuseum, 11. Juni bis 4. Oktober 1992* (Wien: Austria Tabakwerke Aktiengesellschaft, 1992).

8. "Tobacco Trade and Industries," *Encyclopedia Judaica*, 16 vols. (Jerusalem: Encyclopedia Judaica, 1972), 1175–1178. This entry ignores the "legend" of the Jewish origin of tobacco in Europe and stresses only the sociological aspect of this question.

9. Robert N. Proctor, *The Nazi War on Tobacco* (Princeton: Princeton University Press, 1999), p. 235.

10. Hayyim ben Israel Benveniste, *Keneset ha-Godolah* (Constantinople: Bi-defus Yonah [ben] Ya'akov, 1729), pp. 101ff.

11. Clemens Brentano, "Über die Kennzeichen des Judenthums," reproduced as an appendix to Heinz Härtl, "Arnim und Goethe. Zum Goethe-Verständnis der Romantik im ersten Jahrzehnt des 19. Jahrhunderts" (diss., Halle, 1971), pp. 471–90; on tobacco farming, p. 474; on tobacco consumption, p. 473; on the disease of the Jews, pp. 484–6.

12. On the Jewish discussion, I am indebted to Louis Jacobs, "Tobacco and Hasidim," *Polin* 11(1998): 25–30; here, 26.

13. Yaffa Eliach, "The Russian Dissenting Sects and Their Influence on Israel Baal Shem, Founder of Hasidism," *Proceedings of the*

American Academy for Jewish Research 36 (1968): 57–88; here, 80–81.

14. *Solomon Maimon: An Autobiography*, trans. J. Clark Murray (London: Alexander Gardner, 1888), p. 162.

15. Compare the Asian American situation in Xing Guang Chen et al., "Smoking Patterns of Asian-American Youth in California and Their Relationship with Acculturation," *Journal of Adolescent Health* 24 (1999): 321–8.

16. Jacobs, p. 26.

17. Jacobs, p. 27.

18. Jacobs, p. 27.

19. Jacobs, p. 27.

20. Raphael Kohen, *Hut ha-Meshullah* (Odessa: n.p., 1874).

21. His first paper on this topic is Jean Martin Charcot, "Sur la claudication intermittente," *Comptes rendus des séances et mémoires de la société de biologie* (Paris) 1858, Mémoire 1859, 2 series, 5, 25–38. While this is not the first description of the syndrome, it is the one that labels this as a separate disease entity. It is first described by Benjamin Collins Brodie, *Lectures Illustrative of Various Subjects in Pathology and Surgery* (London: Longman, 1846): p. 361. Neither Brodie nor Charcot attempts to provide an etiology for this syndrome. Compare M. S. Rosenbloom et al., "Risk Factors Affecting the Natural History of Intermittent Claudication," *Archive of Surgery* 123 (1989): 867–70.

22. H. Higier, "Zur Klinik der angiosklerotischen paroxysmalen Myasthenie ('claudication intermittente' Charcot's) und der sog. spontanen Gangrän," *Deutsche Zeitschrift für Nervenheilkunde* 19 (1901): 438–67.

23. Heinrich Singer, *Allgemeine und spezielle Krankheitslehre der Juden* (Leipzig: Benno Konegen, 1904), pp. 124–5.

24. Samuel Goldflam, "Weiteres über das intermittierende Hinken," *Neurologisches Centralblatt* 20 (1901): 197–213. See also his "Über intermittierende Hinken ('claudication intermittente' Charcot's) und Arteritis der Beine," *Deutsche medizinische Wochenschrift* 21 (1901): 587–98.

25. See Enfemiuse Herman, "Samuel Goldflam (1852–1932)," in Kurt Kolle, ed., *Grosse Nervenärtze*, 3 vols. (Stuttgart: Thieme, 1963), 3:143–49.

26. Samuel Goldflam, "Zur Ätiologie und Symptomatologie des intermittierenden Hinkens," *Neurologisches Zentralblatt* 22 (1903): 994–6. On tobacco misuse as a primary cause of illness, see the literature overview by Johannes Bresler, *Tabakologia medizinalis: Literarische Studie über den Tabak in medizinischer Beziehung*, 2 vols. (Halle: Carl Marhold, 1911–13).

27. Toby Cohn, "Nervenkrankheiten bei Juden," *Zeitschrift für Demographie und Statistik der Juden*, New Series 3 (1926): 76–85.
28. Kurt Mendel, "Intermitterendes Hinken," *Zentralblatt für die gesamt Neurologie und Psychiatrie* 27 (1922): 65–95.
29. Wilhelm Erb, "Über das 'intermittirende Hinken' und andere nervöse Störungen in Folge von Gefässerkrankungen," *Deutsche Zeitschrift für Nervenheilkunde* 13 (1898): 1–77.
30. Wilhelm Erb, "Über Disbasia angiosklerotika (intermittierendes Hinken)," *Münchener medizinische Wochenschrift* 51 (1904): 905–8.
31. Compare P. C. Waller, S. A. Solomon, and L. E. Ramsay, "The Acute Effects of Cigarette Smoking on Treadmill Exercise Distances in Patients with Stable Intermittent Claudication," *Angiology* 40 (1989): 164–9.
32. Hermann Oppenheim, "Zur Psychopathologie und Nosologie der russisch-jüdischen Bevölkerung," *Journal für Psychologie und Neurologie* 13 (1908): 7.
33. L. v. Frankl-Hochwart, *Die nervösen Erkrankungen der Tabakraucher* (Wien und Leipzig: Alfred Hölder, 1912), pp. 30–31; 48–53.
34. Cited by R. Hofstätter, *Die rauchende Frau: Eine klinische, psychologische und soziale Studie* (Wien/Leipzig: Hölder-Pichler-Tempsky, 1924), pp. 179.
35. Fritz Lickint, *Tabak und Organismus: Handbuch der Gesamten Tabakkunde* (Stuttgart: Hippokrates, 1939), p. 284.
36. See John M. Efron, *Medicine and the German Jews: A History* (New Haven: Yale University Press, 2001), pp. 108–17.
37. Proctor, p. 208.
38. M. A. Gilbert, "Hystérie tabagique," *La Lancette française* 62 (1889): 1173–4; Corti, p. 260.
39. Leopold Löwenfeld, *Pathologie und Therapie der Neurasthenie und Hysterie* (Wiesbaden: J. F. Bergmann, 1894, in the Freud Library, London), p. 46.
40. See the detailed account of the literature compiled by Paul Näcke, "Der Tabak in der Ätiologie der Psychosen, " *Wiener Klinische Rundschau* 23 (1909): 805–7; 821–4, 840–2.
41. Leopold Löwenfeld, *Die moderne Behandlung der Nervenschwäche (Neurasthenie) der Hysterie und verwandten Leiden* (Wiesbaden: J. F. Bergmann, 1887, in the Freud Library, London), p. 28.
42. Felix Deutsch, "Reflections on Freud's One Hundredth Birthday," *Psychosomatic Medicine* 18 (1956): 279.
43. *The Diary of Sigmund Freud 1929–1939: A Record of the Final Decade*, ed. and trans. Michael Molnar (New York: Charles Scribner, 1992), p. 69.

44. Max Schur, *Freud: Living and Dying* (New York: International Universities Press, 1972), p. 86.

45. Cohn, 85.

46. Jacobs, p. 29.

47. Sharon Romm, *The Unwelcome Intruder: Freud's Struggle with Cancer* (New York: Praeger, 1983), p. 38.

48. Maurice Sorsby, *Cancer and Race: A Study of the Incidence of Cancer among Jews* (London: John Bale, Sons & Danielsson, 1931), p. 34. (Sorsby's initial publications on this topic are under the name of Sourasky).

49. I. Rosenwaike, "Causes of Death Among Elderly Jews in New York City, 1979–1981." *International Journal of Epidemiology* (1994) 23: 327–32.

50. Judy Siegel-Itzkovich, "Clearing the Air," *Jerusalem Post* (July 27, 2000).

51. Judy Siegel, "Rabbis Call on Jews to Stop Smoking," *Jerusalem Post* (May 31 2001).

52. Ibid.

CHAPTER 4

1. Tape no. 0026, Chicago Jewish Archives, Spertus Institute of Jewish Studies.

2. Richard W. Saunders, *Metamorphoses of the Proustian Body : A Study of Bodily Signs in à la Recherche du Temps Perdu* (New York: Peter Lang, 1994); Michael R Finn, *Proust, the Body, and Literary Form* (Cambridge: Cambridge University Press, 1999).

3. Marcel Proust, *Remembrance of Things Past, Combray*, trans. C. K. Scott Moncrieff and Terence Kilmartin (Harmondsworth, Eng.: Penguin, 1986) 1:23–24.

4. Albert Sonnenfeld, "Marcel Proust: Anti-Semite?" *French Review* 62 (1988): 25–40, 275–82; Gilles Zenou, "Proust et la judéité," *Europe* 705–6 (1988): 157–64.

5. Proust, 1986, *Cities of the Plain*, 2:639.

6. Proust, 1986, 1: 326.

7. Johann Friedrich Dieffenbach, *Chirurgische Erfahrungen, besonders über die Wiederherstellung zerstörter Theile des menschlichen Körpers nach neuen Methoden*, 4 vols. in 3 and atlas (Berlin: Enslin, 1829–34), 3:39.

8. Robert Gersuny, "Über einige kosmetische Operationen," *Wiener medizinische Wochenschrift* 53 (1903): 2253–8, here, 2253.

9. Frank McDowell, ed., *The Source Book of Plastic Surgery* (Baltimore: Williams & Wilkins, 1977), p. 147.

10. J. Jadassohn, ed., *Handbuch der Haut-und Geschlechtskrankheiten* 23 vols. (Berlin: Julius Springer, 1931), 23:399–400.

11. Joseph Banister, *England under the Jews* (London: [J. Banister], 1907), p. 61.

12. Adolf Hitler, *Mein Kampf*, trans. Ralph Manheim (Boston: Houghton Mifflin, 1943), pp. 325.

13. Thomas Mann, "The Blood of the Walsungs," in *Death in Venice and Seven Other Stories*, trans. H. T. Lowe-Porter (New York: Vintage, 1989), pp. 289–316, here, 290.

14. Amos Elon, *Herzl* (New York: Holt, Rinehart & Winston, 1975), p. 63.

15. Konrad H. Jarausch, *Students, Society and Politics in Imperial Germany: The Rise of Academic Illiberalism* (Princeton: Princeton University Press, 1982), p. 350.

16. W[illiam] O[sler], "Berlin Correspondence," *Canada Medical and Surgical Journal* 2 (1874): 308–15, here, 310.

17. Jarausch, p. 272.

18. Peter Pulzer, *The Rise of Political Anti-Semitism in Germany and Austria* (London: Peter Halband, 1988), p. 246.

19. Ludwig Lévy-Lenz, *Erinnerungen eines Sexual-Arztes: Aus den Memorien eines Sexologen* (Baden-Baden: Wadi-Verlagsbuchhandlung, 1954), p. 460. See also his *Praxis der kosmetischen Chirugie, Fortschritte und Gefahren* (Stuttgart: Hippokrates, 1954).

20. Friedrich Trendelenburg, *Die erste 25 Jahre der Deutschen Gesellschaft für Chirurgie: Ein Beitrag zur Geschichte der Chirurgie* (Berlin: Julius Springer, 1925), p. 197.

21. Stephan Mencke, *Zur Geschichte der Orthopädie* (Munich: Michael Beckstein, 1930), pp. 68–69.

22. Bruno Valentin, *Geschichte der Orthopädie* (Stuttgart: Georg Thieme, 1961), pp. 101–2.

23. Edward T. Ely, "An Operation for Prominence of the Auricles," *Archives of Otology* 10 (1881): 97.

24. Jack E. Davis and Horacio H. Hernandez, "History of the Aesthetic Surgery of the Ear," in Mario González-Ulloa, ed., *The Creation of Aesthetic Plastic Surgery* (New York: Springer, 1976), pp. 115–35.

25. Hans F. K. Günther, *Rassenkunde des jüdischen Volkes* (München: J. F. Lehmann, 1930), p. 218.

26. Telemachus Thomas Timayenis, The *Original Mr. Jacobs* (New York: Minerva Publishing, 1888), p. 21.

27. William H. Luckett, "A New Operation for Prominent Ears Based on the Anatomy of the Deformity," *Surgical Gynecology & Obstetrics* 10 (1910): 635–7.

28. All quotes are from Heinrich Mann, *Man of Straw*, no trans. (Harmondsworth, Eng.: Penguin, 1984).

29. Alan Bullock, *Hitler and Stalin: Parallel Lives* (New York: Knopf-Random House, 1992), p. 537.

30. Alfred Berndorfer, "Aesthetic Surgery as Organopsychic Therapy," *Aesthetic Plastic Surgery* 3 (1979): 143–6, here, 143.

31. John R. Baker, *Race* (New York: Oxford University Press, 1974), p. 238.

32. Jacques Joseph, "Über die operative Verkleinerung einer Nase (Rhinomiosis)," Berliner *klinische Wochenschrift* 40 (1898): 882–5. Translation from "Operative Reduction of the Size of a Nose (Rhinomiosis)," trans. Gustave Aufricht, *Plastic and Reconstructive Surgery* 46 (1970): 178–81, here, 178.

33. Joseph, 180.

34. Jacques Joseph, *Nasenplastik und sonstige Gesichtsplastik, nebst einem Anhang über Mammaplastik und einige weitere Operationen aus dem Gebiete der äusseren Körperplastik: Ein Atlas und ein Lehrbuch* (Leipzig: C. Kabitzsch, 1931). Quotations cited in parentheses are from the translation by Stanley Milstein, Jacques Joseph, *Rhinoplasty and Facial Plastic Surgery with a Supplement on Mammaplasty and Other Operations in the Field of Plastic Surgery of the Body* (Phoenix: Columella Press, 1987), here, p. 34.

35. Blair Rogers, "John Orlando Roe—Not Jacques Joseph—the Father of Aesthetic Rhinoplasty," Aesthetic *Plastic Surgery* 10 (1986): 63–88, here, 81.

36. Trendelenburg, pp. 199–200.

37. John O. Roe, "The Correction of Angular Deformities of the Nose by a Subcutaneous Operation," *Medical Record* (July 18, 1891): 1–7.

38. Robert F. Weir, "On Restoring Sunken Noses without Scarring the Face," *New York Medical Journal* 56 (1892): 449–54.

39. Jacques Joseph, "Nasenverkleinerung (mit Krankenvorstellung)," Deutsche *Medizinische Wochenschrift* 30 (1904): 1095.

40. Rogers, p. 81.

41. See my "Dreyfusens Körper-Kafkas Angst," in Julius H. Schoeps and Hermann Simon, eds., *Dreyfus und die Folgen* (Berlin: Hentrich, 1995), pp. 212–33.

CHAPTER 5

1. Walter H. Sokel, "Freud and the Magic of Kafka's Writing," in J. P. Stern, ed., *The World of Franz Kafka* (New York: Holt, Reinhart & Winston, 1980), pp. 145–58; and Michel Vanoosthuyse, "Récits

de rêve et fiction chez Kafka," *Cahiers d'Études Germaniques* 33 (1997): 137–46. Kafka's library no longer contains his Freud editions. See Jürgen Born, ed., *Kafkas Bibliothek: ein beschreibendes Verzeichnis mit einem Index aller in Kafkas Schriften erwähnten Bücher, Zeitschriften und Zeitschriftenbeitrage* (Frankfurt am Main: Fischer, 1991).

2. These quotes are from Gaspare Guidice and Michael Müller, eds., *Franz Kafka: Träume* (Frankfurt: Fischer, 1993).

3. Karl Erich Grözinger, *Kafka und die Kabbala: Das Jüdische in Werk und Denken von Franz Kafka* (Frankfurt a. M.: Eichborn, 1992), pp. 85–92.

4. Julius Tandler, "Konstitution und Rassenhygiene," *Zeitschrift für angewandte Anatomie und Konstitutionslehre* 1 (1914): 11–26.

5. Rotraut Hackermuller, *Das Leben, das mich stort: eine Dokumentation zu Kafkas letzten Jahren 1917–1924* (Wien: Medusa, 1984), p. 120.

6. Theodor Boveri, *Zur Frage der Entstehung malingner Tumoren* (Jena: Gustav Fischer, 1914).

7. David von Hansemann, *Die mikroskopische Diagnose der bösartigen Geschwülste* (Berlin: Hirschwald, 1897).

8. Jean de Grouchy, "Theodor Boveri et la théorie chromosomique de la cacerogenese," *Nouvelle revue: French Hematology and Blood Cells* 18 (1977): 1–4.

9. See B. Fischer-Wasels, *Die Vererbung der Krebskrankheit* (Berlin: Alfred Metzner, 1935), which appeared in a series edited by the eugenist Günther Just, *Schriften zur Erblehre und Rassenhygiene.*

10. Cesare Lombroso, "Sulla mortalità degli Ebrei di Verona nel Decennio 1855–1864," *Rivista Clinica di Bologna* 6 (1867): 3–37.

11. Maurice Sorsby, *Cancer and Race: A Study of the Incidence of Cancer among Jews* (London: John Bale, Sons & Danielsson, 1931), p.1. Following Sorsby, I. Davidsohn, "Cancer among Jews," *Medical Leaves* 2 (1939): 19–27 surveys this question until the end of the 1930s.

12. M. J. Gutmann, *Über den heutigen Stand der Rasse-und Krankheitsfrage der Juden* (Berlin: Rudolph Müller & Steinecke, 1920), pp. 50–51.

13. See Maurice Fishberg's presentation of the fin-de-siècle material in the essay on "Cancer," *Jewish Encyclopedia*, 12 vols. (New York: Funk & Wagnalls, 1905–1926), 3: 529–31.

14. Anon., "Cancer among Jews," *British Medical Journal* (March 15, 1902): 681–2, here, 681.

15. This debate is outlined in more detail by the Viennese physician Sigismund Peller, "Über Krebssterblichkeit der Juden," *Zeitschrift für Krebsforschung* 34 (1931): 128–47, here, 129–31.

16. Sorsby, p. 77.
17. A. Theilhaber, "Zur Lehre von der Entstehung der Uterustumoren," *Münchener Medizinische Wochenschrift* 56 (1909): 1272–3.
18. See his discussion in Felix Theilhaber, *Die Beschneidung* (Berlin: L. Lamm, 1927). Compare Herbert Lewin, "Geleitwort. Mit einigen biblischen Gedanken in der modernen Medizin," in Ernst Róth and Fritz Bloch, eds., *Festschrift. Dr. I. E. Lichtigfeld, Landesrabbiner von Hessen, zum 70. Geburtstag* (Frankfurt am Main: n.p., 1964), pp. 10–12.
19. Leopold Löwenfeld, *Über die sexuelle Konstitution und andere Sexualprobleme* (Wiesbaden: J. F. Bergmann, 1911), p. 128.
20. A. Theilhaber and S. Greischer, "Zur Aetiologie des Carcinoms," *Zeitschrift für Krebsforschung* 9 (1910): 530–54, here, 548; Felix Theilhaber, *Zur Lehre von dem Zusammenhang der sozialen Stellung und der Rasse mit der Entstehung der Uteruscarcinome* (diss.: Munich, 1910), pp. 11–14; and "Zur Lehre von dem Zusammenhang der sozialen Stellung und der Rasse mit der Entstehung der Uteruscarcinome," *Zeitschrift für Krebsforschung* 8 (1909), 466–88, here, 475–8;
21. Theilhaber, *Zusammenhang*, p. 13.
22. H. N. Vineberg, "The Relative Infrequency of Cancer of the Uterus in Women of the Hebrew Race," *Contributions to Medical and Biological Research Dedicated to Sir William Osler*, 2 vols. (New York: P. B. Hoeber, 1919) 2: 1217–25, here, 1224.
23. M. H. Pejovic and M. Thuaire, "Étiologie des cancers du col de l'uterus. Le point sur 150 ans de rechérché," *Journal de gynécologie, obstétrice, biologie, et reproduction* 15 (1986): 37–43.
24. Wilson I. B. Onuigbo, "Historical Notes on Cancer in Married Couples," *Netherlands Journal of Surgery* 36 (1984): 112–15.
25. Felix A. Theilhaber, "Gesundheitsverhältnisse," *Jüdisches Lexikon*, ed. Georg Herlitz and Bruno Kirschner, 4 vols. in 5 (Berlin: Jüdischer Verlag, 1927–30): 2:1120–41, here, 1138–9.
26. See the discussion of cancer in Peter Charles Remondino, *History of Circumcision from the Earliest Times to the Present. Moral and Physical Reasons for Its Performance, with a History of Eunuchism, Hermaphrodism, etc., and of the Different Operations Practiced upon the Prepuce* (Philadelphia: F. A. Davis, 1891), pp. 226–30.
27. See the case material on circumcision in his periodical, *Archives of Surgery* (London) 2 (1891): 15, 267–9.
28. Jonathan Hutchinson, "The Pre-cancerous Stage of Cancer and the Importance of Early Operations," *British Medical Journal* (1882): 4–7.
29. J. Dellinger Barney, "Epithelioma of the Penis. An Analysis of One Hundred Cases," *Annals of Surgery* 46 (1907): 890–914, here, 894.

30. Benjamin S. Barringer and Archie Dean, "Epithelioma of the Penis," *Journal of Urology* 11 (1924): 497–514, here, 497.

31. Abraham L. Wolbarst, "Is Circumcision a Prophylactic Against Penis Cancer?" *Cancer* 3 (1925–26): 301–9, here, 308.

32. Wolbarst, 302.

33. V. Föderl, "Zur Klinik und Statistik des Peniskarzinomes," *Deutsche Zeitschrift für Chirurgie* 198 (1926): 207–30, here, 208.

34. Sorsby, 65.

35. Jonathan Hutchinson, *Syphilis* (London: Cassell, 1887), p. 512. The German translation is Jonathan Hutchinson, *Syphilis*, trans. Artur Kollmann (Leipzig: Arnold, 1888).

36. A. Theilhaber and Felix Theilhaber, "Zur Lehre vom Zusammenhänge von Krebs und Narbe," *Zeitschrift für Krebsforschung* 9 (1910): 554–69, here, 561.

37. Sorsby, pp. 2–3.

38. Sorsby, pp. 79–80.

39. Peller, 139.

40. Hans Auler, "Rasse und bösartige Gewächse," in Johannes Schottky, ed., *Rasse und Krankheit* (Munich: J. F. Lehmann, 1937), pp. 388–99, here, 395.

41. So for example in the summary by the Bucharest physician M. Schachter, "Cancer et race: a propos du cancer chez les Juifs," *Le Progrès médical* 50 (December 5, 1931): 2213–14.

42. J[ules] Héricourt, *The Social Diseases: Tuberculosis, Syphilis, Alcoholism, Sterility*, trans. with a final chapter by Bernard Miall (London: George Routledge, 1920). Quotations cited in parentheses in text are from this edition. Originally published as *Les maladies des societés: tuberculose, syphilis, alcoolisme et sterilité* (Paris: Flammarion, 1918).

43. N. Haltrecht, "Das Tuberkuloseproblem bei den Juden: Eine rassen-und sozialpathologische Studie," *Beiträge zur Klinik der Tuberkulose* 62 (1925): 442–80. See also the figures from 1910 to 1950 in appendix C in Jean Dubos, *The White Plague: Tuberculosis, Man, and Society* (1952; New Brunswick: Rutgers University Press, 1987), and compare the British discussion summarized in Linda Bryder, "The First World War: Healthy or Hungry?" *History Workshop Journal* 24 (1987): 141–57.

44. Maurice Fishberg, "The Comparative Pathology of the Jews," *New York Medical Journal* 73 (1901): 537–43, 576–82, here, 581.

45. Max Brod, ed., *Letters to Friends, Family, and Editors*, trans. Richard and Clara Winston (New York: Schocken, 1977), here, p. 67.

46. Franz Kafka, *Tagebücher*, ed. Hans-Gerd Koch, Michael Müller, Malcolm Pasley (Frankfurt am Main: S. Fischer, 1990), p. 768.

47. Oskar Panizza, *The Council of Love*, trans. O. F. Pucciani (New York: Viking, 1979), p. 79. See in this context the discussion of Panizza in Claude Quétel, *History of Syphilis*, trans. Judith Braddock and Brian Pike (London: Polity Press, 1990) 45–49.

48. See the first-rate study by Anna Foa, "Il Nuovo e il Vecchio: L'Insorgere della Sifilide (1494–1530)," *Quaderni Storici* 55 (1984): 11–34, trans. by Carole C. Gallucci, in Edward Muir and Guido Ruggiero, *Sex and Gender in Historical Perspective* (Baltimore: Johns Hopkins University Press, 1990), pp. 24–45. On Jews and syphilis, see also Klaus Theweleit, *Male Fantasies*, trans. Erica Carter and Chris Turner, 2 vols. (Minneapolis: University of Minnesota Press, 1987–89), 2:16.

49. Quotations are from the English translation, Otto Weininger, *Sex & Character* (London: William Heinemann, 1906), p. 303. On Weininger, see my *Jewish Self-Hatred: Anti-Semitism and the Hidden Language of the Jews* (Baltimore: Johns Hopkins University Press, 1986) 244–51; Jacques Le Rider, *Der Fall Otto Weininger: Wurzeln des Antifeminismus und Antisemitismus*, trans. Dieter Hornig (Vienna: Löcker Verlag, 1985); Jacques Le Rider and Norbert Leser, eds., *Otto Weininger: Werk und Wirkung* (Vienna: Österreichischer Bundesverlag, 1984); Peter Heller, "A Quarrel over Bisexuality," in Gerald Chapple and Hans H. Schulte, eds., *The Turn of the Century: German Literature and Art, 1890–1915* (Bonn: Bouvier, 1978), pp. 87–116; Franco Nicolino, *Indagini su Freud e sulla Psicoanalisi* (Naples: Liguori editore, n.d.), pp. 103–110.

50. "Das Urteil" in Max Brod, ed., *Erzählungen* (Frankfurt am Main: Fischer, 1989), pp. 43–53; "The Judgment," Franz Kafka, *The Complete Stories*, ed. Nahum N. Glatzer (New York: Schocken: 1971), pp. 77–88, here, p. 77.

51. "Der Landarzt" in Erzählungen, pp. 112–116; "A Country Doctor," in Kafka, *The Complete Stories*, pp. 220–5. While there are a very large number of sources on the general question of Kafka's tale, I have found the following the most useful: Eric Marson and Leopold Keith, "Kafka, Freud, and Ein Landarzt," *German Quarterly* 37 (1964): 146–59; A. P. Foulkes, "Dream Pictures in Kafka's Writings," *Germanic Review* 40 (1965): 17–30; Todd C. Hanlin, "Franz Kafka's Landarzt: 'Und heilt er nicht . . . '" *Modern Austrian Literature* 11(1978): 333–44; Edward Timms, "Kafka's Expanded Metaphors: A Freudian Approach to Ein Landarzt," in J. P. Stern, ed., *Paths and Labyrinths: Nine Papers Read at the Franz Kafka Symposium Held at the Institute of Germanic Studies*, October 20–21, 1983 (London: Institute of Germanic Studies, University

of London, 1985), pp. 66–79; Karen J. Campbell, "Dreams of Interpretation: On the Sources of Kafka's 'Landarzt,'" *German Quarterly* 60 (1987): 420–31; Patricia McGurk, "Cracking the Code in 'A Country Doctor': Kafka, Freud, and Homotextuality," Frederico Pereira, ed., *Literature and Psychology: Proceedings of the Eleventh International Conference on Literature and Psychology*, Sandbjerg (Denmark), June 1994 (Lisbon: Institut Superior de Psicologia Aplicada, 1995): 111–18.

52. M. Courtney, J.C.T. Church, and T.J. Ryan, "Larva Therapy in Wound Management," *Journal of the Royal Society of Medicine* 93 (2000): 72–4.

53. W.S. Baer, "The Treatment of Chronic Osteomyeltis with the Maggot (larva of the blowfly)," *Journal of Bone Joint Surgery* 13 (1931): 438–75.

54. Anthony Northey, *Kafka's Relatives: Their Lives and His Writing* (New Haven: Yale University Press, 1991), p. 85.

55. Sander L. Gilman, *Franz Kafka: The Jewish Patient* (New York: Routledge, 1995). See the notes for a full bibliography of Kafka and Jewishness. See also Harry Stecopoulos and Michael Uebel, eds., *Race and the Subject of Masculinities* (Durham: Duke University Press, 1997).

56. Sander L. Gilman, "Kafka Wept," *Modernism/Modernity* 1 (1994): 17–37.

57. Leopold von Sacher-Masoch, "Zwei Ärtze," in his *Jüdisches Leben* (Mannheim: Bensheimer, 1892), pp. 287–98.

CHAPTER 6

1. Dorothy Nelkin and Laurence R. Tancredi, *Dangerous Diagnostics: The Social Power of Biological Information* (Chicago: University of Chicago Press, 1994); Dorothy Nelkin and M. Susan Lindee, *The DNA Mystique: The Gene As a Cultural Icon* (New York: W. H. Freeman, 1996); Elaine Draper, *Risky Business: Genetic Testing and Exclusionary Practices in the Hazardous Workplace* (Cambridge: Cambridge University Press, 1991); Stephen G. Post and Peter J. Whitehouse, eds., *Genetic Testing for Alzheimer Disease: Ethical and Clinical Issues* (Baltimore: The Johns Hopkins University Press, 1998); Peter Doherty and Agneta Sutton, eds., *Man-made Man: Ethical and Legal Issues in Genetics* (Dublin: Open Air, 1997).

2. Ben Anderson, *Imagined Communities: Reflections on the Origin and Spread of Nationalism* (London: Verso, 1991).

3. Susan Michie and Theresa Marteau, "Knowing too Much or Knowing too Little: Psychological Questions Raised for the Adop-

tive Process by Genetic Testing," in Peter Turnpenny, ed., *Secrets in the Genes: Adoption, Inheritance and Genetic Disease* (London: British Agencies for Adoption and Fostering, 1995), pp. 176–87, here, p. 183.

4. J. A. Raeburn, "Issues of Confidentiality, Disclosure and Non-Disclosure: Medical Perspective," in Turnpenny, *Secrets in the Genes*, pp. 188–93, here, p. 190.

5. T. M. Marteau and T. J. Peters, "Will Genetic Testing for Predisposition for Disease Result in Fatalism?" *Social Science and Medicine* 48 (1999): 1857–60.

6. G. M. Petersen and P. A. Boyd, "Gene Tests and Counseling for Colorectal Cancer Risk: Lessons from Familial Polyposis," *Journal of the National Cancer Institute Monographs* 17 (1995): 67–71.

7. T. J. Wilcke, et al., "Transmitting Genetic Risk Information in Families: Attitudes about Disclosing the Identity of Relatives," *American Journal of Human Genetics* 65 (1999): 902–9. The survey had an unusually high return rate of 82 percent return rate of 1,761 (1,609 or 75 percent actually filled out the questionnaire).

8. www.Darkwing.uoregon.edu/-lfrohn.

9. www.geocities.com/nashville/Opry/1574.

10. www.nfjgd.org.

11. Howard Markel, "One Side Effect of Genetic Testing: Fear," *New York Times* (May 16, 2000): D8.

12. See Lynn Morgan, ed., *Fetal Subjects, Feminist Positions* (Philadelphia: University of Pennsylvania Press, 1999).

13. www.fdvillage.org.

14. fd-net@relay.doit.wisc.edu.

15. Toby Gelfand, "Charcot's Response to Freud's Rebellion," *Journal of the History of Ideas* 50/2 (April-June, 1989): 293–307, here, 304.

16. Toby Gelfand, "'Mon Cher Docteur Freud': Charcot's Unpublished Correspondence to Freud, 1888–1893," *Bulletin of the History of Medicine*, 62 (1988): 563–588, here, 574.

17. Felix Theilhaber Theilhaber, "Zur Sterblichkeit der Juden," *Zeitschrift für die Statistik und Demographie der Juden* 5 (1909): 10.

18. Joseph Jacobs, *Studies in Jewish Statistics* (London: D. Nutt, 1891), p. 32.

19. Maurice Fishberg, *The Jews: A Study of Race and Environment* (New York: Walter Scott, 1911), 25.

20. Arnold Pollatschek, "Zur Aetiologie des Diabetes mellitus," *Zeitschrift für klinische Medizin* 42 (1902): 479.

21. A. M. Cohen, et al., "Change of Diet of Yemenite Jews in Relation to Diabetes and Ischaemic Heart Disease," *Lancet* (1961): 1399–401; and A. M. Cohen, J. Fidel, B. Cohen, et al., "Diabetes,

Blood Lipids, Lipoproteins, and Change of Environment: Restudy of the 'New immigrant Yemenites' in Israel," *Metabolism* 28 (1979): 716–28.

22. Richard M. Goodman, *Genetic Disorders among the Jewish People* (Baltimore: Johns Hopkins, 1979), p. 334–41, citing K. Schmidt-Nielsen, et al., "Diabetes mellitus in the sand rat induced by standard laboratory diets," *Science* 143 (1964): 689.

23. How closely knit groups respond to such psychological pressure is the subject of a number of theories. Psychoanalysis has provided some productive insights into the modalities by which such a disruptive force impacts family dynamics. In the 1970s the French psychoanalysts Nicolas Abraham and Maria Torok (authors of *The Shell and the Kernel: Renewals of Psychoanalysis* [Chicago: University of Chicago Press, 1994]), published three central papers on what they called a theory of the transgenerational phantom. To summarize a rather complex theory in a few sentences, they argued for the existence of real, repressed, often unspoken hidden knowledge within families. They see that its affect is transmitted to the children and to the children's children with ever-diminished presence in the form of concrete psychological disturbances. In the children and grandchildren, analogous psychological symptoms are present without any of the direct cause. The narratives of the children about their experiences parallel those of the parents. Abraham and Torok's theory can be elegantly applied to the survivors of the Shoah, whose children, whether or not they were knowledgeable about their parents' status as survivors, manifested many of the same psychological symptoms as their parents. Their lives revolved unconsciously about the centrality, unspoken but real, in their parents' lives of their often accidental survival. The children sense their own existence as accidental, depending of the accident of their own parents' survival and manifest many of the same symptoms as their parents. This is true in families where the parents' experience remains unspoken or unarticulated as well as those in which it is spoken and placed into a broader narrative. While there is, of course, a copycat effect present, the underlying psychological deformation has been shown to exist in virtually every case of survivors' children. This can be extended even to those families in which the precipitating event is discussed. For the vital fact of the children's existence is both proof of the survival of the parents but can be seen by the children as suddenly drawn into question given the earlier potential for the parent's own death. Our lives are, of course, always tenuous, but to imagine that you exist because of an accident of fate that enabled your parents to

exist, and to have this reinforced by the unspoken phantom present in each family, precipitates a sense of one's own instability. The phantom is the cohort that gives meaning of some type to the experience of the family.

CHAPTER 7

1. Gloria Anzaldúa, *Borderlands/La Frontera: The New Mestiza* (San Francisco: Spinsters/Aunt Lute, 1987), pp. 79–81.
2. Christine Welsh, "Women in the Shadows: Reclaiming a Métis Heritage," *Descant* 24 (1993): 89–103.
3. Barry Gross, "'Intellectual Overlordship': Blacks, Jews and Native Son," *Journal of Ethnic Studies* 5 (1977): 51–9; Evelyn M. Avery, "'Bittersweet Encounter': Blacks and Jews in the Fiction of Ethnic Women," in Edith Blicksilver, ed., *The Ethnic American Woman: Problems, Protests, Lifestyle* (Dubuque: Kendall/Hunt, 1989), pp. 420–5; Michael Galchinsky, "Glimpsing Golus in the Golden Land: Jews and Multiculturalism in America," *Judaism: A Quarterly Journal of Jewish Life and Thought* 43 (1994): 360–8; Emily Miller Budick, *Blacks and Jews in Literary Conversation* (Cambridge: Cambridge University Press, 1998); David Biale, Michael Galchinsky, Susan Heschel, *Insider/Outsider: American Jews and Multiculturalism* (Berkeley: University of California Press, 1998); Milli Heyd, *Mutual Reflections: Jews and Blacks in American Art* (New Brunswick, N.J.: Rutgers University Press, 1999); Adam Zachary Newton, *Facing Black and Jew: Literature as Public Space in Twentieth-Century America* (Cambridge: Cambridge University Press, 1999); Ethan Goffman, *Imagining Each Other: Blacks and Jews in Contemporary American Literature* (Albany: State University of New York Press, 2000).
4. Sander L. Gilman, *The Jew's Body* (New York: Routledge, 1991).
5. Peter Novick, *The Holocaust in American Life* (Boston: Houghton Mifflin, 1999).
6. Quotations from Hanif Kureishi's work cited in parentheses in the text are from "We're Not Jews," *Love in a Blue Time* (London: Faber and Faber, 1997), pp. 41–51. See Stefano Manferlotti, *Dopo l'Impero: Romanzo ed etnia in Gran Bretagna* (Napoli: Liguori, 1995); Ines Karin Böhner, *My Beautiful Laundrette und Sammy and Rosie Get Laid: Filmische Reflexion von Identitätsprozessen* (Frankfurt am Main, New York: Peter Lang, 1996); John Clement Ball, "The Semi-Detached Metropolis: Hanif Kureishi's London," *Ariel* 27 (1996): 7–27; Kenneth C. Kaleta, *Hanif Kureishi: Postcolonial Storyteller* (Austin: University of Texas Press, 1998); Ray Sangeeta, "The Nation in Performance: Bhabha, Mukherjee and Kureishi,"

in Monika Fludernik, ed., *Hybridity and Postcolonialism: Twentieth-Century Indian Literature* (Tübingen: Stauffenburg, 1998), pp. 219–38; Anuradha Dingwaney Needham, *Using the Master's Tools: Resistance and the Literature of the African and South Asian Diasporas* (New York: St. Martin's, 2000).

7. Paul Gilroy, *"There Ain't No Black in the Union Jack": The Cultural Politics of Race and Nation* (Chicago: University of Chicago Press, 1991).

8. Julian Barnes, *Metroland* (London: Cape, 1980), p. 32.

9. Y. Michal Bodemann, "Von Berlin nach Chicago und weiter. Georg Simmel und die Reise seines 'Fremden,'" *Berliner Journal für Soziologie* 8 (1998): 125–42.

10. Sarah Lyall, "Shadowy Party Heats Up British Racial Tensions," *New York Times* (July 4, 2001): A3.

11. Quotations from Achmat Dangor's work in parentheses in the text are from *Kafka's Curse: A Novella & Three Other Stories* (Cape Town: Kwela, 1997), pp. 5–142. See also Loren Kruger, "Black Atlantics, White Indians, and Jews: Locations, Locutions, and Syncretic Identities in the Fiction of Achmat Dangor and Others," *South Atlantic Quarterly* (2001): 111–43.

12. http://www.randomreference.com/boldtype/0399/dangor/interview.html.

13. See Noel Ignatiev, *How the Irish Became White* (New York: Routledge, 1996); Karen Brodkin, *How Jews Became White Folks and What That Says about Race in America* (New Brunswick, N.J.: Rutgers University Press, 1998); Maurice Berger, *White Lies: Race and the Myths of Whiteness* (New York: Farrar, Straus, Giroux, 1999); Matthew Frye Jacobson, *Whiteness of a Different Color: European Immigrants and the Alchemy of Race* (Harvard University Press, 1999); Matthew Frye Jacobson and David Roediger *Special Sorrows: The Diasporic Imagination of Irish, Polish, and Jewish Immigrants in the United States* (Berkeley: University of California Press, 2002).

14. Milton Shain, *The Roots of Antisemitism in South Africa* (Johannesburg: Witwatersrand University Press, 1994), p. 16. Published in the series *Reconsiderations in Southern Africa History* ed. by Jeffrey Butler and Richard Elphick (Charlottesville: University of Virginia Press, 1994).

15. Anatole Leroy-Beaulieu, *Israel Among the Nations: A Study of the Jews and Antisemitism*, trans. Frances Hellman (New York: Putnam's Sons, 1895), pp. 166–7.

16. D. Chwolson, *Die Blutanklage und sonstige mittelalterliche Beschuldigungen der Juden. Eine historische Untersuchung nach den Quellen* (Frankfurt am Main: Kauffmann, 1901), pp. 7, 207–10.

17. Julius Preuss, "Die Beschneidung nach Bibel und Talmud," *Wiener klinische Rundschau* 11 (1897): 708–9; 724–7; J. Alkvist, "Geschichte der Circumcision," *Janus* 30 (1926): 86–104; 152–71; and Samuel Krauss, *Geschichte der jüdischen Ärzte vom frühsten Mittelalter bis zur Gleichberechtigung* (Vienna: A. S. Bettelheim-Stiftung, 1930), pp. 157–8.

18. Sander L. Gilman, *Franz Kafka: The Jewish Patient* (New York: Routledge, 1995).

19. John Ezard, "Double First for Novel Newcomer Zadie Smith," *Guardian* (January 4, 2001).

20. Zadie Smith, *White Teeth* (New York: Random House, 2000), pp. 271–2l.

21. Zadie Smith, *The Autograph Man* (New York: Random House, 2002).

22. Quotations from Senocak's work cited in parentheses in the text are my translation of from Zafer Senocak, *Gefährliche Verwandtschaft* (München: Babel, 1998). See also Roland Dollinger, "Hybride Identitaeten: Zafer Senocaks Roman 'Gefaehrliche Verwandtschaft'," *Seminar: A Journal of Germanic Studies* 38: 59–73; and Katherine Gerstenberger, "Difficult Stories: Generation, Genealogy, Gender in Zafer Senocak's *Gefährliche Verwandtschaft* and Monika Maron's *Pawels Briefe*," Stuart Taberner, ed., *Recasting Identity in Contemporary Germany* (Columbia, S.C.: Camden House, forthcoming).

23. On the German Jewish literary reception of the question of hybridity, see Todd Herzog, "Hybrids and Mischlinge: Translating Anglo-American Cultural Theory into German," *German Quarterly* 70 (1997): 1–17.

24. Rudolf Virchow, "Gesamtbericht über die Farbe der Haut, der Haare und der Augen der Schulkinder in Deutschland," *Archiv für Anthropologie* 16 (1886): 275–475.

25. George L. Mosse, *Toward the Final Solution: A History of European Racism* (New York: Howard Fertig, 1975), pp. 90–91.

26. Daniel Boyarin, *Unheroic Conduct* (Berkeley: University of California Press, 1997), and Judith Butler, *Gender Trouble* (New York, Routledge, 1990).

27. Thomas Meinecke, *Hellblau* (Frankfurt a. M.: Suhrkamp, 2001), pp. 222–3.

28. Quotations from this novel cited in parentheses in the text are from Gish Jen, *Mona in the Promised Land: A Novel* (New York: Vintage, 1996). See Rachel C. Lee, *The Americas of Asian American Literature: Gendered Fictions of Nation and Transnation* (Princeton: Princeton University Press, 1999).

29. Laura Accinelli, "Eye of the Beholder," *Los Angeles Times* (January 23, 1996) E:1.

30. Quotations from this novel cited in parentheses in the text are from Oscar Hijuelos, *A Simple Havana Melody (from when the world was good)* (New York: HarperCollins, 2002). See also Jose Miguel Oviedo, "Six Problems for Oscar Hijuelos: A Conversation with Jose Miguel Oviedo," *Latin American Literature and Arts* 63 (2001) 73–9; Amy Elias, "Oscar Hijuelos's *The Mambo Kings Play Songs of Love*, Ishmael Reed's *Mumbo Jumbo*, and Robert Coover's *The Public Burning*," *Critique: Studies in Contemporary Fiction* 41 (2000):115–28; Alphy J. Plakkoottam, "Popular Fiction or Social Treatise? Oscar Hijuelos' *The Mambo Kings Play Songs of Love*," *Indian Journal of American Studies* 24 (1994): 48–52; Steven G. Kellman, "Oscar Hijuelos Plays Songs of Sisterly Love," *Revista Espanola de Estudios Norteamericanos* 7 (1996): 35–41; Juan Bruce-Novoa, "Hijuelos' Mambo Kings: Reading from Divergent Traditions," *Confluencia: Revista Hispanica de Cultura y Literatura* 10 (1995): 11–22; Ilan Stavans, "Oscar Hijuelos, novelista," *Revista Iberoamericana* 57 (1991): 155–6.

31. Philippe Blasband, *Quand j'étais sumo* (Paris: Le Castor Astral, 2000): 97–110.

32. Philippe Blasband, *De cedres et de fumées* (Paris: Gallimard, 1990).

33. James Atlas, *Bellow: A Biography* (New York: Random House, 2000), pp. 573–4.

34. Gary Shteyngart, *The Russian Debutant's Handbook* (New York: Riverhead, 2002).

35. Daniel Zalewski, "From Russian with Tsoris," *New York Times Magazine* (June 2, 2002): 54–7.

Supplemental Readings

MULTICULTURALISM AND IDENTITY

Anderson, Kay. "Thinking 'Postnationally': Dialogue across Multicultural, Indigenous, and Settler Spaces." *Annals of the Association of American Geographers* 90/2 (2000): 381–91.

Berry, J. W. "A Psychology of Immigration." *Journal of Social Issues* 57/3 (2001): 15–31.

Berting, Jan, and Christiane Villain-Gandossi. "The Significance of Collective Identities in Intergroup Relations." *Journal of Mediterranean Studies* 11/1 (2001): 11–42.

Bhatt, Chetan, and Parita Mukta. "Hindutva in the West: Mapping the Antimonies of Diaspora Nationalism." *Ethnic and Racial Studies* 23/3 (2000): 407–41.

Brubaker, Rogers. "The Return of Assimilation? Changing Perspectives on Immigration and Its Sequels in France, Germany, and the United States." *Ethnic and Racial Studies* 24/4 (2001): 531–48.

Chiao, Chien. "Multiethnicity, Multiculturalism and Cultural Counseling." *Bulletin of the Institute of Ethnology (Taipei)* 89 (2000): 81–91.

Cochran, David Carroll. "A Multicultural Fable (Ethnic Restaurants Go Multicultural)." *Dissent* 48/2 (2000): 101–2.

Cunningham, Stuart, Gay Hawkins, and Audrey Yue. "Multicultural Broadcasting and Diasporic Video as Public Sphericules." *American Behavioral Scientist* 43/9 (2000): 1533–47.

Etzioni, Amitai. "The Monochrome Society." *Policy Review* 105 (2001): 53–70.

Faist, Thomas. "Transnationalization in International Migration: Implications for the Study of Citizenship and Culture." *Ethnic and Racial Studies* 23/2 (2000): 189–222.

Nancy Fraser. "Recognition without Ethics?" *Theory, culture and society* 18/2–3 (2001): 21–42.

Gardenswartz, Lee, and Anita Rowe. "Cross-cultural Awareness."
    HRMagazine 46/3 (2001): 139–42.
Geddes, John, and Julian Beltrame. "Power Games." *Maclean's* 115/4
    (2002): 22–3.
Ginges, Jeremy, and David Cairns. "Social Representations of Multicul-
    turalism: A Faceted Analysis." *Journal of Applied Social Psychology* 30/7
    (2000): 1345–70.
Haidar, Aziz. "The Impact of National Conflict and Peace on the Forma-
    tion of the Image of the Other: How Palestinians in Israel Perceive
    and Are Perceived by Others." *Journal of Mediterranean studies* 11/1
    (2001): 67–87.
Kershen, Anne J. "From Celebrationists to Confrontationists: Some
    Thoughts on British Jewish Historiography in the Twentieth Cen-
    tury." *Immigrants & Minorities* 19/2 (2000): 91–106.
Kuzio, Taras. "The Myth of the Civic State: A Critical Survey of Hans
    Kohn's Framework for Understanding Nationalism." *Ethnic and
    Racial Studies* 25/1 (2001): 20–39.
Lau, Kimberly, J. "Serial Logic: Folklore and Difference in the Age of
    Feel-good Multiculturalism." *Journal of American Folklore* 113/447
    (2000): 70–82.
Lecours, Andre. "Theorizing Cultural Identities: Historical Institutional-
    ism as a Challenge to the Culturalists." *Canadian Journal of Political
    Science* 33/3 (2000): 499–522.
Lemert, Charles. "The Clothes Have No Emperor" (in special section
    "Multiculturalism and intellectuals"). *Theory, Culture and Society* 17/1
    (2000): 97–106.
Martinez Aleman, Ana M. "Community, Higher Education, and the
    Challenge of Multiculturalism." *Teachers College Record* 103/3 (2001):
    485–502.
Meyer, Luanna H. "Multiculturalism and Severe Disabilities." *Journal of
    the Association for Persons with Severe Handicaps* 26/3 (2001): 204–5.
Miklavcic-Brezigar, Inga. "Cultural Identity and Ethnology within the
    Framework of Modern Globalisation." *Glasnik slovenskega etnoloskega
    Drustva* 41/1–2 (2001): 34–40, 167.
Mlekuz, Jernej. "The Role of Space in the Formation and Preservation of
    Ethnic, National and Statehood Identity." *Glasnik slovenskega et-
    noloskega Drustva* 41/1–2 (2001): 55–61, 169.
Osborne, Evan. "Diversity, Multiculturalism, and Ethnic Conflict: A
    Rent-seeking Perspective." *Kyklos* 53/4 (2000): 509–25.
Padolsky, Enoch. "Multiculturalism at the Millennium." *Journal of Cana-
    dian Studies* 35/1 (2000): 138–60.
San Juan, E., Jr. "The Multiculturalist Problematic in the Age of Global-
    ized Capitalism." *Social Justice* 27/1 (2000): 61–75.

Sarat, Austin. "The Micropolitics of Identity/Difference: Recognition and Accommodation in Everyday Life." *Daedalus* 129/4 (2000): 147–68.

Singh, Anita Inder. "Diversity, Human Rights and Peace." *UN Chronicle* 38/2 (2001): 36–7.

Sokefeld, Martin. "Debating Self, Identity, and Culture in Anthropology." *Current Anthropology* 40/4 (1999): 417–47.

Steyn, Mark. "The Slyer Virus: The West's Anti-Westernism." *New Criterion* 20/6 (2002): 4–17.

Tolbert, Caroline J., and Rodney E. Hero. "Dealing with Diversity: Racial/Ethnic Context and Social Policy Change." *Political Research Quarterly* 54/3 (2001): 571–604.

Wagner, Cynthia G. "Transmigrants: Living in Multiple Cultures." *Futurist* 34/5 (2000): 18.

Werbner, Pnina. "Who Sets the Terms of the Debate? Heterotropic Intellectuals and the Clash of Discourses" (in special section "Multiculturalism and intellectuals"). *Theory, Culture and Society* 17/1 (2000): 147–56.

Winter, Elke. "Recasting European and Canadian History: National Consciousness, Migration, Multicultural Lives." *Canadian Ethnic Studies* 32/2 (2000): 115–8.

AT THE FRONTIER

Abbink, J. "Violence and the Crisis of Conciliation: Suri, Dizi and the State in Southwest Ethiopia." *Africa* 70/4 (2000): 527–50.

Abler, Thomas S. "Iroquois Policy and Iroquois Culture: Two Histories and an Anthropological Ethnohistory." *Ethnohistory* 47/2 (2000): 483–91.

Adams, David B. "At the Lion's Mouth: San Miguel de Aguayo in the Defense of Nuevo Leon 1686–1841." *Colonial Latin American Historical Review* 9/3 (2000): 324–46.

Akamine, Jun. "On the Diversification of the Tropical Trepang Resources: A View from the Frontier Society in the Maritime Southeast Asia." *Bulletin of the National Museum of Ethnology (Osaka)* 25/1 (2000): 59–112.

Cisilin, Alessandro. "The Imposition of a Frontier. Society and Ideology in Trieste, between Municipality, Nationality, and Empire, 1717–1914." *Social anthropology* 8/3 (2000): 319–40, 365–6.

Domagala, Bozena. "The German Minority in Varmia and Masuria: Culture and Politics." *Ethnologia polona* 21 (2000): 47–52.

Dupre, Louis. "Philosophy and the Natural Desire for God: An Historical Reflection." *International Philosophical Quarterly* 40/2 (2000): 141–8.

Ensel, Remco. "Dirty Harry in Nador and Muhammad in Amsterdam: Notes on the Migration of People and Ideas." *Focaal* 38 (2001): 163–70.

Holland, Alison. "The Campaign for Women Protectors: Gender, Race and Frontier Between the Wars." *Australian Feminist Studies* 16/34 (2001).

Hopwood, Keith. "Living on the margin—Byzantine Farmers and Turkish Herders." *Journal of Mediterranean Studies* 10/1–2 (2000): 93–105.

Howitt, Richie. "Frontiers, Borders, Edges: Liminal Challenges to the Hegemony of Exclusion." *Australian Geographical Studies* 39/2 (2001): 233–44.

Ingram, Penelope. "Racializing Babylon: Settler Whiteness and the 'New Racism'." *New Literary History* 32/1 (2001): 157–76.

Jersild, Austin. "Faith, Custom, Ritual in the Borderlands: Orthodoxy, Islam, and the 'Small Peoples' of the Middle Volga and the North Caucasus." *Russian Review* 59/4 (2000): 512–29.

Johnson, Benjamin. "Engendering Nation and Race in the Borderlands." *American Research Review* 37/1 (2002): 259–71.

Kabzinska, Iwona. "Space-Memory-Identity: Elements of Space (Places) in the Remembrance of the Eastern Frontier Expatriates." *Literatura ludowa* 44/2 (2000): 3–23.

King, Charles, and Neil J. Melvin. "Diaspora Politics." *International Security* 24/3 (2000): 108–40.

Krohn-Hansen, Christian. "A Tomb for Columbus in Santo Domingo. Political Cosmology, Population and Racial Frontiers." *Social anthropology* 9/2 (2001): 165–92, 237–9.

Lugo, Alejandro. "Theorizing Border Inspections." *Cultural Dynamics* 12/3 (2000): 353–73.

Morris-Suzuku, Tessa. "'Northern lights': The Making and Unmaking of Karafuto Identity." *Journal of Asian Studies* 60/3 (2001): 645–71.

Pollins, Harold. "Jewries at the Margin." *Jewish Journal of Sociology* 42/1–2 (2000): 90–100.

Sassen, Saskia. "How Should the Left Respond to Globalization." *Dissent* 48/1 (2001): 13–14.

Sassen, Saskia. "Excavating Power: In Search of Frontier Zones and New Actions." *Theory, Culture and Society* 17/1 (2000): 163–70.

Sherman, Joseph. "Serving the Natives: Whiteness as the Price of Hospitality in South African Yiddish Literature." *Journal of Southern African Studies* 26/3 (2000): 505–21.

Sutton, Donald S. "Myth Making on an Ethnic Frontier." *Modern China* 26/4 (2000): 448–97.

Wrzesinska, Katarzyna. "The Belorussian Minority in the Press Coverage of the Poznan Conservatives in the Years 1918–1939." *Ethnologia polona* 21 (2000): 35–45.

Index